OMNISCIENCE™: THE BASIC GAME OF KNOWLEDGE IN BOOK FORM

By John P. Campbell

Campbell's High School/College Quiz Book

Campbell's Potpourri I of Quiz Bowl Questions

Campbell's Potpourri II of Quiz Bowl Questions

Campbell's Middle School Quiz Book #1

Campbell's Potpourri III of Quiz Bowl Questions

Campbell's Middle School Quiz Book #2

Campbell's Elementary School Quiz Book #1

Campbell's 2001 Quiz Questions

Campbell's Potpourri IV of Quiz Bowl Questions

Campbell's Middle School Quiz Book #3

The 500 Famous Quotations Quiz Book

Campbell's 2002 Quiz Questions

Campbell's 210 Lightning Rounds

Campbell's 175 Lightning Rounds

Campbell's 2003 Quiz Questions

Campbell's 211 Lightning Rounds

OMNISCIENCE™: The Basic Game of Knowledge in Book Form (Revised Edition)

Campbell's 2004 Quiz Questions

Campbell's 212 Lightning Rounds

Campbell's Elementary School Quiz Book #2

Campbell's 176 Lightning Rounds

Campbell's 213 Lightning Rounds

Campbell's Potpourri V of Quiz Bowl Questions

Campbell's Mastering the Myths in a Giant Nutshell Quiz Book

Campbell's 3001 Quiz Questions

Campbell's 2701 Quiz Questions

Campbell's Quiz Book on Explorations and U.S. History to 1865

Campbell's Accent Cubed: Humanities, Math, and Science

Campbell's 2501 Quiz Questions

Campbell's Accent on the Alphabet Quiz Book

Campbell's U.S. History 1866 to 1960 Quiz Book

Campbell's 177 Lightning Rounds

Campbell's 214 Lightning Rounds

Campbell's Accent on Numbers Quiz Book

OMNISCIENCE™: THE BASIC GAME OF KNOWLEDGE IN BOOK FORM

by John P. Campbell

SECOND EDITION,
REVISED AND UPDATED

PATRICK'S PRESS

Columbus, Georgia

Printed in the United States of America

CIP data suggested by the author

Campbell, John P., 1942-
Omniscience: The Basic Game of Knowledge in Book Form
2nd ed., rev. and updated

Includes index.
Summary: Questions and answers on a wide-range of topics—U.S. geography; history; literature; entertainment; sports and games; science and nature; world geography; leaders and government; music and rhymes; language; arts, religion, and culture; and potpourri—are arranged into two sets of questions on alternate pages.
1. Questions and answers. [1. Questions and answers]
I. Title II. Title: Omniscience: The Basic Game of Knowledge in Book Form.
III. Title: The Basic Game of Knowledge in Book Form.

AG195.C290 2000 031'.02

ISBN (International Standard Book Number): 0-944322-12-3

First Edition
First Printing, September, 1992
Second Edition Revised and Updated
First Printing, September, 2000

ACKNOWLEDGEMENTS

I am once again very indebted to Rinda Brewbaker for her editing ability and suggestions.

I appreciate Todd Huber's diligence in rechecking the material and the efforts of those workers who did the initial work when the questions were part of a board game. I also thank my office staff for the help they gave, especially Saundra Voter for naming the game and Kim Baxley for proofreading it.

I also thank David Taggart for his help in updating this book's material and Sherry Tomblin for her help in rereading it.

I would also like to thank Jackie Taylor for her typesetting services.

To

Those students willing to put in the extra time required for successful quiz bowl competition and to their coaches who seek out materials to help them reach their goals.

PREFACE

This book is intended as a source of basic quiz bowl questions not only for the coach of an Academic Bowl team to use in conducting practices but also for individual team members to use as study material.

Your suggestions and comments will be appreciated. Please send them to me care of PATRICK'S PRESS, Box 5189, Columbus, Georgia, 31906.

John Campbell

OMNISCIENCE™: THE BASIC GAME OF KNOWLEDGE IN BOOK FORM

Rules of Play

The game of 392 pages, 12 categories, and 2,352 questions with multiple parts for a total of 7,056 possible answers.

OBJECT OF THE GAME

Players correctly answer questions to become the first to score 100 points (or any goal mutually agreed upon).

NUMBER OF PLAYERS

Two or more, individually or in teams.

PREPARATION

Cut out 14 category cards, shuffle, and stack face down.

START OF PLAY

Players decide who goes first. Play continues in a clockwise direction. The player with the first turn draws a card from the top of the category deck. The player is then asked a question from the category listed on the back side of the card and has 30 seconds to give his answers (players may agree on 60 seconds). If the category card reads "Lady Luck," the player chooses any category, but if it reads "Hard Luck," the player with the least number of points chooses the category.

All questions have 3 parts. A player receives 1 point for the first correct answer, 2 points for the second, and 3 points for the third. Players need to give their best answer first as any incorrect answer stops the turn for that player.

KNOW-IT-ALL OPTION

A player may attempt to earn **10 points** on his turn. If so, he announces his intention **after** picking the category card. In this case, he must answer the question correctly in its entirety (the 3 required parts).

If the player chooses this option and is unable to answer all parts correctly, he loses 5 points.

CONCLUSION

Once a player is within 10 points of the set game total (e.g., 90 or more points in a game of 100), a player must answer all three parts of the question on an all-or-nothing basis for a total of 3 points per turn. (For younger players, the all or nothing requirement for the last few points can be eliminated.)

U.S. GEOGRAPHY

What are the capitals of Alabama, Alaska, and Arizona?

Answer: Montgomery / Juneau / Phoenix.

HISTORY

Which war was fought in the U.S. from 1861 to 1865, and which names other than North and South designate the 2 sides in the war?

Answer: Civil War (War Between the States) / Union (accept United States) / Confederacy (accept Confederate States of America).

LITERATURE

Which notorious one-legged person leads the pirates in *Treasure Island*, aboard which ship under Captain Smollett's command do they hunt for the treasure, and who is the author of this work?

Answer: Long John Silver / *Hispaniola* / Robert Louis Stevenson.

ENTERTAINMENT

Identify any 3 of the following: cities for the Asian Disneyland and the U.S.'s Disneyland and Walt Disney World, and the country in which the European Disneyland opened in 1992.

Answer: Tokyo / Anaheim (California) / Orlando (Florida) / France.

SPORTS AND GAMES

Arrange the medals, silver, gold, and bronze, in the order in which they would be awarded to the 1st, 2nd, and 3rd place finishers in a contest.

Answer: Gold / silver / bronze.

SCIENCE AND NATURE

What are the 3 "kingdoms" or categories of nature, especially as used in the game of *Twenty Questions*?

Answer: Animal / vegetable / mineral.

WORLD GEOGRAPHY

What are the capitals of Argentina, Australia, and the Czech Republic?

Answer: Buenos Aires / Canberra / Prague.

LEADERS & GOVERNMENT

What title is given to the chief executive of the U.S., what title is given to this person's wife, and what title is given to the chief executive of a U.S. state?

Answer: The President / First Lady / Governor.

MUSIC & RHYMES

In the song "Yankee Doodle," which words complete the lines: "Yankee Doodle went (came) to town / Riding on a _____, / He stuck a _____ in his cap (hat) / And called it _____"?

Answer: "pony" / "feather" / "macaroni."

LANGUAGE

What are the 3 traditional principal parts of regular and irregular verbs?

Answer: Present (present infinitive) / past tense (1st person singular) / past participle.

ARTS, RELIGION, & CULTURE

Which 3 words, each beginning with the prefix *omni-*, are used by most religions to describe their god as being "all knowing," "all powerful," and "present in all places at the same time"?

Answer: Omniscient / omnipotent / omnipresent.

POTPOURRI

Traditionally, which number is considered unlucky, especially in a building; which animal's foot do some carry for good luck; and which animal is considered bad luck if it crosses your path?

Answer: 13 / rabbit's foot / black cat.

U.S. GEOGRAPHY
What are the capitals of Arkansas, California, and Colorado?
Answer: Little Rock / Sacramento / Denver.

HISTORY
Which side won the American Civil War, and which leader surrendered to which leader to end the war?
Answer: Union (the North) / Robert E. Lee / Ulysses S. Grant.

LITERATURE
Who is the young narrator in *Treasure Island*, which inn did his parents own, and whose treasure is being sought?
Answer: Jim Hawkins / Admiral Benbow Inn / Captain Flint's (the story was inspired by the tales of Captain Kidd's treasure).

ENTERTAINMENT
Name 3 of the 4 "Worlds" or "Lands" of Disneyland.
Answer: Fantasyland / Adventureland / Frontierland (accept Westernland) / Tomorrowland (accept Discoveryland).

SPORTS AND GAMES
Name the 3 races that comprise the Triple Crown of thoroughbred horseracing.
Answer: Kentucky Derby / Preakness Stakes / Belmont Stakes.

SCIENCE AND NATURE
Give the name for inflammation of the appendix, spell the name for the operation that removes it, and give the name for inflammation of the tonsils.
Answer: Appendicitis / A-P-P-E-N-D-E-C-T-O-M-Y / tonsillitis.

WORLD GEOGRAPHY

What is the capital of Belgium, and what are its 2 official languages?

Answer: Brussels / Dutch (accept Flemish) / French.

LEADERS & GOVERNMENT

George Washington and John Adams were the first 2 U.S. Presidents. Name the 3rd, 4th, and 5th Presidents.

Answer: Thomas Jefferson / James Madison / James Monroe.

MUSIC & RHYMES

In the song "Yankee Doodle," which words complete: "Yankee Doodle keep it up, / Yankee Doodle dandy; / Mind the _____ and the _____, / And with the _____ be handy"?

Answer: "music" / "step" / "girls."

LANGUAGE

Complete each of the following sayings: "All's well that ends _____," "A friend in _____ is a friend indeed," and "Great oaks from little _____ grow."

Answer: "well" / "need" / "acorns."

ARTS, RELIGION, & CULTURE

Who was the oldest man in the Bible, in which book is he mentioned in verse 5:21, and how is his name spelled?

Answer: Methuselah / Genesis / M-E-T-H-U-S-E-L-A-H.

POTPOURRI

What is the most common name given to the pirate flag, what color is its field, and what are the 2 white symbols commonly featured on it?

Answer: Jolly Roger / black / skull and crossbones.

U.S. GEOGRAPHY
What are the capitals of Connecticut, Delaware, and Florida?
Answer: Hartford / Dover / Tallahassee.

HISTORY
At which village in which Southern state in which year did the Confederate Army surrender on April 9 to end the U.S. Civil War?
Answer: Appomattox Court House / Virginia / 1865 (fighting continued, however).

LITERATURE
Which words complete the following lines sung by Bill Bones in *Treasure Island*: "_____ men on the _____ man's chest / Yo-ho-ho and a bottle of _____"?
Answer: "Fifteen" / "dead" / "rum" ("Drink and the devil had done for the rest" / Yo-ho-ho, and a bottle of rum").

ENTERTAINMENT
What kind of animals are Bambi, Flower, and Thumper in the Disney film *Bambi*?
Answer: Deer (fawn) / skunk / rabbit.

SPORTS AND GAMES
In which 3 states are the thoroughbred horseraces of the Triple Crown held?
Answer: Kentucky / Maryland / New York.

SCIENCE AND NATURE
Which reptile is known as the "King of the Dinosaurs," during which age or era did the dinosaurs live, and which one had 3 sharp horns with which to defend itself?
Answer: Tyrannosaurus Rex / Mesozoic Era / triceratops.

WORLD GEOGRAPHY
Which river flows through the center of Paris, into which major body of water does it empty near Le Havre, and which French valley is noted for its elegant châteaux?
Answer: Seine River / English Channel / Loire Valley.

U.S. LEADERS & GOVERNMENT
John Quincy Adams and Andrew Jackson were the 6th and 7th U.S. Presidents. Arrange the following in the order of 8th through 10th: William H. Harrison, John Tyler, and Martin Van Buren.
Answer: Martin Van Buren / William H. Harrison / John Tyler.

MUSIC & RHYMES
In the song "Take Me Out to the Ball Game," which 2 purchases are requested, and which word completes, "Let me root, root, root for the _____ team"?
Answer: "some peanuts" / "Cracker Jacks" / "home."

LANGUAGE
Complete the following phrases: "Hitch your _____ to a star," "Laugh and the _____ laughs with you; weep, and you weep alone," and "The more the _____."
Answer: "wagon" / "world" / "merrier."

ARTS, RELIGION, & CULTURE
To which garden outside Jerusalem did Jesus go to pray, which apostle betrayed him there to the high priests, and with which act did he do so?
Answer: Garden of Gethsemane / Judas (Iscariot) / with a kiss.

POTPOURRI
Which ancient sign of good luck was adopted by Hitler as a Nazi emblem about 1920; and to prevent bad luck, what do superstitious people knock on and what do they avoid walking under?
Answer: Swastika / wood / a ladder.

U.S. GEOGRAPHY

What are the capitals of Georgia, Hawaii, and Idaho?

Answer: Atlanta / Honolulu / Boise.

HISTORY

Identify the U.S. Presidents in office at the end of World War I, World War II, and the Korean War.

Answer: Woodrow Wilson / Harry S Truman / Dwight D. Eisenhower.

LITERATURE

Identify Long John Silver's parrot in *Treasure Island*, give the phrase the parrot keeps repeating, and name the eccentric pirate who put the treasure in his own cave.

Answer: Captain Flint / "Pieces of eight, pieces of eight" / Ben Gunn.

ENTERTAINMENT

In the Disney film *Bambi*, with whom does Bambi fall in love, which animal is "very brave, and very wise," and from which catastrophe do these animals leap over a waterfall to safety?

Answer: (Little) Faline / Great Prince (the old stag, Bambi's father) / forest fire.

SPORTS AND GAMES

In American professional football, one or two points are awarded for a conversion after a touchdown. How many points are awarded for a touchdown, for a field goal, and for a safety?

Answer: 6 / 3 / 2.

SCIENCE AND NATURE

Which chemical elements are identified by their symbols B, C, and F?

Answer: Boron / carbon / fluorine.

WORLD GEOGRAPHY

What are the capitals of the Canadian provinces of Alberta, British Columbia, and Manitoba?

Answer: Edmonton / Victoria / Winnipeg.

LEADERS & GOVERNMENT

James K. Polk and Zachary Taylor were the 11th and 12th U.S. Presidents. Arrange the following in the order of 13th through 15th: Franklin Pierce, James Buchanan, and Millard Fillmore.

Answer: Millard Fillmore / Franklin Pierce / James Buchanan.

MUSIC & RHYMES

Complete the following lines to the "Star-Spangled Banner": "Oh! say, can you see, by the _____'s early light, / What so proudly we hailed at the _____'s last _____?"

Answer: "dawn" / "twilight" / "gleaming."

LANGUAGE

What are the Italian and Hawaiian words for "Hello" and "Goodbye," and which French word can be used upon greeting and departing for "Good Morning" or "Good Day"?

Answer: ***Ciao / Aloha / Bonjour.***

ARTS, RELIGION, & CULTURE

What title is given to the spiritual ruler of the Roman Catholic Church, which body of religious leaders elects him, and which officials of this church administer a district called a diocese?

Answer: Pope / College of Cardinals / Bishops.

POTPOURRI

What are the B, the L, and the T in a BLT sandwich?

Answer: Bacon / lettuce / tomato.

U.S. GEOGRAPHY

What are the capitals of Illinois, Indiana, and Iowa?

Answer: Springfield / Indianapolis / Des Moines.

HISTORY

Identify the U.S. capital, the motto the U.S. adopted on July 30, 1956, and this country's national anthem.

Answer: Washington, D.C. / In God We Trust / "The Star-Spangled Banner."

LITERATURE

Identify the deformed blind man in *Treasure Island* who comes to the inn, the pirates' death notice he brings, and the person to whom he gives it.

Answer: Blind Pew / the Black Spot / Billy Bones.

ENTERTAINMENT

Which word completes "Love Is a _____," the opening song of the Disney film *Bambi*; who is the new "Prince of the Forest"; and who brings danger and death to the forest?

Answer: "Song" / Bambi / "Man."

SPORTS AND GAMES

How many playing cards are there in a deck without the 2 jokers, what are the 2 red suits, and what are the 2 black suits?

Answer: 52 / hearts and diamonds / spades and clubs.

SCIENCE AND NATURE

Which chemical elements are identified by their symbols H, I, and N?

Answer: Hydrogen / iodine / nitrogen.

WORLD GEOGRAPHY

What are the capitals of the Canadian provinces of New Brunswick, Newfoundland, and Nova Scotia?

Answer: Fredericton / St. John's / Halifax.

LEADERS & GOVERNMENT

Abraham Lincoln and Andrew Johnson were the 16th and 17th U.S. Presidents. Arrange the following in the order of 18th through 20th: James A. Garfield, Rutherford B. Hayes, and Ulysses S. Grant.

Answer: Ulysses S. Grant / Rutherford B. Hayes / James A. Garfield.

MUSIC & RHYMES

Complete the following to the "Star-Spangled Banner": "Whose broad stripes and _____ stars, thro' the perilous fight, / O'er the _____ we watched, were so _____ streaming?"

Answer: "bright" / "ramparts" / "gallantly."

LANGUAGE

Complete the following sayings: "It's _____ over till it's over," "It's never too late to _____," and "It's put up or _____ up."

Answer: "never" ("ain't") / "mend" / "shut."

ARTS, RELIGION, & CULTURE

How many commandments are there, to whom did God give these commandments, and on which mountain did he do so?

Answer: 10 / Moses / Mount Sinai.

POTPOURRI

What is the nickname of the Loch Ness monster, in which division of Great Britain is Loch Ness, and what is a "loch"?

Answer: "Nessie" / Scotland / a lake.

U.S. GEOGRAPHY

What are the capitals of Kansas, Kentucky, and Louisiana?

Answer: Topeka / Frankfort / Baton Rouge.

HISTORY

Which American is credited with saying, "Go West, young man, go west," which one said, "Give me liberty or give me death," and which one wrote, "These are the times that try men's souls"?

Answer: Horace Greeley / Patrick Henry / Thomas Paine.

LITERATURE

Identify the legendary cup that Jesus Christ used at the Last Supper, King Arthur's knights who went searching for it, and the "noblest of these knights" who found it.

Answer: Holy Grail / Knights of the Round Table / Sir Galahad.

ENTERTAINMENT

Which Disney film features the song "Bibbidi Bobbidi Boo!"; which word completes "Salaga doola, / Menchicka _____"; and which charming old lady character sings these magical words?

Answer: ***Cinderella*** **/ "boola" / the Fairy Godmother.**

SPORTS AND GAMES

Which professional leagues are known by the initials NFL, NHL, and NBA?

Answer: National Football League / National Hockey League / National Basketball Association.

SCIENCE AND NATURE

Which chemical elements are identified by their symbols O, P, and S?

Answer: Oxygen / phosphorus / sulfur.

WORLD GEOGRAPHY

Quebec (City) is the capital of Quebec. What are the capitals of the Canadian provinces of Ontario, Prince Edward Island, and Saskatchewan?

Answer: Toronto / Charlottetown / Regina.

LEADERS & GOVERNMENT

Chester Arthur and Grover Cleveland were the 21st and 22nd Presidents. Arrange the following in the order of 23rd through 25th: William McKinley, Grover Cleveland (who served twice), and Benjamin Harrison.

Answer: Benjamin Harrison / Grover Cleveland / William McKinley.

MUSIC & RHYMES

Complete the following to the "Star-Spangled Banner": "And the _____'s red glare, the _____ bursting in _____."

Answer: "rocket" / "bombs" / "air."

LANGUAGE

According to the sayings, what is "the thief of time," with what is "the road to hell paved," and what "burns a hole in your pocket"?

Answer: Procrastination / good intentions / money.

ARTS, RELIGION, & CULTURE

Complete the Biblical commandments: "Thou shalt not take the name of the Lord thy God in _____," "Remember the _____ day, to keep it holy," and "Thou shalt not commit _____."

Answer: "vain" / "Sabbath" / "adultery."

POTPOURRI

In which U.S. state are the Luray Caverns, and what are the names for the icelike formations hanging from a cave's ceiling and those rising from the cave's floor?

Answer: Virginia / stalactites / stalagmites.

U.S. GEOGRAPHY

What are the capitals of Maine, Maryland, and Massachusetts?

Answer: Augusta / Annapolis / Boston.

HISTORY

On which great national holiday on which date does France celebrate the people's attack on a fortress used as a prison, and in which year did this attack occur?

Answer: Bastille Day / July 14 / 1789.

LITERATURE

Which medieval chieftain was the "King of the Round Table," what was the name of the sword he removed from a block of stone, and who was the magician and seer who helped him?

Answer: King Arthur / Excalibur / Merlin.

ENTERTAINMENT

Which kind of birds awaken Cinderella with their singing in the Disney film *Cinderella*, and what are the names of her 2 mean stepsisters?

Answer: Bluebirds / Anastasia / Drizella (daughters of Lady Tremaine).

SPORTS AND GAMES

Which major league player for which team hit 60 home runs in 1927, and what nickname was given to Frank Baker, who led the American League in home runs every year from 1911 to 1914?

Answer: Babe Ruth / New York Yankees / "Home Run."

SCIENCE AND NATURE

Which chemical elements are identified by their symbols K, W, and U?

Answer: Potassium / tungsten / uranium.

WORLD GEOGRAPHY

What are the capitals of Chile, El Salvador, and Luxembourg?

Answer: Santiago / San Salvador / Luxembourg.

LEADERS & GOVERNMENT

Theodore Roosevelt and William H. Taft were the 26th and 27th U.S. Presidents. Arrange the following in the order of 28th through 30th: Woodrow Wilson, Calvin Coolidge, and Warren G. Harding.

Answer: Woodrow Wilson / Warren G. Harding / Calvin Coolidge.

MUSIC & RHYMES

Complete the following to the "Star-Spangled Banner": "Gave _____ thro' the _____ that our _____ was still there."

Answer: "proof" / "night" / "flag."

LANGUAGE

Which words designate "eaters of any type of food," "eaters of flesh," and "eaters of grass or other plants"?

Answer: Omnivores / carnivores / herbivores.

ARTS, RELIGION, & CULTURE

Name the only 2 commandments which have just one word following the words "Thou shalt not," and complete the commandment, "Thou shalt not bear false _____ against thy neighbor."

Answer: "Thou shalt not kill" / "Thou shalt not steal" / "witness."

POTPOURRI

Which monument in which city bears the names of more than 58,000 Americans who died in a war, and how many servicemen are portrayed in the bronze sculpture that is part of this memorial?

Answer: Vietnam Veterans Memorial / Washington, D.C. / 3.

U.S. GEOGRAPHY

What are the capitals of Michigan, Minnesota, and Mississippi?

Answer: Lansing / St. Paul / Jackson.

HISTORY

Which Dutch colonial governor bought which island from the Indians in 1626, and about how much did he pay them for it?

Answer: Peter Minuit / Manhattan Island / about $24 (60 Dutch guilders).

LITERATURE

Which Greek slave is famous for his fables, which insect in one of his fables stored up food all summer, and which one in this same fable played all summer and had nothing to eat in winter?

Answer: Aesop / the ant / the grasshopper.

ENTERTAINMENT

What is the name of one of the 2 mice who star in the Disney film *Cinderella*, what is the name of the friendly dog, and what is the name of the stepmother's mean cat?

Answer: Jaq (or Jacques) or Gus (Octavian) / Bruno / Lucifer.

SPORTS AND GAMES

In which college sports are the Naismith Trophy, the Heisman Trophy, and the Hermann Trophy awarded annually?

Answer: Basketball / football / soccer.

SCIENCE AND NATURE

Which chemical elements are identified by their symbols Al, Ar, and As?

Answer: Aluminum / argon / arsenic.

WORLD GEOGRAPHY

What are the capitals of Taiwan, Colombia, and Costa Rica?

Answer: Taipei / Bogotá / San José.

LEADERS & GOVERNMENT

Herbert C. Hoover and Franklin D. Roosevelt were the 31st and 32nd U.S. Presidents. Arrange the following in the order of 33rd through 35th: John F. Kennedy, Harry S Truman, and Dwight D. Eisenhower.

Answer: Harry S Truman / Dwight D. Eisenhower / John F. Kennedy.

MUSIC & RHYMES

Complete the following to the "Star-Spangled Banner": "Oh! say, does that star-spangled banner yet _____ / O'er the land of the _____ and the home of the _____?"

Answer: "wave" / "free" / "brave."

LANGUAGE

Complete the following sayings: "Once bitten, twice _____," "The proof of the _____ is in the eating," and "Seeing is _____."

Answer: "shy" / "pudding" / "believing."

ARTS, RELIGION, & CULTURE

"Amen" is the last word of the Bible. Give its first 3 words and its first and last books.

Answer: "In the beginning" / Genesis / Revelation.

POTPOURRI

Give the meaning of DST regarding time, and complete the saying for remembering how to set the clocks for seasonal time changes: "_____ forward, _____ back."

Answer: Daylight-saving time / "Spring" / "fall."

U.S. GEOGRAPHY

What are the capitals of Missouri, Montana, and Nebraska?

Answer: Jefferson City / Helena / Lincoln.

HISTORY

Which American in which plane made the first solo nonstop flight across the Atlantic on May 20-21, 1927, and in which city did he land after leaving New York?

Answer: Charles A. Lindbergh / *The Spirit of St. Louis* / Paris.

LITERATURE

"Slow but sure wins the race" is the moral of an Aesop fable. Which 2 animals are involved in a race won by the slower one, and what does the faster one do that causes him to lose?

Answer: The hare / the tortoise / lies down and takes a nap.

ENTERTAINMENT

In the Disney film, after the Fairy Godmother changes a pumpkin into Cinderella's carriage, which animals become the 4 horses, which one becomes the coachman, and which one becomes the footman?

Answer: Mice / horse (Major) / dog (Bruno).

SPORTS AND GAMES

Identify 3 of the following 4 events in the decathlon: the 2 that include the word "jump" in their names and the 2 that include the word "throw."

Answer: Long jump / high jump / discus throw / javelin throw.

SCIENCE AND NATURE

Which chemical elements are identified by their symbols Cl, Cu, and He?

Answer: Chlorine / copper / helium.

WORLD GEOGRAPHY

What are the capitals of Bulgaria, Burma or Myanmar, and New Zealand?

Answer: Sofia / Rangoon (or Yangon) / Wellington.

LEADERS & GOVERNMENT

Lyndon B. Johnson and Richard M. Nixon were the 36th and 37th U.S. Presidents. Name the U.S. Presidents numbered 38 through 40.

Answer: Gerald R. Ford / James E. Carter Jr. / Ronald W. Reagan.

MUSIC & RHYMES

Which words complete the titles of songs by Stephen Collins Foster: "Old _____ at Home," "My Old _____ Home," and "_____ with the Light Brown Hair"?

Answer: "Folks" / "Kentucky" / "Jeanie."

LANGUAGE

How many lines are there in a limerick, in a sonnet, and in a Haiku?

Answer: 5 / 14 / 3.

ARTS, RELIGION, & CULTURE

What type of crown did the Roman soldiers put on Jesus' head at the Crucifixion, what did they force Him to carry like a common criminal, and on which hill was He crucified?

Answer: Crown of thorns / the cross / Calvary (or Golgotha).

POTPOURRI

Traditionally, if a boat is sinking, which 2 groups get in the lifeboats first, and who goes down with the ship?

Answer: Women / children / the captain.

U.S. GEOGRAPHY

What are the capitals of Nevada, New Hampshire, and New Jersey?

Answer: Carson City / Concord / Trenton.

HISTORY

What was the last major battle of the American Revolutionary War, in which state did it take place, and which British general surrendered to George Washington on October 19, 1781?

Answer: Yorktown / Virginia / Lord Cornwallis.

LITERATURE

In *Alice's Adventures in Wonderland*, who is usually screaming, "Off with her head!"; what is the name of the turtle who was once a real turtle; and which creature takes Alice to see him?

Answer: Queen of Hearts / Mock Turtle / Gryphon.

ENTERTAINMENT

At what time is the spell broken on Cinderella's evening at the ball, what does she lose on the steps as she leaves the ball, and which animals help her escape from her room by stealing the key in the Disney film?

Answer: Midnight / her glass slipper / the 2 mice.

SPORTS AND GAMES

For which college football team did the "Four Horsemen" play from 1922 to 1924, in which state is this school, and what is the nickname of its athletic teams?

Answer: Notre Dame / Indiana / "(Fighting) Irish."

SCIENCE AND NATURE

Which chemical elements are identified by their symbols Mg, Ne, and Ni?

Answer: Magnesium / neon / nickel.

WORLD GEOGRAPHY
What are the capitals of the Dominican Republic, Ecuador, and Egypt?
Answer: Santo Domingo / Quito / Cairo.

LEADERS & GOVERNMENT
Which U.S. Presidents are known as the "Father of His Country," the "Father of American Independence," and the "Father of the Declaration of Independence"?
Answer: George Washington / John Adams / Thomas Jefferson.

MUSIC & RHYMES
According to a popular song, which animal is "in the window," what kind of a tail does he have, and which 2 words begin the question about the cost of this animal?
Answer: Dog ("doggie") / "waggly" / "How much."

LANGUAGE
The names of which animals complete the sayings, "To take the _____ by the horns," "To flog a dead _____," and "To kill the _____ that lays the golden eggs"?
Answer: "bull" / "horse" / "goose."

ARTS, RELIGION, & CULTURE
According to Genesis, who were the first man and woman, and in which garden did they live?
Answer: Adam / Eve / Garden of Eden.

POTPOURRI
Identify the American frontiersman whose rifle was known as "(Old) Betsy," the one whose favorite rifle was named "Tick-Licker," and the knife known as a "Genuine Arkansas Toothpick."
Answer: Davy Crockett / Daniel Boone / Bowie knife.

U.S. GEOGRAPHY
What are the capitals of New Mexico, New York, and North Carolina?
Answer: Santa Fe / Albany / Raleigh.

HISTORY
Which Civil War leader was described as "standing like a stone wall," and which ones said: "Damn the torpedoes—full speed ahead!" and "The war is over—the rebels are our countrymen again"?
Answer: Thomas "Stonewall" Jackson / Admiral David G. Farragut / Ulysses S. Grant.

LITERATURE
How many nights are in the subtitle of *The Arabian Nights*, which boy finds a magic lamp in one of the stories, and whom does he summon to do his bidding?
Answer: 1,001 (*The Thousand and One Nights*) / Aladdin / genie (or jinni).

ENTERTAINMENT
What are the names of the husband and wife the cocker spaniel Lady lives with in the Disney film *Lady and the Tramp*, and when does she arrive at their home?
Answer: Jim Dear / Darling / Christmas Eve.

SPORTS AND GAMES
Which game, a forerunner of parchesi, has an inner, outer, and home table; which one features pawns and a queen; and which one offers Marvin Gardens and Boardwalk?
Answer: Backgammon / chess / Monopoly.

SCIENCE AND NATURE
Which chemical elements are identified by their symbols Ra, Si, and Zn?
Answer: Radium / silicon / zinc.

WORLD GEOGRAPHY

What are the legislative and the administrative capitals of South Africa, and what is the country's official language besides English?

Answer: Cape Town / Pretoria / Afrikaans.

LEADERS & GOVERNMENT

Which U.S. Presidents are known as "Long Tom," "Honest Abe," and "Old Grover"?

Answer: Thomas Jefferson / Abraham Lincoln / Grover Cleveland.

MUSIC & RHYMES

In the song about Casper, which kind of ghost is he, how do grownups "look at him," and which word completes the line, "The _____ all love him so"?

Answer: Friendly ghost / "with fright" / "children."

LANGUAGE

According to the sayings, how many "words is a picture worth," what "must go on," and what "heals all wounds"?

Answer: Thousand / The show / Time.

ARTS, RELIGION, & CULTURE

According to Genesis, who are the 3 children of the parents of the human race?

Answer: Cain / Abel / Seth.

POTPOURRI

Who is the commonly accepted personification of the U.S., what type of hat does he wear, and from which object is his red, white, and blue suit made?

Answer: Uncle Sam / top hat / American flag.

U.S. GEOGRAPHY

What are the capitals of North Dakota, Ohio, and Oklahoma?

Answer: Bismarck / Columbus / Oklahoma City.

HISTORY

In which year at which site in Massachusetts did the Pilgrims first establish their colony in the New World, and on which ship did they sail?

Answer: 1620 / Plymouth / *Mayflower*.

LITERATURE

In *The Arabian Nights*, which poor man finds the treasure of the thieves in a cave, what is his occupation, and how many thieves are there?

Answer: Ali Baba / woodcutter / 40.

ENTERTAINMENT

Name the Scottish terrier and the bloodhound who are Lady's friends in the Disney film *Lady and the Tramp*, and identify the mongrel who "never gets caught by the dogcatcher."

Answer: Jock (real name is Heather Lad o'Glencairn) / Trusty / Tramp.

SPORTS AND GAMES

Which NFL football quarterbacks are known as "Broadway Joe," "Roger the Dodger," and "The Scrambler"?

Answer: Joe Namath / Roger Staubach / Fran Tarkenton.

SCIENCE AND NATURE

Which chemical elements are identified by their symbols Au, Fe, and Pb?

Answer: Gold / iron / lead.

WORLD GEOGRAPHY

What are the capitals of Germany, Finland, and Greece?

Answer: Berlin / Helsinki / Athens.

LEADERS & GOVERNMENT

Which U.S. Presidents are known as "Little Ben," "Silent Cal," and "Give 'Em Hell Harry"?

Answer: Benjamin Harrison / Calvin Coolidge / Harry S Truman.

MUSIC & RHYMES

Which words complete these song lines: "Rubber _____, you're the one; / You make _____ time lots of fun," and "When I _____ you, you make noise"?

Answer: "Duckie" / "bath" / "squeeze."

LANGUAGE

The names of which body parts complete the sayings, "Hope springs eternal in the human _____," "Don't look a gift horse in the _____," and "To wear one's _____ on one's sleeve"?

Answer: "breast" / "mouth" / "heart."

ARTS, RELIGION, & CULTURE

What is the name for the Christian period of fasting and penitence from Ash Wednesday to Easter, how many days does it last, and what is the name of the week preceding Easter?

Answer: Lent / 40 days / Holy Week.

POTPOURRI

Which flags are known as "Old Glory," the "Stars and Bars," and the "Union Jack"?

Answer: The U.S. flag / the Confederate flag / Great Britain's flag.

U.S. GEOGRAPHY

What are the capitals of Oregon, Pennsylvania, and Rhode Island?

Answer: Salem / Harrisburg / Providence.

HISTORY

Which Americans said: "We must all hang together, or assuredly we shall all hang separately"; "I only regret that I have but one life to lose for my country"; and "We can afford both guns and butter"?

Answer: Benjamin Franklin / Nathan Hale / Lyndon Johnson.

LITERATURE

In *The Arabian Nights*, which words does Ali Baba use to open the cave door, which female servant discovers the thieves' hiding place, and what hot liquid does she pour on them?

Answer: "Open Sesame" / Morgiana / oil.

ENTERTAINMENT

What is the meaning of the word *bairn* in the Disney film *Lady and the Tramp*, which aunt comes to help take care of the *bairn*, and which animals does she bring with her?

Answer: "baby" / Aunt Sarah / Siamese cats (named Si and Am).

SPORTS AND GAMES

How many players are in the starting lineup on each team at the start of a match in professional ice hockey, in Olympic volleyball, and in rugby?

Answer: 6 / 6 / 13 (accept 15).

SCIENCE AND NATURE

Which chemical elements are identified by their symbols Hg, Ag, and Na?

Answer: Mercury / silver / sodium.

WORLD GEOGRAPHY

What are the capitals of Guatemala, Haiti, and Honduras?

Answer: Guatemala City / Port-au-Prince / Tegucigalpa.

LEADERS & GOVERNMENT

Which U.S. Presidents are known as "Ike," "Jack," and "Dutch"?

Answer: Dwight Eisenhower / John F. Kennedy / Ronald Reagan.

MUSIC & RHYMES

Complete the words to the song "Dixie": "I wish I was in the land of _____, / Old times there are not _____ / Look away, Look away, Look away Dixie _____."

Answer: "cotton" / "forgotten" / "Land."

LANGUAGE

Complete the following phrases: "_____ not, want not," "As the _____ flies," and "_____ said than done."

Answer: "Waste" / "Crow" / "Easier."

ARTS, RELIGION, & CULTURE

In which palace in which city does the Pope of the Roman Catholic Church live, and which city surrounds this city?

Answer: Vatican Palace / Vatican City / Rome.

POTPOURRI

Give the colloquial term for "persons who went to California in the 1849 gold rush," name the pro football team with this term as a nickname, and identify the carpenter who discovered gold at Sutter's Mill in 1848.

Answer: Forty-niners / San Francisco (49ers) / James W. Marshall.

U.S. GEOGRAPHY

What are the capitals of South Carolina, South Dakota, and Tennessee?

Answer: Columbia / Pierre / Nashville.

HISTORY

Which general is called the "George Washington of South America," what is the translation of his nickname *El Libertador*, and from which country did he help 5 countries gain their independence?

Answer: Simón Bolívar / "The Liberator" / Spain.

LITERATURE

Who is the Sultan's bride who tells the tales to save her life in *The Arabian Nights*, who is the sailor and adventurer, and how many voyages does he make?

Answer: Scheherazade / Sinbad / 7 voyages.

ENTERTAINMENT

What does the Aunt buy for Lady at the pet shop in the Disney film *Lady and the Tramp*, where does Tramp take Lady to get it removed, and which animal removes it?

Answer: A muzzle / the zoo / the beaver.

SPORTS AND GAMES

In the game of chess, which 2 pieces are moved in castling, which one of these 2 is always moved 2 spaces in castling, and what is the correct name for the horse?

Answer: King and rook (or the castle) / king / knight.

SCIENCE AND NATURE

Which chemical elements were named after Poland, California, and Europe?

Answer: Polonium / californium / europium.

WORLD GEOGRAPHY

What are the capitals of Hungary, Iceland, and Ireland?

Answer: Budapest / Reykjavik / Dublin.

LEADERS & GOVERNMENT

Which U.S. Presidents are known as "Tricky Dick," "Big Bill," and "Landslide Lyndon"?

Answer: Richard Nixon / William Taft / Lyndon Johnson.

MUSIC & RHYMES

Complete the words to the song "Dixie": "In Dixie Land Where I was _____ in, / Early on one _____ mornin' / Look away . . . / Away, Away, away down _____ in Dixie."

Answer: "born" / "frosty" / "South."

LANGUAGE

According to the sayings, what kind of tears does one shed when pretending to act sad, what kind of feet does one have when nervous about making an important decision, and what kind of pie does one eat when admitting an embarrassing mistake?

Answer: Crocodile tears / Cold feet / Humble pie.

ARTS, RELIGION, & CULTURE

Genesis and Deuteronomy are the first and fifth books of the Bible. Name the 2nd, 3rd, and 4th.

Answer: Exodus / Leviticus / Numbers.

POTPOURRI

Identify the 2 objects carried by the symbolic figure Father Time, and identify the mythological god of time.

Answer: Hourglass / scythe / Cronus (or Kronos).

U.S. GEOGRAPHY

What are the capitals of Texas, Utah, and Vermont?

Answer: Austin / Salt Lake City / Montpelier.

HISTORY

Which Roman leader was assassinated on the Ides of March, what is this date, and in which year did the assassination take place?

Answer: Julius Caesar / March 15 / 44 B.C.

LITERATURE

In which language was *The Arabian Nights* originally written, whom does its heroine Morgiana marry, and by which means of transportation are the characters magically transported?

Answer: Arabic / Ali Baba's son / magic carpet.

ENTERTAINMENT

What does Lady see sneaking into the house in the Disney film *Lady and the Tramp*, who kills this invader before it can attack the baby, and who comes to take away this hero afterwards?

Answer: A rat / Tramp / the dog catcher.

SPORTS AND GAMES

In which professional sports are the Super Bowl, the Masters at Augusta National, and the Stanley Cup played?

Answer: Football / golf / ice hockey.

SCIENCE AND NATURE

Which chemical elements were named after Albert Einstein, Alfred Nobel, and Marie Curie?

Answer: Einsteinium / nobelium / curium.

WORLD GEOGRAPHY

What are the capitals of Indonesia, Iran, and Iraq?

Answer: Jakarta / Teheran / Baghdad.

LEADERS & GOVERNMENT

Identify the U.S. Presidents whose initials are FDR, HST, and DDE.

Answer: Franklin D. Roosevelt / Harry S Truman / Dwight D. Eisenhower.

MUSIC & RHYMES

Which words complete the song lines: "Oh where, oh where has my little _____ gone? / . . . With his _____ cut short and his _____ cut long, / Oh where, oh where can he be"?

Answer: "dog" / "ears" / "tail" ("ears" and "tail" can be reversed).

LANGUAGE

Choose the correct form in the parentheses: "He (rose, raised) the window," "She (rang, rung) the bell," and "They (set, sat) the book on the table."

Answer: raised / rang / set.

ARTS, RELIGION, & CULTURE

Complete the following song lines: "Good _____ we bring to you and your _____; / We wish you a Merry _____ And a Happy New Year."

Answer: "tidings" / "kin" / "Christmas."

POTPOURRI

Give the traditional colors for each of the following: a quarantine flag, a "Go ahead" flag, and a flag indicating danger or stop.

Answer: Yellow / green / red.

U.S. GEOGRAPHY

What are the capitals of Washington, West Virginia, and Wisconsin?

Answer: Olympia / Charleston / Madison.

HISTORY

Which war was fought from 1939 to 1945, which country invaded Poland in 1939 to start the war, and who was the leader of the invading country?

Answer: World War II / Germany / Adolf Hitler.

LITERATURE

Which word completes the title of Maurice Sendak's *Where the _____ Things Are*, what is the name of the boy sent to his room without dinner, and which type of suit is he wearing?

Answer: *Wild* / Max / a wolf suit.

ENTERTAINMENT

Identify the following characters in Disney's 1994 film *The Lion King*: the king, the queen, and their son the prince who is presented to the other animals soon after he is born.

Answer: King Mufasa / Queen Sarabi / Prince Simba.

SPORTS AND GAMES

Name the 2 major leagues in American professional baseball, and give the name of the championship series played to determine the best team in both divisions.

Answer: American League / National League / World Series.

SCIENCE AND NATURE

Which element is contained in all organic compounds, which form of this element is the "lead" in pencils, and which amorphous form of it is produced by partially burning wood?

Answer: Carbon / graphite / charcoal (accept soot).

WORLD GEOGRAPHY

What are the capitals of Israel, Jamaica, and Jordan?

Answer: Jerusalem (most countries maintain their embassy in Tel Aviv) / Kingston / Amman.

LEADERS & GOVERNMENT

Which U.S. Presidents are known as JFK, LBJ, and RN?

Answer: John F. Kennedy / Lyndon B. Johnson / Richard M. Nixon.

MUSIC & RHYMES

Complete the words to the song lines: "O, Columbia! the _____ of the ocean, / The home of the _____ and the _____."

Answer: "gem" / "brave" / "free."

LANGUAGE

Complete the following sayings: "Beat around the _____," "Clean bill of _____," "Give the _____ his due."

Answer: "bush" / "health" / "devil."

ARTS, RELIGION, & CULTURE

Name the 3 gifts of the Three Wise Men.

Answer: Gold / frankincense / myrrh.

POTPOURRI

Of which country is Saint Patrick the patron saint, which animals did he allegedly charm into the sea so that they drowned, and on which day in March is his feast celebrated?

Answer: Ireland / snakes / 17th.

U.S. GEOGRAPHY
What are the capitals of Virginia and Wyoming, and which historic city between the James and York rivers served as Virginia's capital from 1776 to 1780?
Answer: Richmond / Cheyenne / Williamsburg.

HISTORY
Which war was fought from 1914 to 1918, which event involving Francis Ferdinand prompted Austria-Hungary to declare war, and who was the President when the U.S. entered the war in 1917?
Answer: World War I / his assassination / Woodrow Wilson.

LITERATURE
Complete the titles of these works by English authors: H.G. Wells' *The War of the* _____, Charles Dickens' *David* _____, and George Orwell's *Animal* _____.
Answer: *Worlds / Copperfield / Farm.*

ENTERTAINMENT
Identify the Oscar-winning song in the 1964 movie *Mary Poppins*, and give the professions of both Mary Poppins and Bert.
Answer: "Chim Chim Cheree" / nanny / chimney sweep (accept pavement artist).

SPORTS AND GAMES
Name 3 of the 4 railroads in the game of *Monopoly*.
Answer: Reading / B. & O. / Short Line / Pennsylvania.

SCIENCE AND NATURE
Give the medical names for both the "voice box" and the "windpipe," and give the more common name for *halitosis*.
Answer: Larynx / trachea / bad breath.

WORLD GEOGRAPHY

Identify the 3 objects on the flag of the former Soviet Union.

Answer: Hammer / sickle / star.

LEADERS & GOVERNMENT

Which U.S. Presidents are known as the "Sage of Mount Vernon," the "Sage of Montpelier," and the "Sage of the Hermitage"?

Answer: George Washington / James Madison / Andrew Jackson.

MUSIC & RHYMES

In the song "I'm Popeye the Sailor Man," what does Popeye say he eats, and which words complete the line "I'm one tough _____ / Which hates all _____"?

Answer: Spinach / "gazookus" / "palookas."

LANGUAGE

Which letter begins the most words in English, which one begins the fewest words, and which one is the least used?

Answer: S / X / Q.

ARTS, RELIGION, & CULTURE

Which words complete these song lines: "Mine eyes have seen the _____ of the coming of the _____; / He is trampling out the vintage where the _____ of wrath are stored"?

Answer: "glory" / "Lord" / "grapes" (from "The Battle Hymn of the Republic").

POTPOURRI

Which planets were named after the Roman gods of war, agriculture, and the sea?

Answer: Mars / Saturn / Neptune.

U.S. GEOGRAPHY

The postal abbreviation for Alabama is AL. What are the postal abbreviations for Alaska, Arizona, and Arkansas?

Answer: AK / AZ / AR.

HISTORY

In which month on which day in which year was an armistice signed to end World War I?

Answer: November / 11 / 1918.

LITERATURE

Complete the following lines from "Paul Revere's Ride": "Listen, my children, and you shall hear / Of the _____ ride of Paul Revere, / On the eighteenth of _____, in _____."

Answer: "midnight" / "April" / "seventy-five" (1775).

ENTERTAINMENT

In which city is the Disney film *Mary Poppins* set, for which family does Mary Poppins work, and what are the names of the 2 children?

Answer: London / (Mr. & Mrs. George) Banks family / Jane and Michael.

SPORTS AND GAMES

What are the names of the major league baseball teams in Baltimore, Boston, and Cleveland?

Answer: Orioles / Red Sox / Indians.

SCIENCE AND NATURE

Which name is used for most male deer, which one for most female deer, and which one for most young deer?

Answer: Buck / doe / fawn.

WORLD GEOGRAPHY
What are the capitals of Kenya, North Korea, and South Korea?
Answer: Nairobi / Pyongyang / Seoul.

LEADERS & GOVERNMENT
Which U.S. Presidents are known as the "Hero of Appomattox," the "Hero of New Orleans," and the "Hero of San Juan Hill"?
Answer: Ulysses S. Grant / Andrew Jackson / Theodore Roosevelt.

MUSIC & RHYMES
Which words complete these song lines: "Carry me back to old _____, / That's where the _____ and the _____ and 'tatoes grow"?
Answer: "Virginny" / "cotton" / "corn."

LANGUAGE
Give the plural form of each of the following: cupful, baby sitter, and father-in-law.
Answer: Cupfuls / baby sitters / fathers-in-law.

ARTS, RELIGION, & CULTURE
Which word completes the song lines: "Glory, Glory _____! . . . / His truth is marching on!," and which song's chorus written by which composer includes these words?
Answer: "Hallelujah" / "Battle Hymn of the Republic" / Julia Ward Howe.

POTPOURRI
In which state was the "Monkey Trial" held in 1925, whose theory of evolution was the basis for the case, and which high school teacher taught this theory?
Answer: Tennessee / Charles Darwin's / (John T.) Scopes.

U.S. GEOGRAPHY
What are the postal abbreviations for Connecticut, Hawaii, and Iowa?
Answer: CT / HI / IA.

HISTORY
In which year did the Great Depression begin; which nickname designates, Tuesday, October 29, the day the stock market crashed; and which President's policies relieved the situation?
Answer: 1929 / "Black Tuesday" / Franklin Roosevelt's.

LITERATURE
Complete the following titles: Cervantes' *Don* _____, Geoffrey Chaucer's *Canterbury* _____, and William Shakespeare's *Antony and* _____.
Answer: *Quixote* / *Tales* / *Cleopatra*.

ENTERTAINMENT
On which street does the family live in the film *Mary Poppins*, what does Admiral Boom shoot off to mark the time, and what happens to all the nannies in front of the house?
Answer: (17) Cherry Tree Lane / a cannon / a strong wind blows them away.

SPORTS AND GAMES
What are the names of the major league baseball teams in Detroit, Milwaukee, and Toronto?
Answer: Tigers / Brewers / Blue Jays.

SCIENCE AND NATURE
Name the 3 planets nearest the sun.
Answer: Mercury / Venus / Earth (listed in order from the sun).

WORLD GEOGRAPHY

What are the capitals of Lebanon, Liberia, and Libya?

Answer: Beirut / Monrovia / Tripoli.

LEADERS & GOVERNMENT

Which 20th-century U.S. Presidents are known as "Uncle Cornpone," "Mr. Clean," and the "Peanut Farmer"?

Answer: Lyndon Johnson / Gerald Ford (accept Ronald Reagan) / Jimmy Carter.

MUSIC & RHYMES

Which words complete the titles of the following songs by Irving Berlin: "God Bless _____," "There's No Business Like _____ Business," and "Easter _____"?

Answer: "America" / "Show" / "Parade."

LANGUAGE

Which word means "to arrange in alphabetical order," which 3 letters are often used to designate the basic facts or principles of a given subject, and which letters are used to designated an injection given directly into a vein or veins?

Answer: Alphabetize / ABC (as in *the ABC of*) / IV (for intravenous).

ARTS, RELIGION, & CULTURE

Which words complete these song lines from "The Battle Hymn of the Republic": "He hath loos'd the fateful _____ of His _____ swift _____"?

Answer: "lightning" / "terrible" / "sword."

POTPOURRI

Traditionally, what should the U.S. flag never touch, how is it flown as a signal of mourning, and what name is given to the persons who carry the flag in a parade?

Answer: The ground / at half-mast / color guard (accept colorbearer).

U.S. GEOGRAPHY

What are the postal abbreviations for Kansas, Kentucky, and Maine?

Answer: KS / KY / ME.

HISTORY

Which country did the Nazis control from 1933 to 1945, who was this country's leader, and 6 million of which group of people were killed by the Nazis during the destruction called the Holocaust?

Answer: Germany / Adolf Hitler / Jewish people.

LITERATURE

Which word completes the first line of an Edgar Allan Poe poem, "Once upon a _____ dreary," which bird is used as the poem's title, and what is the bird's one-word refrain?

Answer: "midnight" / a raven ("The Raven") / "Nevermore."

ENTERTAINMENT

Give the coined nonsense word used as the title of a song in the film *Mary Poppins*, spell this word, and complete Mary Poppins' saying, "Well begun is half _____."

Answer: Supercalifragilisticexpialidocious / S-U-P-E-R-C-A-L-I-F-R-A-G-I-L-I-S-T-I-C-E-X-P-I-A-L-I-D-O-C-I-O-U-S / "done."

SPORTS AND GAMES

What are the names of the major league baseball teams in Kansas City, Minnesota, and Oakland?

Answer: Royals / Twins / Athletics (or A's).

SCIENCE AND NATURE

Name the 4th, 5th, and 6th planets nearest the sun.

Answer: Mars / Jupiter / Saturn (listed in order from the sun).

WORLD GEOGRAPHY

What is the capital of The Netherlands (or Holland), what is its seat of government, and what is its official language?

Answer: Amsterdam / The Hague / Dutch.

LEADERS & GOVERNMENT

Which U.S. Presidents are known as the "Man of Independence," "That Wit in the White House," and the "Teflon President"?

Answer: Harry S Truman / John F. Kennedy / Ronald Reagan.

MUSIC & RHYMES

In the rhyme of "Little boy blue, come blow your horn," where are the sheep, where is the cow, and "where is the boy . . . fast asleep"?

Answer: "in the meadow" / "in the corn" / "under the haystack."

LANGUAGE

Give the 3 traditional principal parts of the verbs *lay*, *lie* (to tell a falsehood), and *lie* (to recline).

Answer: Lay, laid, laid / lie, lied, lied / lie, lay, lain.

ARTS, RELIGION, & CULTURE

Which words complete the song title, "Put a Little _____ in Your Heart" and its line, "It's getting late, oh, please don't _____," and what kind of hand do you lend "your fellow man"?

Answer: "Love" / "hesitate" / "a helping hand."

POTPOURRI

Which word was used as a title by the emperors of Rome from Augustus to Hadrian, and which German and Russian imperial titles are both derived from this word?

Answer: Caesar / kaiser / tsar (tzar or czar).

U.S. GEOGRAPHY

What are the postal abbreviations for Maryland, Massachusetts, and Montana?

Answer: MD / MA / MT.

HISTORY

In which country was the Berlin Wall erected in 1961, which 2 cities or zones were divided by this wall, and in which year did the wall fall?

Answer: East Germany (German Democratic Republic) / (Communist) East Berlin and (non-Communist) West Berlin / 1989.

LITERATURE

Name Peter Rabbit's 3 sisters.

Answer: Flopsy / Mopsy / Cottontail.

ENTERTAINMENT

Which animals serve as waiters to Mary and Bert in the teashop in the film *Mary Poppins*, on which type of horse does Mary win a horse race, and which word completes the film's song title "Spoonful of _____"?

Answer: Penguins / merry-go-round horse / "Sugar."

SPORTS AND GAMES

What are the names of the major league baseball teams in Seattle, Montreal, and Philadelphia?

Answer: Mariners / Expos / Phillies.

SCIENCE AND NATURE

Name the 7th, 8th, and 9th planets away from the sun.

Answer: Uranus / Neptune / Pluto (Pluto and Neptune sometimes change positions).

WORLD GEOGRAPHY

What are the capitals of Norway, Sweden, and Denmark?

Answer: Oslo / Stockholm / Copenhagen.

LEADERS & GOVERNMENT

Which U.S. Presidents are known as the "Sage of Monticello," the "Era of Good Feelings President," and the "Great Emancipator"?

Answer: Thomas Jefferson / James Monroe / Abraham Lincoln.

MUSIC & RHYMES

Complete the rhyme: "Pease-porridge _____, pease-porridge _____, / Pease-porridge in the pot, _____ days old."

Answer: "hot" / "cold" / "nine."

LANGUAGE

Give the compound words beginning with "moon" for: "to hold a second regular job after one's regular job," "illicitly distilled whiskey," and "mentally deranged" or "crazed."

Answer: Moonlight / moonshine / moonstruck.

ARTS, RELIGION, & CULTURE

Identify the character in *A Christmas Carol* whose name means today "a greedy, miserly person"; the character in the story who says, "God bless us, every one"; and the author of this story.

Answer: (Ebenezer) Scrooge / Tiny Tim / Charles Dickens.

POTPOURRI

Identify the machine that separates cotton fiber from the seed, the inventor of this machine, and the harmful beetle that damages cotton plants by laying its eggs inside the seed pods.

Answer: Cotton gin / Eli Whitney / boll weevil.

U.S. GEOGRAPHY

What are the postal abbreviations for Minnesota, Mississippi, and Missouri?

Answer: MN / MS / MO.

HISTORY

Complete the names of King Louis _____ and Queen Marie _____, the king and queen of France who were executed in 1793, and identify the means of execution.

Answer: Louis XVI / Marie Antoinette / guillotine (accept beheading).

LITERATURE

Who wrote *The Tale of Peter Rabbit*, into whose garden were the children told not to go, and into which food was Peter's father put by the wife of the garden's owner?

Answer: Beatrix Potter / Mr. McGregor's / pie.

ENTERTAINMENT

In which country is the Disney film *Bedknobs and Broomsticks* set, in which practice is Eglantine Price an amateur, and who are the rulers of the fantasy Isle of Naboombu?

Answer: England / witchcraft / animals (accept King Leonidas).

SPORTS AND GAMES

What are the names of the major league baseball teams in Pittsburgh, St. Louis, and Cincinnati?

Answer: Pirates / Cardinals / Reds.

SCIENCE AND NATURE

Which chemical elements were named after the 7th planet from the sun, after the Greek god of the sun, and after the Greek god of the dead and underworld?

Answer: Uranium / helium / plutonium.

WORLD GEOGRAPHY
What are the capitals of Panama, Paraguay, and Peru?
Answer: Panama (City) / Asunción / Lima.

LEADERS & GOVERNMENT
Which U.S. Presidents are known as the "Sage of Springfield," "Unconditional Surrender," and the "Rough Rider"?
Answer: Abraham Lincoln / Ulysses S. Grant / Theodore Roosevelt.

MUSIC & RHYMES
Complete the rhyme: "Ding dong bell, / Pussy's in the _____. / Who put her in? / Little Tommy _____." / Who pulled her out? / Little Johnny _____."
Answer: "well" / "Green" / "Stout."

LANGUAGE
Which 3 letters of the alphabet sound like words designating the following: an elevated railroad, an interrogative adverb, and one's former spouse?
Answer: L (for *el*, short for *elevated*) / Y (sounds the same as *why*) / Ex (pronounced as *X*).

ARTS, RELIGION, & CULTURE
Name Ebenezer Scrooge's late partner, and then name 2 of the 3 other ghosts who visit Scrooge on Christmas Eve in *A Christmas Carol*.
Answer: Jacob Marley / Ghost of Christmas Past / Ghost of Christmas Present / Ghost of Christmas Yet to Come (accept Future).

POTPOURRI
Which famous statue was designed by Frenchman Frédéric Auguste Bartholdi, which French engineer designed the steel skeletal framework for it, and what is this statue's official name?
Answer: Statue of Liberty / Gustave Eiffel / "Liberty Enlightening the World" (or in French, *La Liberté Eclairant le Monde*).

U.S. GEOGRAPHY

What are the postal abbreviations for Tennessee, Nevada, and Pennsylvania?

Answer: TN / NV / PA.

HISTORY

What is the meaning of the *V* in VE-Day and VJ-Day, and which countries surrendered on these days in 1945?

Answer: Victory / Germany / Japan.

LITERATURE

In Mark Twain's *The Adventures of Huckleberry Finn*, which family member locks Huck in a cabin, which runaway slave accompanies Huck on his raft, and down which river do they travel?

Answer: His father / Jim / Mississippi River.

ENTERTAINMENT

Identify the following concerning Disney's 1994 film *The Lion King*: the rock on which Prince Simba is presented to the other animals, the wise animal named Rafiki who presented him to the kingdom, and Prince Simba's uncle who killed Simba's father.

Answer: Pride Rock / baboon / Scar.

SPORTS AND GAMES

What are the names of the major league baseball teams located in Los Angeles, San Diego, and San Francisco?

Answer: Dodgers / Padres / Giants.

SCIENCE AND NATURE

Give the number of tentacles for an octopus, the number of arms for a squid, and the number of feet for a platypus.

Answer: 8 / 10 / 4.

WORLD GEOGRAPHY
What are the capitals of The Philippines, Poland, and Portugal?
Answer: Manila / Warsaw / Lisbon.

LEADERS & GOVERNMENT
Which U.S. Presidents are known as "Old Hickory," "Old Tippecanoe," and "Old Rough and Ready"?
Answer: Andrew Jackson / William Henry Harrison / Zachary Taylor.

MUSIC & RHYMES
Which words complete the lines from "America, the Beautiful": "O beautiful, for _____ skies, / For _____ waves of _____"?
Answer: "spacious" / "amber" / "grain."

LANGUAGE
According to the sayings, what "is broken" when something friendly is done to make shy people feel more comfortable in a social setting, what "is buried" when an agreement is made to end a quarrel or fight, and what bird must one "eat" when admitting wrong?
Answer: The ice / The hatchet / Crow.

ARTS, RELIGION, & CULTURE
Which names complete Clement Moore's "'Twas the Night Before Christmas": "Now, Dasher! / now Dancer! / now Prancer / and Vixen! / On Comet! / on ________! / on ________ / and ________!"
Answer: "Cupid" / "Donder" / "Blitzen."

POTPOURRI
Traditionally, how many years of bad luck does one face for breaking a mirror, what will happen if there is a ring around the moon, and which part of the body do people cross to ensure good luck?
Answer: 7 / it will rain (accept snow) / the fingers.

U.S. GEOGRAPHY

Identify 3 of the 4 states named after kings.

Answer: Georgia (George II) / Louisiana (Louis XIV) / North Carolina / South Carolina (both named for Charles I).

HISTORY

In which country were the Medici involved in politics in Florence, in which one was the Mogul Empire founded in 1526, and in which one were the *samurai* the hereditary warrior class?

Answer: Italy / India / Japan.

LITERATURE

Who wrote *The Adventures of Tom Sawyer*, who is Tom's aunt, and who is the young girl Tom loves?

Answer: Mark Twain (Samuel Langhorne Clemens) / Aunt Polly / Becky Thatcher.

ENTERTAINMENT

Which Disney film features the song "When I See an Elephant Fly," and which words complete the line, "I saw a front porch _____, heard a diamond _____"?

Answer: *Dumbo* / "swing" / "ring."

SPORTS AND GAMES

Identify 3 of the following 4: the names of the 2 major league baseball teams located in Chicago and the 2 located in New York.

Answer: White Sox / Cubs / Yankees / Mets.

SCIENCE AND NATURE

Name the 3 diseases against which a DPT shot will protect a child.

Answer: Diphtheria / pertussis (or whooping cough) / tetanus (lockjaw).

WORLD GEOGRAPHY

Identify the capitals of Morocco, Romania, and Senegal.

Answer: Rabat / Bucharest / Dakar.

LEADERS & GOVERNMENT

Which U.S. Presidents are known as the "Bachelor President," the "Railsplitter," and the "Father of the Constitution"?

Answer: James Buchanan / Abraham Lincoln / James Madison.

MUSIC & RHYMES

Which words complete the lines from "America, the Beautiful": "For _____ mountain _____, / Above the _____ plain"?

Answer: "purple" / "majesties" / "fruited."

LANGUAGE

Complete the following sayings: "To eat someone out of house and _____," "To make _____ meet," and "To steal someone's _____."

Answer: "home" / "ends" / "thunder."

ARTS, RELIGION, & CULTURE

Complete the lines from the Clement C. Moore poem: " 'Twas the night before Christmas, When all through the _____, / Not a creature was _____, not even a _____."

Answer: "house" / "stirring" / "mouse."

POTPOURRI

Traditionally, which type of clover brings good luck, where does one throw spilled salt to cancel bad luck, and how many cigarettes should not be lit on the same match?

Answer: 4-leaf clover / over the left shoulder / 3.

U.S. GEOGRAPHY

Name the 3 states named after queens.

Answer: Maryland (Henrietta Maria) / Virginia / West Virginia (both for Elizabeth I, the "Virgin Queen").

HISTORY

Which English leaders said: "I have nothing to offer but blood, toil, tears, and sweat"; "England expects that every man will do his duty"; and "We shall not flag or fail. We shall go on to the end"?

Answer: Winston Churchill / Lord Nelson / Winston Churchill.

LITERATURE

Which tropical birds serve as the mallets and which animals resembling porcupines serve as the balls in the croquet game in *Alice's Adventures in Wonderland*, and which characters serve as the arches or wickets?

Answer: Flamingoes / hedgehogs / soldiers (accept the cards).

ENTERTAINMENT

Complete the following lines sung in the Disney film *Dumbo*, "I saw a peanut _____, heard a rubber _____; / I saw a needle that winked its _____."

Answer: "stand" / "band" / "eye."

SPORTS AND GAMES

What are the names of the major league baseball teams in Arlington, Texas; Houston, Texas; and Anaheim, California?

Answer: (Texas) Rangers / (Houston) Astros / (Anaheim) Angels.

SCIENCE AND NATURE

Give both the Fahrenheit measure and its Celsius equivalent for normal body temperature in man, and give the term for what scientists consider the lowest possible temperature -273.15 degrees Celsius.

Answer: 98.6 degrees / 37 degrees / absolute zero.

WORLD GEOGRAPHY

What is the capital of Spain, what was its basic monetary unit before the Euro, and what is this country's major religion?

Answer: Madrid / peseta / Roman Catholicism.

LEADERS & GOVERNMENT

Which U.S. Presidents were married to Martha Dandridge Custis, Abigail Smith, and Dolley Payne Todd?

Answer: George Washington / John Adams / James Madison.

MUSIC & RHYMES

Which words complete the lines from "America, the Beautiful": "America! America! / God shed His _____ on thee / And crown thy good with _____ / From sea to _____ sea"?

Answer: "grace" / "brotherhood" / "shining."

LANGUAGE

According to the sayings, what kind of "water are you in" if you are in deep trouble, to which "land" do you go when you fall asleep, and what do you "turn over" when you change your behavior for the better?

Answer: Hot / (Land of) Nod / new leaf.

ARTS, RELIGION, & CULTURE

Complete the lines from the Clement C. Moore poem: "The _____ were hung by the _____ with care, / In hopes that St. _____ soon would be there."

Answer: "stockings" / "chimney" / "Nicholas" (from "'Twas the Night Before Christmas").

POTPOURRI

Traditionally, on a sidewalk what does a person avoid stepping on to prevent bad luck, which jumping insect in a house brings good luck to the owners, and which type of shoe if found brings good luck?

Answer: Cracks / cricket / horseshoe.

U.S. GEOGRAPHY

Identify 3 of the 4 states named for people other than kings and queens.

Answer: Delaware / New York / Pennsylvania / Washington (accept Hawaii).

HISTORY

In which country did the Gunpowder Plot fail to blow up the House of Commons in 1605, in which one did a revolution occur in 1917, and in which one was there a Civil War from 1936 to 1939?

Answer: England / Russia / Spain.

LITERATURE

Identify the cat that appears and disappears, leaving behind only a grin, the animal that smokes and sits on a mushroom, and Alice's cat in *Alice's Adventures in Wonderland.*

Answer: Cheshire cat / (blue) caterpillar / Dinah.

ENTERTAINMENT

Which Disney films feature the songs "Hi-Diddle-Dee-Dee" and "I'm Wishing," and which short film features the song "Who's Afraid of the Big Bad Wolf"?

Answer: *Pinocchio / Snow White and the Seven Dwarfs / The Three Little Pigs.*

SPORTS AND GAMES

What are the names of the NFL teams in Dallas, Philadelphia, and Arizona?

Answer: Cowboys / Eagles / Cardinals.

SCIENCE AND NATURE

How many pairs of chromosomes, how many bones, and how many permanent teeth are usually found in the human body?

Answer: 23 / 206 / 32.

WORLD GEOGRAPHY

What are the capitals of Switzerland, Syria, and Thailand?

Answer: Bern / Damascus / Bangkok.

LEADERS & GOVERNMENT

Which U.S. Presidents were married to Rachel Donelson Robards, Mary Todd, and Anna Eleanor Roosevelt?

Answer: Andrew Jackson / Abraham Lincoln / Franklin Roosevelt.

MUSIC & RHYMES

Which words complete the song lines: "A-tisket, a-_____ / A _____ and yellow _____ / . . . On the way I dropped it"?

Answer: "tasket" / "green" / "basket."

LANGUAGE

Which words beginning with the Greek *philo-* or *phil-* literally mean "loving music," "a person who loves mankind," and "a lover of wisdom"?

Answer: Philharmonic / philanthropist / philosopher.

ARTS, RELIGION, & CULTURE

Complete the lines from the Clement C. Moore poem: "The children were _____ all snug in their _____, / While visions of _____ danced through their heads."

Answer: "nestled" / "beds" / "sugar-plums" (from "'Twas the Night Before Christmas").

POTPOURRI

Traditionally, kissing which stone in which country brings that person the gift of flattery and convincing speech, and which birthstone brings good luck to those born in April?

Answer: Blarney Stone / Ireland / diamond.

U.S. GEOGRAPHY

Name 3 of the 4 states bordering Lake Michigan.

Answer: Michigan / Illinois / Wisconsin / Indiana.

HISTORY

In which country did the Bolsheviks lead the Revolution, who became head of the Soviet state in late 1917, and to which city was the capital moved in 1918?

Answer: Russia / V.I. Lenin / Moscow.

LITERATURE

Which animal does Alice follow down a hole in *Alice's Adventures in Wonderland*, what does he pull out of his waist-coat-pocket, and whom would this animal upset if he were late?

Answer: White Rabbit / watch / the Duchess.

ENTERTAINMENT

Which words complete the lines from Disney's *The Three Little Pigs*: "I play on my _____, / And dance all kinds of jigs" and "I'll _____ and I'll _____, and I'll blow your house in!"

Answer: "fiddle" / "huff" / "puff."

SPORTS AND GAMES

What are the names of the Washington, Chicago, and Detroit NFL teams?

Answer: Redskins / Bears / Lions.

SCIENCE AND NATURE

What is the world's tallest grass, and which bear-like animal from which country eats this grass as its favorite food?

Answer: Bamboo / panda / China.

WORLD GEOGRAPHY

What are the capitals of Tunisia, Turkey, and the United Kingdom?

Answer: Tunis / Ankara / London.

LEADERS & GOVERNMENT

Which U.S. Presidents were married to Elizabeth Virginia Wallace, Mamie Geneva Doud, and Thelma Catharine (Pat) Ryan?

Answer: Harry S Truman / Dwight D. Eisenhower / Richard M. Nixon.

MUSIC & RHYMES

In the rhyme, where did the old woman live who "had so many children she didn't know what to do," what did she give them "without any bread," and where did she put them after a sound whipping?

Answer: "in a shoe" / "some broth" / "She put them to bed."

LANGUAGE

Give the correct form of the pronoun "who" in the following: "_____ do you love the most?" "_____ do you think said so?" and "I told him _____ I felt made the best cake."

Answer: Whom / Who / who.

ARTS, RELIGION, & CULTURE

Complete Clement C. Moore's description of St. Nicholas: "He was dressed all in fur," "His cheeks were like _____, his nose like a _____," and "His eyes—how they _____."

Answer: "roses" / "cherry" / "twinkled" (from "'Twas the Night Before Christmas").

POTPOURRI

Which diviners claim they can find underground water, which ones claim they can predict events by reading the lines on a hand, and which deck of pictured cards is used to tell the future?

Answer: Dowsers / palmists / tarot cards.

U.S. GEOGRAPHY
Which U.S. national park includes the lowest point in the Western Hemisphere, and in which 2 states is this park located?
Answer: Death Valley National Park / California / Nevada.

HISTORY
In which state was the Battle of Gettysburg fought in 1863, which side won this battle, and what are the first 5 words of Lincoln's 1863 Gettysburg Address?
Answer: Pennsylvania / Union (North) / "Fourscore and seven years ago."

LITERATURE
Veruca (Salt) and Violet (Beauregarde) are 2 of the 5 children who are invited to visit the factory in Roald Dahl's *Charlie and the Chocolate Factory*. Give the first names of the 3 boys who accompany them.
Answer: Augustus (Gloop) / Mike (Teavee) / Charlie (Bucket).

ENTERTAINMENT
Name the princess who is *The Little Mermaid* in a Disney film; name her father, the god of the sea; and name the crab, who is the castle's music director.
Answer: Ariel / (King) Triton / Sebastian.

SPORTS AND GAMES
What are the names of the Minnesota, Green Bay, and Tampa Bay NFL teams?
Answer: Vikings / Packers / Buccaneers.

SCIENCE AND NATURE
How many degrees are in a circle, which instrument with 2 legs is used to draw a circle, and which Greek letter is used to represent the ratio of the circumference of a circle to its diameter?
Answer: 360 degrees / compass / *pi*.

WORLD GEOGRAPHY

What are the capitals of Northern Ireland, Scotland, and Wales?

Answer: Belfast / Edinburgh / Cardiff.

LEADERS & GOVERNMENT

Which U.S. Presidents were married to Lucy Ware Webb, Jacqueline Lee Bouvier, and Claudia Alta Taylor?

Answer: Rutherford B. Hayes / John F. Kennedy / Lyndon B. Johnson.

MUSIC & RHYMES

Which words complete these lines from the song "America": "My country! 'tis of thee, / _____ land of _____, / Of thee I _____"?

Answer: "Sweet" / "liberty" / "sing."

LANGUAGE

Give the positive, comparative, and superlative of the following: good, bad, and well.

Answer: Good, better, best / bad, worse, worst / well, better, best.

ARTS, RELIGION, & CULTURE

According to Biblical tradition, whom did Paul refer to as the "Beloved Physician," which country was known as the "Land of Bondage," and which place was known as the "Promised Land"?

Answer: Luke / Egypt / Canaan (Palestine).

POTPOURRI

What kind of "eye" supposedly harms people merely by looking at them, which name is given to a charm that supposedly can protect against this force, and what is the name for a male witch?

Answer: Evil eye / amulet (accept talisman) / warlock.

U.S. GEOGRAPHY

Name the 3 states besides Texas and Florida that border the Gulf of Mexico.

Answer: Louisiana / Mississippi / Alabama.

HISTORY

How many major civilizations developed in river valleys from about 3500 to 1100 B.C., in which one of them did the Sumerian civilization begin about 3500 B.C., and in which modern-day country is most of this area today?

Answer: 4 / Mesopotamia / Iraq.

LITERATURE

Complete the titles of these Dr. Seuss books: _____ *Hatches the Egg*; *Oh Say Can You* _____; and *Hunches in* _____.

Answer: *Horton / Say? / Bunches.*

ENTERTAINMENT

Identify the 3 chipmunks created by David Seville.

Answer: Alvin / Simon / Theodore.

SPORTS AND GAMES

What are the names of the NFL teams in St. Louis, Oakland, and Atlanta?

Answer: Rams / Raiders / Falcons.

SCIENCE AND NATURE

How many are in a baker's dozen, how many in a gross, and how many in a score?

Answer: 13 / 144 / 20.

WORLD GEOGRAPHY
What are the capitals of Nicaragua, Uruguay, and Venezuela?
Answer: Managua / Montevideo / Caracas.

LEADERS & GOVERNMENT
Which U.S. Presidents were married to Elizabeth Bloomer Warren, Rosalynn Smith, and Jane Wyman and Nancy Davis?
Answer: Gerald Ford / James E. Carter Jr. / Ronald W. Reagan.

MUSIC & RHYMES
Which words complete these lines from the song "America": "Land where my _____ died / Land of the _____s' pride, / From every mountain side, let freedom _____"?
Answer: "fathers" / "Pilgrim" / "ring!"

LANGUAGE
Complete the following sayings: "Can't hold a _____ to," "Like a _____ out of water," and "Out of the _____ pan into the fire."
Answer: "candle" / "fish" / "frying."

ARTS, RELIGION, & CULTURE
Complete the following song lines: "Joy to the world! The Lord is come: / Let earth receive her _____; / Let every _____ prepare him room, / And heav'n and nature _____."
Answer: "King" / "heart" / "sing."

POTPOURRI
Which U.S. President is said to be the White House Ghost, and what are the words for "a ghost responsible for mysterious disturbances" and "a person who supposedly can call a ghost back to earth"?
Answer: Abraham Lincoln / poltergeist / medium.

U.S. GEOGRAPHY

Name 3 of the 4 states that touch at the point known as the "Four Corners."

Answer: New Mexico / Arizona / Utah / Colorado.

HISTORY

Identify the countries in which the early civilizations of the Nile River, Indus River, and the Hwang Ho, or Yellow River, valleys began.

Answer: Egypt / India / China.

LITERATURE

Who wrote *Charlotte's Web*, and which kinds of animals are Charlotte and Wilbur in this work?

Answer: E.B. White / spider / pig.

ENTERTAINMENT

What song does Dorothy sing at the beginning of the film *The Wizard of Oz*, who comes to the house to complain about the dog, and out of which container does the dog jump to escape?

Answer: "Over the Rainbow" / Miss (Elmira) Gulch / a basket (on the back of a bicycle).

SPORTS AND GAMES

What are the names of the New Orleans, Carolina, and Cincinnati NFL teams?

Answer: Saints / Panthers / Bengals.

SCIENCE AND NATURE

Convert 220 minutes to hours and minutes, give the number of minutes in 3 quarters of an hour, and give the more common reading for 2240 military time.

Answer: 3 hours 40 minutes / 45 minutes / 10:40 p.m.

WORLD GEOGRAPHY
What are the capitals of Vietnam, Yugoslavia, and the Democratic Republic of the Congo?
Answer: Hanoi / Belgrade / Kinshasa.

LEADERS & GOVERNMENT
What are the middle names of U.S. Presidents Gerald R. Ford, James E. Carter Jr., and Ronald W. Reagan?
Answer: Rudolph / Earl / Wilson.

MUSIC & RHYMES
Complete the song: "Over hill, over _____, we have hit the dusty _____ / And those _____ go rolling along. / In and out hear them shout: 'Counter march! And right about.'"
Answer: "dale" / "trail" / "caissons."

LANGUAGE
According to the sayings, which "hour" is the latest possible time at which something can be accomplished, what do you put "in your cap" when you have made a great accomplishment, and where is "there a tempest" when a great commotion is made over a minor problem?
Answer: Eleventh / feather / teapot.

ARTS, RELIGION, & CULTURE
Which head and which body does the mythological Sphinx have, and in which country is there a huge limestone statue of this monster near Giza?
Answer: Head of a man (accept woman) / body of a lion / Egypt.

POTPOURRI
Proverbially, what is the moon supposed to be made of, who has been imprisoned there for stealing or for breaking the Sabbath, and who was the Roman goddess of the moon and the hunt?
Answer: Green cheese / man in the moon / Diana.

U.S. GEOGRAPHY

Name 3 of the 4 time zones of the contiguous 48 states.

Answer: Eastern Time / Central Time / Mountain Time / Pacific Time.

HISTORY

Arrange the Bronze Age, the Iron Age, and the Stone Age in chronological order.

Answer: Stone Age / Bronze Age / Iron Age.

LITERATURE

Name the author who became the first Englishman to receive the Nobel Prize for literature, and complete the titles of his *Just So* _____ and *The Jungle* _____.

Answer: Rudyard Kipling / *Stories* / *Book(s)*.

ENTERTAINMENT

What does the Professor consult at the start of the film *The Wizard of Oz*, where does everyone on the farm hide when the twister arrives, and where is Dorothy when she is knocked unconscious?

Answer: Crystal ball / in the storm cellar / in the house (bedroom).

SPORTS AND GAMES

What are the names of the Tennessee, Cleveland, and Pittsburgh NFL teams?

Answer: Titans / Browns / Steelers.

SCIENCE AND NATURE

What is the branch of science that deals with living organisms and the life processes of plants and animals, and what are the branches dealing with plant life and animal life?

Answer: Biology / botany / zoology.

WORLD GEOGRAPHY

Identify the 2 independent countries of South America whose names begin with the letter *B* and the one whose name begins with the letter *A*.

Answer: Bolivia / Brazil / Argentina.

LEADERS & GOVERNMENT

What are the middle names of U.S. Presidents John F. Kennedy, Lyndon B. Johnson, and Richard M. Nixon?

Answer: Fitzgerald / Baines / Milhous.

MUSIC & RHYMES

Which words complete the titles of works by American composer George Gershwin: *Rhapsody in* _____, "I Got _____," and *Strike Up the* _____?

Answer: *Blue* / "Rhythm" / *Band*.

LANGUAGE

Alpha is the first letter of the Greek alphabet and epsilon is the 5th. Give the 2nd, 3rd, and 4th letters of this alphabet.

Answer: Beta / gamma / delta.

ARTS, RELIGION, & CULTURE

On which day of the week was Jesus Christ crucified, what name do Christians give to this day in memory of His suffering, and how many were present at the Last Supper?

Answer: Friday / Good Friday / 13.

POTPOURRI

Which color symbolizes evil and wickedness; in mythology from whose box did all the evils of the world escape; and in which country did the Gestapo, the secret police, commit atrocities?

Answer: Black / Pandora's / Germany.

U.S. GEOGRAPHY

Name the 3 largest New England states in area.

Answer: Maine / Vermont / New Hampshire (listed from largest to smallest).

HISTORY

Give the title of the later kings of ancient Egypt, name the triangular structures in which they were buried, and give the word for "a dead body preserved by embalming."

Answer: Pharaohs / pyramids / mummy.

LITERATURE

In which city does the Wizard live in *The Wonderful Wizard of Oz*, what color are the bricks which pave the road to this city, and what color glasses does the Wizard require all to wear in the city?

Answer: Emerald City (or City of Emeralds) / yellow / green.

ENTERTAINMENT

In which land and on whom does Dorothy's house land in the film *The Wizard of Oz*, and which witch then appears to Dorothy?

Answer: Munchkinland (or Land of Oz) / Wicked Witch (of the East) / Glinda (the Good Witch of the North).

SPORTS AND GAMES

What are the names of the NFL teams in Buffalo, Indianapolis, and Miami?

Answer: Bills / Colts / Dolphins.

SCIENCE AND NATURE

Which animal is known as the "King of the Jungle," which one is the "Ship of the Desert," and which one is the "Poor Man's Cow"?

Answer: Lion / camel / goat.

WORLD GEOGRAPHY

Identify the 2 independent countries of South America whose names begin with the letter *C* and the one whose name begins with the letter *E*.

Answer: Chile / Colombia / Ecuador.

LEADERS & GOVERNMENT

What are the middle names of U.S. Presidents Franklin D. Roosevelt, Harry S Truman, and Dwight D. Eisenhower?

Answer: Delano / the S does not stand for a particular name / David.

MUSIC & RHYMES

In the song about the Big Bad Wolf, which words complete the pig's words, "Not by the _____ of my _____-chin-chin," and how did the wolf enter the brick house before he was killed?

Answer: "hair" / "chinny" / chimney.

LANGUAGE

According to the sayings, what "are you on" if you are very angry and ready to act, what part of your body "is out of joint" if you are offended by someone else, especially that person's success, and what "are you sitting on" if you are refusing to take sides in an argument?

Answer: Warpath / nose / fence.

ARTS, RELIGION, & CULTURE

Complete the following song lines: "Deck the hall(s) with _____ of holly, / Tis the season to be _____, / Don we now our gay _____, / Troll the ancient yuletide carol."

Answer: "boughs" / "jolly" / "apparel."

POTPOURRI

Give the French word for the peace pipe smoked by North American Indians, the Spanish word for Indian corn, and the Indian word for small beads used as money.

Answer: Calumet / maize / wampum.

U.S. GEOGRAPHY

Name the 3 smallest New England states in area.

Answer: Rhode Island / Connecticut / Massachusetts (listed from smallest to largest).

HISTORY

Which eastern Mediterranean people left their alphabet to the Western world, what name identifies the Sumerian wedge-shaped writing system, and what name is given to the "sacred carving" picture symbols of ancient Egypt?

Answer: Phoenicians / cuneiform / hieroglyphics.

LITERATURE

From which areas do the Good Witches come in *The Wonderful Wizard of Oz*, from which areas do the Wicked Witches come, and what is the name of the Great Wizard?

Answer: North and South / East and West / Oz.

ENTERTAINMENT

What color slippers is the dead Witch wearing when she dies in the film *The Wizard of Oz*, which tree throws fruit at the scarecrow and Dorothy, and which field puts Dorothy to sleep?

Answer: Ruby (or red) / apple tree / poppy field.

SPORTS AND GAMES

What are the names of the 2 NFL teams whose names start with New York and the one whose name starts with New England?

Answer: Jets / Giants / Patriots.

SCIENCE AND NATURE

Through which tubes in the body does blood flow from the heart, through which ones does it return, and what is the name for the minute blood vessels that connect the two?

Answer: Arteries / veins / capillaries.

WORLD GEOGRAPHY
Identify the 2 independent countries of South America whose names begin with the letter *P* and the one whose name begins with the letter *G*.
Answer: Paraguay / Peru / Guyana.

LEADERS & GOVERNMENT
How many consecutive times may a person be elected President of the U.S., how often are the elections held for the Presidency, and what is the maximum number of years a President may serve?
Answer: 2 times / every 4 years / 10 years.

MUSIC & RHYMES
Which words complete the rhyme: "Pussy-cat, pussy-cat, where have you been? / I've been to _____ to visit the _____ / . . . I frightened a little _____ under her chair"?
Answer: "London" / "queen" / "mouse."

LANGUAGE
Identify the correct answer from the choices in parentheses: "He has (already, all ready) eaten," "The family was (altogether, all together) at lunch," and "The dog ate (its, it's) bone."
Answer: already / all together / its.

ARTS, RELIGION, & CULTURE
In the song, who is "the most famous reindeer of all," what would you say about his "very shiny nose . . . if you ever saw it," and what would the other reindeer not let this "poor" reindeer do?
Answer: Rudolph, the Red-Nosed Reindeer / "you would even say it glows" / "join in any reindeer games."

POTPOURRI
Which word designates "a corpse that becomes reanimated and leaves its grave to suck the blood of sleeping persons at night," and which type of water and what object driven through its heart can kill it?
Answer: Vampire / holy water / wooden stake.

U.S. GEOGRAPHY

Identify Alaska's largest city by population; its largest one by area; and its "Golden Heart City," the second most populous and the terminus of the Alaska Highway.

Answer: Anchorage / Juneau / Fairbanks.

HISTORY

Identify the 2 towns near Boston which on April 19 were the sites of the battles that touched off the American Revolutionary War, and give the year of these battles.

Answer: Lexington / Concord / 1775.

LITERATURE

Identify Dorothy's little black dog and the aunt and uncle with whom she lives in *The Wonderful Wizard of Oz*.

Answer: Toto / Aunt Em / Uncle Henry.

ENTERTAINMENT

Which phrase designates the horse in the film *The Wizard of Oz*, in which forest is Dorothy captured, and what substance does Dorothy throw on the Wicked Witch of the West to melt her?

Answer: Horse of a Different Color / Haunted Forest / water.

SPORTS AND GAMES

What are the names of the NFL teams in Denver, Kansas City, and Seattle?

Answer: Broncos / Chiefs / Seahawks.

SCIENCE AND NATURE

What are the names for animals with and without a backbone, and of what does the spinal column of a shark consist?

Answer: Vertebrates / invertebrates / cartilage.

WORLD GEOGRAPHY
Identify the independent countries of South America whose names begin with the letters *S*, *U*, and *V*.
Answer: Suriname / Uruguay / Venezuela.

LEADERS & GOVERNMENT
Of which cities did Tom Bradley, Harold Washington, and Coleman Young become the first black mayors?
Answer: Los Angeles / Chicago / Detroit.

MUSIC & RHYMES
Which words complete these lines from the rhyme: "There was a crooked _____, and he walked a crooked _____, / He found a crooked _____ against a crooked stile"?
Answer: "man" / "mile" / "sixpence."

LANGUAGE
Identify the crimes named from the Latin for "to burn"; and "to fabricate," as in to sign someone else's name; and from the French for "to imitate," as in to copy money.
Answer: Arson / forgery / counterfeiting.

ARTS, RELIGION, & CULTURE
Which words complete these song lines: "All things bright and _____, / All creatures great and _____, / All things wise and _____; / The Lord God made them all"?
Answer: "beautiful" / "small" / "wonderful."

POTPOURRI
Which plant of the lily family do vampires by legend hate, which Christian symbol with the figure of Christ do vampires fear, and which TV character with the epithet "The Vampire Slayer" does Sarah Michelle Gellar play?
Answer: Garlic / crucifix / Buffy.

U.S. GEOGRAPHY
Identify the 2 state capitals named after the same explorer, and identify the only state named after a U.S. President.
Answer: Columbus (Ohio) / Columbia (South Carolina) / Washington.

HISTORY
What was the first major battle of the American Revolutionary War on June 17, 1775, in which city did it occur, and which New York battle of October 7, 1777, was the turning point of the war?
Answer: Bunker Hill (or Breed's Hill) / Boston / Saratoga (or Freeman's Farm).

LITERATURE
Name the first 3 novels in the Harry Potter series created by British author J.K. Rowling about a bespectacled orphaned student wizard.
Answer: *Harry Potter and the Sorcerer's Stone* (or *Harry Potter and the Philosopher's Stone*) / *Harry Potter and the Chamber of Secrets* / *Harry Potter and the Prisoner of Azkaban*.

ENTERTAINMENT
In which 1939 film did "Over the Rainbow" win the Academy Award for Best Song, what flies "over the rainbow," and which word completes the song line "Why then, oh why can't _____"?
Answer: *The Wizard of Oz* / birds (accept bluebirds) / "I."

SPORTS AND GAMES
In which cities are the Rose Bowl, Sugar Bowl, and Orange Bowl football games played?
Answer: Pasadena / New Orleans / Miami.

SCIENCE AND NATURE
Give the more common names for nitrous oxide, solid carbon dioxide, and sodium chloride.
Answer: Laughing gas / dry ice / table salt.

WORLD GEOGRAPHY
Identify the independent countries of Central America whose names begin with the letters *C*, *E*, and *G*.
Answer: Costa Rica / El Salvador / Guatemala.

LEADERS & GOVERNMENT
Which of John Kennedy's brothers became a senator from Massachusetts, which one served as Attorney General, and which state did the latter also represent as a U.S. senator?
Answer: Edward Kennedy / Robert Kennedy / New York.

MUSIC & RHYMES
Which words complete these lines from the song: "There was a _____ who had a _____, / And _____ was his name-o"?
Answer: "farmer" / "dog" / "Bingo."

LANGUAGE
Identify the correct answer from the choices in parentheses: "What is your (principal, principle) goal?" "Do you know (who's, whose) going?" and "He has (fewer, less) books than they."
Answer: principal / who's / fewer.

ARTS, RELIGION, & CULTURE
Complete the following song lines: "Silent night! Holy night! / All is _____, all is bright / Round yon _____ Mother and Child, / Holy _____ so tender and mild."
Answer: "calm" / "Virgin" / "Infant" ("Sleep in heavenly peace").

POTPOURRI
In which Caribbean country was voodoo started, on which day of the year did witches in ancient times allegedly assemble to worship the devil, and in which U.S. state were witches hunted at Salem?
Answer: Haiti / October 31 / Massachusetts.

U.S. GEOGRAPHY

Identify the states in which the ski resorts of Jackson Hole, Sun Valley, and Squaw Valley are located.

Answer: Wyoming / Idaho / California.

HISTORY

Which American said in 1944, "I have returned"; which country's forces did he defeat in the Pacific during WWII; and which President removed him from his U.N. command in 1951?

Answer: General Douglas MacArthur / Japan's / President Truman.

LITERATURE

What did the Scarecrow, the Tin Woodman, and the Cowardly Lion want from the Wizard in *The Wonderful Wizard of Oz*?

Answer: Brains / heart / courage.

ENTERTAINMENT

What does Dorothy take back to the Wizard in the film *The Wizard of Oz*, who unveils the Wizard behind his curtain, and how does the Wizard plan to take Dorothy back to her home?

Answer: The Witch's broom / Dorothy's dog (Toto) / in a balloon.

SPORTS AND GAMES

In which cities are the Fiesta Bowl, Cotton Bowl, and Gator Bowl football games played?

Answer: Tempe / Dallas / Jacksonville.

SCIENCE AND NATURE

Give the words for "the vast Russian grasslands," "the vast, nearly treeless plains of the arctic regions," and "the coniferous evergreen forests of subarctic regions."

Answer: Steppe / tundra / taiga.

WORLD GEOGRAPHY

Identify the independent countries of Central America whose names begin with the letters *H*, *N*, and *P*.

Answer: Honduras / Nicaragua / Panama.

LEADERS & GOVERNMENT

Who were the Vice Presidents under Dwight D. Eisenhower, John F. Kennedy, and Lyndon B. Johnson?

Answer: Richard Nixon / Lyndon Johnson / Hubert Humphrey.

MUSIC & RHYMES

Complete the rhyme: "March _____ and April _____ / Bring forth May _____."

Answer: "winds" / "showers" / "flowers."

LANGUAGE

Give the first person singular, 3rd person singular, and first person plural forms of the present tense of the verb "to be."

Answer: I am / he (she, it) is / we are.

ARTS, RELIGION, & CULTURE

Give the art terms for "painting with water colors on wet plaster," "a picture drawn with colored chalk sticks," and "an opaque, water-base paint often used for posters."

Answer: Fresco / pastel / tempera.

POTPOURRI

Which street in which city is the main financial center in the U.S., and in which year in the 1920s did the stock market suffer the "Great Crash"?

Answer: Wall Street / New York / 1929 (also called the "Wall Street Crash").

U.S. GEOGRAPHY

Name the 2 states separated by a river that begins in British Columbia and flows into the Pacific Ocean, name this river, and then name the largest river that rises in the Rocky Mountains and flows into the Gulf of Mexico.

Answer: Washington and Oregon / Columbia River / Colorado River.

HISTORY

Which explorer is credited with the discovery of the North Pole on April 6, 1909, what is his nationality, and which black, his chief assistant, reached it with him?

Answer: Robert Edwin Peary / American / Matthew Henson.

LITERATURE

Who said and in which book by which author after clapping the heels of her shoes together, "Take me home to Aunt Em!"

Answer: Dorothy / *The Wonderful Wizard of Oz* / L. Frank Baum.

ENTERTAINMENT

In the film *The Wizard of Oz*, which words complete, "Then close your eyes and tap your _____ together _____ times. And think to yourself 'There's no place like _____' "?

Answer: "heels" / "three" / "home" (said by the Good Witch to Dorothy).

SPORTS AND GAMES

In which cities are the Alamo Bowl, Peach Bowl, and Citrus Bowl football games played?

Answer: San Antonio / Atlanta / Orlando.

SCIENCE AND NATURE

Which parts of the skeletal system are called the sternum, the clavicle, and the scapula?

Answer: Breastbone / collarbone / shoulder blade.

WORLD GEOGRAPHY

In which country is Imhotep's Step Pyramid, in which country did the Etruscans build the Temple of Jupiter, and in which South American country did the Mochica Indians build The Temple of the Sun?

Answer: Egypt / Italy / Peru.

LEADERS & GOVERNMENT

Who defeated Richard Nixon in a presidential election, and who were Nixon's 2 Vice Presidents once he took office?

Answer: John F. Kennedy / Spiro Agnew / Gerald Ford.

MUSIC & RHYMES

Complete the rhyme: "Jack and Jill went up the _____ / To fetch a pail of _____; / Jack fell down and broke his _____, / And Jill came tumbling after."

Answer: "hill" / "water" / "crown."

LANGUAGE

Choose the correct form in the parentheses: "They should have (rang, rung) the doorbell," "He (swam, swum) the English Channel," and "We should have (knew, known) the answer."

Answer: "rung" / "swam" / "known."

ARTS, RELIGION, & CULTURE

Give the art terms for "the coarse cloth on which an oil painting is made," "the tripod that holds an artist's painting," and "the thin board on which an artist mixes his paints."

Answer: Canvas / easel / palette.

POTPOURRI

Which mythical animal has a single horn in the middle of its head, which animal does it most resemble, and from which animal does its tail come?

Answer: Unicorn / horse / lion.

U.S. GEOGRAPHY
In which city is the "Golden Triangle" located near the confluence of 3 rivers, and which 2 rivers join there to form the Ohio River?
Answer: Pittsburgh / Monongahela / Allegheny.

HISTORY
Which explorer is credited with the discovery of the South Pole on December 14, 1911, what is his nationality, and which country's expedition did he beat there by 5 weeks?
Answer: Roald Amundsen / Norwegian / British (led by Robert Scott).

LITERATURE
Identify Dorothy's home state in *The Wonderful Wizard of Oz*, the type of storm that carries her away, and the name of the "queerest people she had ever seen" who greet her after she lands and call her a sorceress.
Answer: Kansas / a cyclone (accept tornado) / Munchkins.

ENTERTAINMENT
In the 1939 film *The Wizard of Oz*, which word completes the message up in the sky, "_____ Dorothy," who writes these words, and with what does she do so?
Answer: "Surrender" / The Wicked Witch of the West / her broom.

SPORTS AND GAMES
What are the names of the Boston, New Jersey, and New York NBA teams?
Answer: Celtics / Nets / Knicks.

SCIENCE AND NATURE
How many sides does a pentagon have, which polygon has the fewest possible number of sides, and how many sides does a dodecagon have?
Answer: 5 / triangle / 12.

WORLD GEOGRAPHY

The largest of the 3 Pyramids at Giza was built for King Khufu. What is the Greek name for Khufu, what common name is given to his pyramid, and which sage, the first Greek historian, wrote about its construction more than 2,000 years after it was completed?

Answer: Cheops / The Great Pyramid / Herodotus.

LEADERS & GOVERNMENT

Who served as Vice Presidents to Gerald Ford, James E. Carter, and Ronald Reagan?

Answer: Nelson Rockefeller / Walter Mondale / George Bush.

MUSIC & RHYMES

Complete the rhyme: "I do not like thee, Doctor Fell, / The _____ why I cannot _____; / But this I know, and know full _____, / I do not like thee, Doctor Fell."

Answer: "reason" / "tell" / "well."

LANGUAGE

Choose the correct form in the parentheses: "We have (ate, eaten) a good meal," "They have (saw, seen) no one," and "They have (wrote, written) a nice letter."

Answer: "eaten" / "seen" / "written."

ARTS, RELIGION, & CULTURE

Who painted the ceiling of the Sistine Chapel, which Frenchman is noted for his paintings of ballet dancers, and which Dutch painter is known for cutting off part of his ear?

Answer: Michelangelo / Edgar Degas / Vincent van Gogh.

POTPOURRI

Which mythical marine creature was half woman and half fish; which one was half man and half fish; and which mythological sea nymph, half woman and half bird, enticed seamen to their deaths?

Answer: Mermaid / Merman / Siren.

U.S. GEOGRAPHY
On which river near which capital city is Three Mile Island, and in which state is this nuclear facility, site of a 1979 accident?
Answer: Susquehanna River / Harrisburg / Pennsylvania.

HISTORY
Which canal across New York to the Hudson River was completed in 1825, which Central American canal linking 2 oceans was completed in 1914, and which Egyptian canal was completed in 1869?
Answer: Erie Canal / Panama Canal / Suez Canal.

LITERATURE
Which "Bear of Very Little Brain" was created by A.A. Milne, what is the real name of this teddy bear, and who is the human friend of this bear?
Answer: Winnie-The-Pooh / Edward Bear / Christopher Robin (the author's son).

ENTERTAINMENT
Complete this song title from *The Wizard of Oz*, "Ding-_____! The _____ is Dead," and complete the line, "She's not merely dead, she's really most _____ dead."
Answer: "Dong" / "Witch" / "sincerely."

SPORTS AND GAMES
What are the names of the Philadelphia, Washington, and Atlanta NBA teams?
Answer: 76ers / Wizards / Hawks.

SCIENCE AND NATURE
To which heavenly bodies do *solar* and *lunar* refer, and which heavenly body is identified by the prefix *aster*-?
Answer: Sun / moon / star.

WORLD GEOGRAPHY

In which European cities do Neapolitans, Muscovites, and Glaswegians live?

Answer: Naples / Moscow / Glasgow.

LEADERS & GOVERNMENT

Which U.S. Presidents are known as "Father Abraham," "Teddy," and "Jerry"?

Answer: Abraham Lincoln / Theodore Roosevelt / Gerald R. Ford.

MUSIC & RHYMES

Match the musicals *Fiddler on the Roof*, *Hello, Dolly!*, and *My Fair Lady* with these songs: "The Rain in Spain," "Matchmaker, Matchmaker," and "It Takes a Woman."

Answer: ***My Fair Lady / Fiddler on the Roof / Hello, Dolly!***

LANGUAGE

Choose the correct form in the parentheses: "The tree should have (fell, fallen)," "She should have (went, gone) to the show," and "I should have (did, done) my homework."

Answer: fallen / gone / done.

ARTS, RELIGION, & CULTURE

Give the nationalities of artists Andy Warhol, Henri Matisse, and Francisco Goya.

Answer: American / French / Spanish.

POTPOURRI

Name the oldest university in the U.S., the state in which it is located, and the century it which it was founded.

Answer: Harvard / Massachusetts / 17th century (in 1636).

U.S. GEOGRAPHY
In which state is the Grand Canyon, which river flows through this canyon, and whose expedition in 1540 was the first to see it?
Answer: Arizona / Colorado River / Francisco Coronado's (accept Lopez de Cardenas, who was part of this expedition).

HISTORY
Excluding the *Enterprise* (a trainer) and *Challenger* (which blew up), name 3 of the other 4 U.S. space shuttles.
Answer: *Columbia* / *Discovery* / *Atlantis* / *Endeavour*.

LITERATURE
Which doctor who talks to the animals was created by Hugh Lofting, and in which town in which country does this doctor live?
Answer: Dr. John Dolittle / Puddleby-on-the-Marsh / England.

ENTERTAINMENT
According to the "Ballad of Davy Crockett," which Indians did Davy fight till they "was whipped," where did he go off to "serve a spell," and which bell's crack did he patch up?
Answer: Creek "Injuns" / Congress / Liberty Bell's.

SPORTS AND GAMES
What are the names of the National Basketball Association teams in Chicago, Cleveland, and Detroit?
Answer: Bulls / Cavaliers / Pistons.

SCIENCE AND NATURE
Which heavenly bodies derive their name from the Greek word meaning "wanderers," and what are the scientific names for "shooting stars" and "minor planets"?
Answer: Planets / meteors / asteroids.

WORLD GEOGRAPHY

In which U.S. state is Mount Washington, the world's windiest spot, and on which continents are the Atacama Desert, the world's driest spot, and Libya, site of the hottest recorded temperature?

Answer: New Hampshire / South America (Chile) / Africa.

LEADERS & GOVERNMENT

Which U.S. Presidents are known as "The Big Chief," "The Chief," and "The Great Communicator"?

Answer: William H. Taft / Herbert Hoover / Ronald Reagan.

MUSIC & RHYMES

Complete the rhyme: "The King of France went up the hill / With _____ thousand men; / The King of France came down the hill, / And _____ went up _____."

Answer: "forty" / "ne'er" (never) / "again."

LANGUAGE

Choose the correct form in the parentheses: "They should have (come, came) to the party," "We should have (run, ran) harder," and "You should have (taken, took) the money."

Answer: come / run / taken.

ARTS, RELIGION, & CULTURE

Complete the following song lines: "God rest ye merry _____, / Let nothing you _____, / For Jesus Christ our _____ / Was born upon this day, / To save us all from Satan's power."

Answer: "gentlemen" / "dismay" / "Savior" ("When we were gone astray").

POTPOURRI

In which state is Princeton University, what is the nickname of the school's athletic teams, and which U.S. President was this school's president?

Answer: New Jersey / "Tigers" / Woodrow Wilson.

U.S. GEOGRAPHY

Name the 3 states whose names have just 4 letters.

Answer: Iowa / Ohio / Utah.

HISTORY

Which 2 countries fought the famous 16th-century battle involving one country's *Invincible Armada* against a much smaller fleet of ships, and in which year was the battle fought?

Answer: Spain / England / 1588.

LITERATURE

Identify the 3 characters Alice joins at the table at the Mad Tea-Party in *Alice's Adventures in Wonderland*.

Answer: The March Hare / the Mad Hatter / a sleepy Dormouse.

ENTERTAINMENT

Complete these lines from the "Ballad of Davy Crockett": "Born on a mountaintop in _____, / _____ state in the Land of the Free," and "kilt him a b'ar when he was only _____."

Answer: "Tennessee" / "Greenest" / "3."

SPORTS AND GAMES

What are the names of the National Basketball Association teams in Indiana, Milwaukee, and Dallas?

Answer: Pacers / Bucks / Mavericks.

SCIENCE AND NATURE

What is another name for the *centigrade scale*, and what are the freezing and boiling points of water on this scale?

Answer: Celsius scale / 0 degrees for freezing / 100 for boiling.

WORLD GEOGRAPHY
Identify the 3 independent European countries whose names begin with the letter *I*.
Answer: Iceland / Ireland / Italy.

LEADERS & GOVERNMENT
Which U.S. Presidents are known as the "Cowboy President," the "Eagle Scout President," and the "Movie Star President"?
Answer: Theodore Roosevelt / Gerald Ford / Ronald Reagan.

MUSIC & RHYMES
Complete the rhyme: "Jack be _____, / Jack be _____, / Jack jump over / The _____."
Answer: "nimble" / "quick" / "candlestick."

LANGUAGE
Choose the correct form in the parentheses: "He spent the weekend (laying, lying) in bed," "He (lay, laid) down on the couch," and "I (did, done) my chores."
Answer: lying / lay / did.

ARTS, RELIGION, & CULTURE
Complete the following song lines: "The first _____ the angel did say. / Was to certain poor _____ in fields as they lay; / In fields where they lay keeping their _____."
Answer: "Noël" / "shepherds" / "sheep" ("On a cold winter's night that was so deep . . . Born is the king of Israel").

POTPOURRI
Which President founded the University of Virginia in 1819, in which city is this university located, and what is the nickname for the school's athletic teams?
Answer: Thomas Jefferson / Charlottesville / "Cavaliers" (accept "Wahoos").

U.S. GEOGRAPHY

On the boundary of which 2 states is the highest peak in the Great Smoky Mountains, and what is this peak's name?

Answer: Tennessee / North Carolina / Clingmans Dome.

HISTORY

Which brothers on which hill succeeded in making the first flight in a heavier-than-air craft on December 17, 1903, and in which state at Kitty Hawk did this flight occur?

Answer: Orville and Wilbur Wright / Kill Devil Hill / North Carolina.

LITERATURE

Which word completes Wilson Rawls' title *Where the ____ Fern Grows*, which animals are hunted by Billy Coleman's dogs, and over which graves does the fern grow?

Answer: *Red* / coons (raccoons) / the graves of his dogs (or the grave of the Indian children).

ENTERTAINMENT

Name the fish that is Ariel's best friend in the Disney film *The Little Mermaid*, the sea gull who tries to impress her with his false knowledge of humans, and the handsome prince she later rescues during a storm.

Answer: Flounder / Scuttle / Prince Eric.

SPORTS AND GAMES

What are the names of the National Basketball Association teams in Denver, Houston, and Sacramento?

Answer: Nuggets / Rockets / Kings.

SCIENCE AND NATURE

Which instrument measures temperature, and what are the freezing and boiling points of pure water on the Fahrenheit scale?

Answer: Thermometer / 32° / 212°.

WORLD GEOGRAPHY

Name 3 of the 4 South American countries bordering the Pacific Ocean.

Answer: Colombia / Ecuador / Peru / Chile.

LEADERS & GOVERNMENT

Which U.S. Presidents were the tallest, the shortest, and the heaviest?

Answer: Abraham Lincoln / James Madison / William H. Taft.

MUSIC & RHYMES

Which words complete these lines from a song: "Old _____ had a farm, / _____, / And on his farm he had a _____ / With a moo-moo here and a moo-moo there"?

Answer: "MacDonald" / "E-I-E-I-O" / "cow."

LANGUAGE

Complete each of the following sayings: "Absence makes the heart grow _____," "Actions speak louder than _____," and "Accidents will _____ in the best regulated families."

Answer: "fonder" / "words" / "happen."

ARTS, RELIGION, & CULTURE

What are the nationalities of artists Salvador Dali, Michelangelo, and Norman Rockwell?

Answer: Spanish / Italian / American.

POTPOURRI

Identify the U.S. Presidents whose portraits are on the 1-cent, 5-cent, and 10-cent coins.

Answer: Abraham Lincoln / Thomas Jefferson / Franklin Roosevelt.

U.S. GEOGRAPHY

In which states are the Buffalo Bill Historical Center in the town of Cody, the Henry Ford Museum in the town of Dearborn, and the Mystic Seaport Museum in the town of Mystic?

Answer: Wyoming / Michigan / Connecticut.

HISTORY

Who was the first English child born in America, on which island in North Carolina did her parents settle in 1587, and of which "colony" that disappeared were they a part?

Answer: Virginia Dare / Roanoke Island / "Lost Colony."

LITERATURE

Which 4 words begin most fairy tale stories, which 7 words end most of them, and which opening line is repeatedly used by Snoopy in *Peanuts* when he tries to write a story?

Answer: "Once upon a time" / "And they all lived happily ever after" / "It was a dark and stormy night."

ENTERTAINMENT

What color are the Smurfs, where do they live, and how big is a Smurf?

Answer: Blue / in mushrooms (or toadstools) / 3 apples high.

SPORTS AND GAMES

What are the names of the San Antonio, Portland, and Utah NBA teams?

Answer: Spurs / Trail Blazers / Jazz.

SCIENCE AND NATURE

Which colorless, odorless, and tasteless gas is exhaled by human beings, which similar but poisonous gas is produced by automobile engines, and what are the chemical formulas of both gases?

Answer: Carbon dioxide / carbon monoxide / CO_2 and CO.

WORLD GEOGRAPHY

What is the name of the world's largest bay, in the northern part of which ocean is it, and which country borders this bay to the west?

Answer: Bay of Bengal / Indian Ocean / India (accept Sri Lanka).

LEADERS & GOVERNMENT

Identify the only court specifically created by the U.S. Constitution, give the minimum age for justices on this court, and give the term of office these justices serve.

Answer: Supreme Court / there is none / life.

MUSIC & RHYMES

Complete the rhyme: "Hickory, dickory, _____, / The mouse ran up the clock. / The clock struck _____, / The mouse ran down, / Hickory, dickory, _____."

Answer: "dock" / "one" / "dock."

LANGUAGE

Complete each of the following proverbs: "All _____ lead to Rome," "When in Rome, do as the _____ do," and "Rome was not built in a _____."

Answer: "roads" / "Romans" / "day."

ARTS, RELIGION, & CULTURE

Who are the artists of the *Mona Lisa*, *Starry Night*, and *American Gothic*?

Answer: Leonardo da Vinci / Vincent van Gogh / Grant Wood.

POTPOURRI

Identify the U.S. Presidents whose portraits are on the $1, $2, and $5 bills.

Answer: George Washington / Thomas Jefferson / Abraham Lincoln.

U.S. GEOGRAPHY

Which cities split by the Mississippi River are known as the "Twin Cities," and in which state are they located?

Answer: Minneapolis / St. Paul / Minnesota.

HISTORY

In which century was the telephone invented, who invented it, and which assistant's name completes the first sentence ever heard over the telephone, "Mr. _____, come here. I want you!"

Answer: 19th century (1876) / Alexander Graham Bell / "Watson."

LITERATURE

What is the nationality of the boys in William Golding's *Lord of the Flies*, in which type of accident are they involved, and where are they stranded?

Answer: British / plane crash / on a deserted island.

ENTERTAINMENT

Which animal completes the nickname of the Warner Brothers' cartoon character "The Fastest _____ in all of Mexico," what is his name, and in which city does he live?

Answer: "Mouse" / Speedy Gonzales / Guadalajara.

SPORTS AND GAMES

What are the names of the 2 National Basketball Association teams in the Greater Los Angeles area, and what is the name of the team called Golden State?

Answer: Clippers / Lakers / Warriors.

SCIENCE AND NATURE

Name the 2 largest planets, and then identify the smallest planet.

Answer: Jupiter / Saturn / Pluto.

WORLD GEOGRAPHY

San Marino, Slovakia, and Slovenia are 3 of the 6 independent European countries whose names begin with the letter *S*. Name the other 3.

Answer: Spain / Sweden / Switzerland.

LEADERS & GOVERNMENT

Give the date of the 50th anniversary of the Declaration of Independence, and identify the 2 U.S. Presidents who died that day.

Answer: July 4, 1826 / John Adams / Thomas Jefferson.

MUSIC & RHYMES

Which words complete: "I'm a little _____, short and stout. / Here is my _____; here is my _____. / When I get all steamed up, then I shout, / 'Tip me over and pour me out'"?

Answer: "teapot" / "handle" / "spout."

LANGUAGE

Complete each of the following: "As you make your bed so you must _____ in it," "(Life is not always) a bed of _____," and "_____ makes strange bedfellows."

Answer: "lie" / "roses" / "adversity" (accept "politics").

ARTS, RELIGION, & CULTURE

Complete the following lines: "Good King _____ looked out / On the Feast of _____, / When the _____ lay round about, / Deep, and crisp, and even; / Brightly shone the moon that night."

Answer: "Wenceslas" / "Stephen" / "snow."

POTPOURRI

Identify the famous Americans whose portraits are on the $10, $20, and $50 bills.

Answer: Alexander Hamilton / Andrew Jackson / Ulysses S. Grant.

U.S. GEOGRAPHY

Which very populous cities are nicknamed "The Big Apple," "The City of Angels," and "The Windy City"?

Answer: New York / Los Angeles / Chicago.

HISTORY

Which war involving the U.S. began in 1957 and ended in 1975, which country did the U.S. support, and what was the name of the Communist-trained rebels in the south?

Answer: Vietnam War / South Vietnam / Viet Cong.

LITERATURE

Complete Lewis Carroll's lines: "Of shoes—and ships—and _____ wax— / Of _____—and kings— / And why the sea is boiling hot— / And whether _____ have wings."

Answer: "sealing" / "cabbages" / "pigs."

ENTERTAINMENT

Which large Warner Brothers' cartoon bird is known for saying, "Beep! Beep!"; what is the name of the desert scavenger who tries to catch him; and which company's devices does this scavenger use?

Answer: Road Runner / Wile E. Coyote / Acme's.

SPORTS AND GAMES

Give the name for the 50-yard line, the 2 rows of lines that parallel the sidelines, and the area 10 yards beyond each goal line on an American football field.

Answer: Midfield / hash marks / end zone.

SCIENCE AND NATURE

Name the thigh bone, the kneecap, and the large bone, or shinbone, of the lower leg.

Answer: Femur / patella / tibia.

WORLD GEOGRAPHY

Which ancient monument is located on the Salisbury Plain in Wiltshire, in which country is Wiltshire, and in which country is Carnac, site of another famous group of megaliths?

Answer: Stonehenge / England / France.

LEADERS & GOVERNMENT

Identify the U.S. President who allegedly threw a silver dollar across the Rappahannock, the one whose wife used the White House's East Room for hanging laundry, and the red-haired one who was known as the "Red Fox."

Answer: George Washington / John Adams / Thomas Jefferson.

MUSIC & RHYMES

Complete the song: "Daisy, Daisy, . . . / I'm half crazy / . . . It won't be a stylish _____ / I can't afford a _____ / But you'll look sweet up on a seat of a _____ built for two."

Answer: "marriage" / "carriage" / "bicycle."

LANGUAGE

Complete each of the following: "His _____ is worse than his bite," "He has a _____ in his bonnet," and "He has a screw _____."

Answer: "bark" / "bee" / "loose" (accept "missing").

ARTS, RELIGION, & CULTURE

Which artists painted *The Blue Boy* and *The Gleaners*, and which one is well known for incorporating Campbell Soup cans into his paintings?

Answer: Thomas Gainsborough / Jean François Millet / Andy Warhol.

POTPOURRI

Give the name for the following U.S. coins: 1-cent, 5-cent, and 10-cent.

Answer: Penny / nickel / dime.

U.S. GEOGRAPHY

Which river is "The Father of Waters," which one is "The Big Muddy," and which New York river did the Indians call Shatemuc, meaning "the river that flows two ways"?

Answer: Mississippi River / Missouri River / Hudson River.

HISTORY

Which country is considered to be the birthplace of Western civilization, which of its cities had the most advanced democracy, and who led this country during its Golden Age, 461-430 B.C.?

Answer: Greece / Athens / Pericles.

LITERATURE

Which 3 words complete the following lines in a Mary Howitt poem: "'Will you walk into my parlor?' said the _____ to the _____; / ''Tis the prettiest little parlor that ever you did _______'"?

Answer: Spider / Fly / spy.

ENTERTAINMENT

Which cartoon rabbit is known for his, "Eh . . . what's up, Doc?"; what is his favorite food; and which pig is known for his, "Th-Th-That's all, folks" at the end of *Looney Tunes* cartoons?

Answer: Bugs Bunny / carrots / Porky Pig.

SPORTS AND GAMES

Give the nicknames of the athletic teams at Louisville, Memphis State, and the University of Nevada at Las Vegas.

Answer: Cardinals / Tigers / Rebels (or Running Rebels).

SCIENCE AND NATURE

Which laboratory equipment was named after Robert Bunsen, which rays were discovered by Wilhelm Roentgen in 1895, and which machine that detects radiation was named after Hans Geiger?

Answer: Bunsen burner / X rays (accept Roentgen rays) / Geiger counter.

WORLD GEOGRAPHY
Identify the old fortress in the Russian capital of Moscow that was the center of the Soviet government from 1918 to 1991, the square on which it is located, and the founder of the Communist Party whose preserved body is there in a mausoleum.
Answer: Kremlin / Red Square / V.I. Lenin.

LEADERS & GOVERNMENT
What is the name for the introduction to the U.S. Constitution, and how many articles and how many amendments does this document contain?
Answer: Preamble / 7 / 27.

MUSIC & RHYMES
In the song "Do-Re-Mi" from *The Sound of Music*, what kind of a deer is the "Doe," what kind of a drop of sun is the "Ray," and which word completes, "Me, a name I call _____"?
Answer: "a female deer" / "a drop of golden sun" / "myself."

LANGUAGE
Complete each of the following: "Beauty is only _____ deep," "Beauty is in the _____ of the beholder," and "The best things in life are _____."
Answer: "skin" / "eye" / "free."

ARTS, RELIGION, & CULTURE
Name the 3 primary colors of paints or pigments.
Answer: Red / yellow / blue.

POTPOURRI
Name the U.S. 25-cent piece and the 50-cent piece, and identify one of the Presidents portrayed on them.
Answer: Quarter / half-dollar / George Washington or John Kennedy.

U.S. GEOGRAPHY

Which states are nicknamed the "Evergreen State," the "Mountain State," and "America's Dairyland"?

Answer: Washington / West Virginia / Wisconsin.

HISTORY

On which island in which sea did the first major civilization in the region of Greece arise about 2500 B.C., and what name was given to this culture?

Answer: Crete / Mediterranean Sea (accept Aegean Sea in this historical context) / Minoan culture (after King Minos).

LITERATURE

In the poem "The Owl and the Pussycat," what do these animals dine on besides "slices of quince," with which type of spoon do they eat it, and by the light of which object do they dance?

Answer: "mince" / "runcible spoon" / "light of the moon."

ENTERTAINMENT

What kind of cartoon animal with a Southern accent is known for saying, "Listen to me, Son!," what is his name, and what is his favorite song?

Answer: Rooster / Foghorn Leghorn / "Camptown Races."

SPORTS AND GAMES

Which colleges are known by the initials UCLA, LSU, and UNLV?

Answer: University of California at Los Angeles / Louisiana State University / University of Nevada at Las Vegas.

SCIENCE AND NATURE

Into which artery does the body's blood flow from the right ventricle, into which respiratory organs does it then flow, and into which artery does it flow after leaving the left atrium and the left ventricle?

Answer: Pulmonary artery / lungs / aorta.

WORLD GEOGRAPHY

Name the only Communist country in which the U.S. has a naval base, one leased in 1903 for $2,000 a year; name the base; and identify the country in which Subic Bay Naval Base was once located.

Answer: Cuba / Guantánamo Bay Naval Base / Philippines.

LEADERS & GOVERNMENT

What are the first 3 words of the U.S. Constitution, which part of this document describes the fundamental liberties of the people of the U.S., and how many amendments are in this part?

Answer: "We, the people" / Bill of Rights / 10.

MUSIC & RHYMES

In the rhyme of the 3 kittens, which words complete: "Oh, mother dear, we sadly _____ / That we have lost our _____," and what does their mother say they shall not then have?

Answer: "fear" / "mittens" / "Then you shall have no pie."

LANGUAGE

Complete each of the following: "The bigger they come (are), the _____ they fall," "When the going gets tough, the _____ get going," and "No pain, no _____."

Answer: "harder" / "tough" / "gain."

ARTS, RELIGION, & CULTURE

Complete Martin Luther's "Cradle Hymn": "Away in a _____, / No _____ for a bed, / The little Lord Jesus / Laid down his sweet _____."

Answer: "manger" / "crib" / "head."

POTPOURRI

Which animals are measured in hands, which items are measured in carats, and what unit of measure originally designated the area a yoke of oxen could plow in a single day?

Answer: Horses / precious stones (or gems) / acre.

U.S. GEOGRAPHY

Which states are nicknamed the "Lone Star State," the "Beehive State," and the "Green Mountain State"?

Answer: Texas / Utah / Vermont.

HISTORY

What is the Spanish word for "conqueror," and which Indian people in which country did Hernando Cortes conquer in 1519-1521?

Answer: *Conquistador* / Aztecs / Mexico.

LITERATURE

Complete these lines from *The Song of Hiawatha*: "By the shores of Gitche _____, / By the Shining Big-Sea-_____, / Stood the _____ of Nokomis."

Answer: "Gumee" / "Water" / "wigwam" (by Henry Wadsworth Longfellow).

ENTERTAINMENT

What is the name of the cartoon animal with a French accent, what kind of animal is he, and which word completes his song, "Toujours, _____, toujours"?

Answer: Pepe LePew / skunk / "l'amour" ("Always, love!").

SPORTS AND GAMES

Which Alexander organized baseball in 1845, which Abner is often erroneously credited with inventing this game, and in which state was the first organized baseball game played in Hoboken in 1846?

Answer: Alexander Cartwright / Abner Doubleday / New Jersey.

SCIENCE AND NATURE

What are the 2 charges possible in an electric current, and what are the meanings of the initials AC and DC in the field of electricity?

Answer: Positive and negative / alternating current / direct current.

WORLD GEOGRAPHY

Identify the arch in Paris begun by Napoleon to commemorate his military victories, the number of avenues that radiate from it, and the commemorative symbol surmounting the tomb of the unknown soldier beneath this arch.

Answer: ***Arc de Triomphe*** **(Arch of Triumph) / 12 / perpetual flame.**

LEADERS & GOVERNMENT

Which representative legislative body met for the first time in America on July 30, 1619, and in which town in which present-day state did it convene?

Answer: **House of Burgesses / Jamestown / Virginia.**

MUSIC & RHYMES

What was the nationality of the popular group the Beatles, in which decade did they become famous, and which word completes their album title *Sgt. _____'s Lonely Hearts Club Band*?

Answer: **English / 1960s / *Pepper*.**

LANGUAGE

Complete the following proverbs: "A _____ in the hand is worth two in the bush" and "You can lead a horse to _____, but you can't make him _____."

Answer: **"bird" / "water" / "drink."**

ARTS, RELIGION, & CULTURE

Which colors are produced when the following pigments are mixed: blue and red; yellow and blue; and red and yellow?

Answer: **Violet (accept purple) / green / orange.**

POTPOURRI

Identify the system of escape that helped slaves reach Canada, the 19th-century reformers who sought to end black slavery, and the literary character whose name today designates a black too deferential to whites.

Answer: **Underground railroad / abolitionists / Uncle Tom.**

U.S. GEOGRAPHY

Which states are nicknamed the "Palmetto State," the "Jayhawker State," and the "Volunteer State"?

Answer: South Carolina / Kansas / Tennessee.

HISTORY

Which explorer from which country searched for the "Fountain of Youth," and which present-day U.S. state did he explore in 1513 while seeking this imaginary spring?

Answer: Juan Ponce de León / Spain / Florida.

LITERATURE

Identify the 2 characters whose names refer today to "a person who is alternately completely good and completely evil," and identify the author of the 1886 tale of a doctor with a dual personality.

Answer: Dr. Jekyll / Mr. Hyde (in *The Strange Case of Dr. Jekyll and Mr. Hyde*) / Robert L. Stevenson.

ENTERTAINMENT

Identify the Warner Brothers' cartoon character known for saying "Thuffering Thucotash," and give the name and the type of bird known for saying, "I tawt I taw a puddy tat."

Answer: Sylvester the Cat (Sylvester P. Pussycat) / Tweety Pie / canary.

SPORTS AND GAMES

To which city did baseball's Boston Braves move in 1953, to which one did the St. Louis Browns move in 1954, and to which one did the Kansas City Athletics move in 1968?

Answer: Milwaukee / Baltimore / Oakland.

SCIENCE AND NATURE

On a global map, which imaginary lines run east and west, which ones run north and south, and which ones form the boundaries of the tropics?

Answer: Parallels or lines of latitude / meridians or lines of longitude / Tropic of Cancer and Tropic of Capricorn.

WORLD GEOGRAPHY

Between which 2 South American countries does the statue of Christ of the Andes stand as a symbol of perpetual peace, and in which Brazilian city is the statue of Christ the Redeemer located?

Answer: Chile / Argentina / Rio de Janeiro.

LEADERS & GOVERNMENT

William Henry Harrison and Benjamin Harrison are 2 of the U.S. Presidents whose surnames begin with the letter *H*. Name the other 3.

Answer: Rutherford B. Hayes / Warren Harding / Herbert Hoover.

MUSIC & RHYMES

Complete the rhyme: "Old Mother _____, / Went to the ________, / To get her poor dog a _____, / But when she got there, / [It] was bare, / And so the poor dog had none."

Answer: "Hubbard" / "cupboard" / "bone."

LANGUAGE

Complete each of the following: "A chip off the old _____," "To have a chip on one's _____," and "Let the chips _____ where they may."

Answer: "block" / "shoulder" / "fall."

ARTS, RELIGION, & CULTURE

Complete the following song lines: "Amazing _____, how sweet the sound, / That saved a wretch like me! / I once was lost but now I am found, / Was _____, but now I _____."

Answer: "Grace" / "blind" / "see."

POTPOURRI

Which 2 countries went to war over the Falkland Islands in 1982, and in which ocean are these islands located?

Answer: Argentina / Great Britain / Atlantic Ocean.

U.S. GEOGRAPHY

Which states are nicknamed the "Beaver State," the "Keystone State," and the "Ocean State"?

Answer: Oregon / Pennsylvania / Rhode Island.

HISTORY

Which Indian people were conquered after a bloody war in Peru from 1532-1533, and which conqueror from which country defeated them?

Answer: Incas / Francisco Pizarro / Spain.

LITERATURE

How many years does Rip Van Winkle sleep, and in which mountains in which state does he do so in a Washington Irving story?

Answer: 20 / Catskill Mountains / New York.

ENTERTAINMENT

Which Warner Brothers' cartoon character is known for saying, "I'm gonna kill dat wascally wabbit," which one wears an oversized cowboy hat, and what is the color of his beard and mustache?

Answer: Elmer Fudd / Yosemite Sam / red.

SPORTS AND GAMES

How many total pieces are used in a chess match, how many squares are on a chess board, and what is the meaning of the notation 0-0?

Answer: 32 / 64 / castles (kingside; 0-0-0 is queenside).

SCIENCE AND NATURE

Give the word for "any 2 places directly opposite each other on the earth," and name the 2 countries identified in this way because of their geographic relationship to England.

Answer: Antipodes / Australia / New Zealand.

WORLD GEOGRAPHY

On which continents are North and South Korea, the Ivory Coast, and French Guiana?

Answer: Asia / Africa / South America.

LEADERS & GOVERNMENT

Identify the 3 U.S. Presidents besides Truman whose surnames begin with the letter *T*.

Answer: John Tyler / Zachary Taylor / William H. Taft.

MUSIC & RHYMES

Which words complete the song: "John Jacob _____ _____, / His name is my name too. / Whenever we go out / The people always _____"?

Answer: "Jingleheimer" / "Schmidt" / "shout."

LANGUAGE

Complete each of the following: "To call a spade a _____," "Let bygones be _____," and "To catch as _____ can."

Answer: "spade" / "bygones" / "catch."

ARTS, RELIGION, & CULTURE

Complete the following: "I pledge allegiance to the flag of the United States of America and to the _____ for which it stands, one _____ under God, _____, with liberty and justice for all."

Answer: "Republic" / "Nation" / "indivisible."

POTPOURRI

Identify the following: the conqueror whose horse was named Bucephalus, the Civil War general who rode Traveller, and the film star who rode Trigger.

Answer: Alexander the Great / Robert E. Lee / Roy Rogers.

U.S. GEOGRAPHY
Which states are nicknamed the "Flickertail State," the "Buckeye State," and the "Boomer State"?
Answer: North Dakota / Ohio / Oklahoma.

HISTORY
Who made the first English voyage to North America in 1497, which French explorer led the first European expedition up the St. Lawrence River in 1535, and for which passage did Henry Hudson search in 1609 for the Dutch East India Company?
Answer: John Cabot / Jacques Cartier / Northwest Passage.

LITERATURE
What is the surname of Astrid Lindgren's 9-year-old Pippi _____, who does this character believe has become king of the cannibals, and with which 2 animals does she live?
Answer: Longstocking / her father / a monkey (named Mr. Nilsson) and a horse.

ENTERTAINMENT
Which Disney film features "The Unbirthday Song," how many unbirthdays is it said there are during the year, and how many people are present at the party besides the young girl?
Answer: *Alice in Wonderland* / 364 / 3.

SPORTS AND GAMES
Which sport is played on a "gridiron," which one on a "diamond," and which one on a "hardwood"?
Answer: Football / baseball / basketball.

SCIENCE AND NATURE
In a computer, what are the only 2 possible numerical values of a bit, from which words is the term bit derived, and how many bits are there in a byte?
Answer: 0 and 1 / *bi*nary digi*t* / 8.

WORLD GEOGRAPHY
On which 3 European rivers whose names begin with the letter *T* are national capitals located?
Answer: Thames (London) / Tagus (Lisbon) / Tiber (Rome).

LEADERS & GOVERNMENT
Identify the 3 U.S. Presidents whose surnames begin with the letter *M*.
Answer: James Madison / James Monroe / William McKinley.

MUSIC & RHYMES
Which words complete these lines from a Dr. Seuss work: "I do so like green _____ and _____! Thank you! Thank you! Sam-I-_____!"?
Answer: "eggs" / "ham" / "am."

LANGUAGE
Complete each of the following: "Cold hands, warm _____," "Finders keepers, losers _____," and "Here today, gone _____."
Answer: "heart" / "weepers" / "tomorrow."

ARTS, RELIGION, & CULTURE
Which of the earliest stringed instruments spans 6 1/2 octaves, which one is the largest and the lowest-pitched, and which one is the most widely used of all orchestral instruments?
Answer: Harp / bass / violin.

POTPOURRI
Name the doll whose boyfriend is Ken, the type of cap worn by Davy Crockett, and the plastic ring swung around the body by hip action.
Answer: Barbie / coonskin cap (from a raccoon) / hula hoop.

U.S. GEOGRAPHY

Which states are nicknamed the "Land of Enchantment," the "Empire State," and the "Tar Heel State"?

Answer: New Mexico (accept Montana) / New York / North Carolina.

HISTORY

Which explorer from which country founded the Canadian city of Quebec in 1608, and what name was given to the colony he founded with Quebec and Montreal at its center?

Answer: Samuel de Champlain / France / New France.

LITERATURE

Who is the author of *The Legend of Sleepy Hollow*, in which state is it set, and who is the town's schoolmaster?

Answer: Washington Irving / New York / Ichabod Crane.

ENTERTAINMENT

In the Disney song "It's A Small World," which 2 words follow "It's a small world"; which word completes "There is just _____ moon, / And _____ golden sun"; and what "means friendship to everyone"?

Answer: "after all" / "one" / "a smile."

SPORTS AND GAMES

In the game of chess, each side has just 2 pieces of 3 different kinds. Name these 3 kinds.

Answer: Rooks (or castles) / bishops / knights.

SCIENCE AND NATURE

Which planet is known for its Great Red Spot, which one is known as the Red Planet, and which one, the brightest planet seen from Earth, is known as Earth's "twin"?

Answer: Jupiter / Mars / Venus.

WORLD GEOGRAPHY

Just west of which Canadian city are the Plains of Abraham; in which city is Mount Royal Park; and in which city is the Canadian National Tower, the world's tallest free-standing structure?

Answer: Quebec / Montreal / Toronto.

LEADERS & GOVERNMENT

Identify the 3 U.S. Presidents besides Thomas Jefferson whose surnames begin with the letter *J*.

Answer: Andrew Jackson / Andrew Johnson / Lyndon Johnson.

MUSIC & RHYMES

Which words complete these lines: "Three blind _____, see how they run! / They all ran after the farmer's _____, / Who cut off their _____ with a carving knife"?

Answer: "mice" / "wife" / "tails."

LANGUAGE

Complete each of the following: "Haste makes _____," "Leave well enough _____," and "Let sleeping dogs _____."

Answer: "waste" / "alone" / "lie."

ARTS, RELIGION, & CULTURE

Complete these lines from the song "Jingle Bells": "Dashing through the _____ / In a one horse open _____, / O'er the fields we go, / _____ all the way."

Answer: "snow" / "sleigh" / "Laughing."

POTPOURRI

What color carpet is rolled out to give royal treatment, what gesture is used in the military to show an officer respect, and what kind of gun salute is usually given to honor a foreign leader?

Answer: Red carpet / (military) salute / 21-gun salute.

U.S. GEOGRAPHY
Which states are nicknamed the "Heart of Dixie," the "Last Frontier," and the "Grand Canyon State"?
Answer: Alabama / Alaska / Arizona.

HISTORY
Which sea captain and explorer discovered a sailing route around Africa in 1488, what is the present name for the Cape he called the "Cape of Storms," and what was his nationality?
Answer: Bartolomeu Dias / Cape of Good Hope / Portuguese.

LITERATURE
Who is Ichabod Crane's rival for Katrina Van Tassel in *The Legend of Sleepy Hollow*, which kind of horseman chases Ichabod out of town, and which broken vegetable is found near Ichabod's hat?
Answer: Brom Bones (or Brom Van Brunt) / headless Horseman / pumpkin.

ENTERTAINMENT
In the Disney song "It's A Small World," which 3 worlds follow "It's a world of laughter"?
Answer: "world of tears" / "world of hopes" / "world of fears."

SPORTS AND GAMES
Name 3 of the 4 feats that an athlete has accomplished when he "hits for the cycle."
Answer: A single / a double / a triple / a home run (in the sport of baseball).

SCIENCE AND NATURE
Give the Arabic equivalents of the Roman numerals *X*, *C*, and *L*.
Answer: 10 / 100 / 50.

WORLD GEOGRAPHY

What do Hindus regard as India's most sacred river, into which bay does it empty, and what is the largest city located on the Hooghly River, this sacred river's tributary?

Answer: Ganges / Bay of Bengal / Calcutta.

LEADERS & GOVERNMENT

Identify the 3 U.S. Presidents whose surnames begin with the letter *A*.

Answer: John Adams / John Quincy Adams / Chester Arthur.

MUSIC & RHYMES

Complete the rhyme: "If wishes were _____, / Then _____ would ride; / If turnips were _____, / I'd wear one by my side."

Answer: "horses" / "beggars" / "watches."

LANGUAGE

Complete the following: "If at _____ you don't _____, try, try again," and "If you can't stand the heat, get out of the _____."

Answer: "first" / "succeed" / "kitchen."

ARTS, RELIGION, & CULTURE

Complete these lines from the song "Jingle Bells": "Bells on _____ ring, / Making _____ bright, / What fun it is to ride and sing a _____ song tonight."

Answer: "Bobtail" / "spirits" / "sleighing."

POTPOURRI

Give the meaning of the terms *pseudonym*, *maiden name*, and *surname*.

Answer: Fictitious name (or pen name) / the last name of a woman before her marriage / last name (accept inherited name or family name).

U.S. GEOGRAPHY

Which states are nicknamed the "Land of Opportunity," the "Golden State," and the "Cavalier State"?

Answer: Arkansas / California / Virginia.

HISTORY

Which sea captain and explorer commanded the first fleet to travel to India from Europe in 1498, around which continent did he sail, and what was his nationality?

Answer: Vasco da Gama / Africa / Portuguese.

LITERATURE

Name the 3 kinds of materials the 3 little pigs use to build their houses to protect themselves from the big bad wolf.

Answer: Straw / sticks / bricks.

ENTERTAINMENT

Identify the following in the *Star Wars* films: the ancient traditional weapon of the Jedi Knight, the mercenary pirate and smuggler captain, and the name of his YT-1300 light freighter.

Answer: Light saber / Han Solo / *Millennium Falcon*.

SPORTS AND GAMES

In golf, par on a hole is the standard score by an expert. Give the term for one stroke under par, one stroke over par, and 2 strokes under par.

Answer: Birdie / bogey / eagle.

SCIENCE AND NATURE

Give the words for "a spring where a river begins," "the stream or streams that flow from the river's beginning," and "the part of a river where its waters are emptied into the sea."

Answer: Source / headwater(s) / mouth.

WORLD GEOGRAPHY

Identify the 3 independent North American countries whose names begin with the letter *C*.

Answer: Canada / Costa Rica / Cuba.

LEADERS & GOVERNMENT

Identify 3 of the 4 U.S. Presidents whose surnames begin with the letter *C*.

Answer: Grover Cleveland / Calvin Coolidge / James E. Carter / William J. Clinton.

MUSIC & RHYMES

Which words complete the rhyme: "Simple Simon met a pieman / Going to the _____; / Says Simple Simon to the pieman, / 'Let me _____ your _____'"?

Answer: "fair" / "taste" / "ware."

LANGUAGE

Complete each of the following: "He's treading on thin _____," "He who hesitates is _____," and "Honesty is the best _____."

Answer: "ice" / "lost" / "policy."

ARTS, RELIGION, & CULTURE

In the song "Put Your Hand in the Hand," which words complete: "of the man who stilled the _____," "of the man who calmed the _____," and "of the man from-a _____"?

Answer: "water" / "sea" / "Galilee."

POTPOURRI

Who is the dragon-slaying patron saint of Britain, what is the country's national anthem, and what is its basic monetary unit?

Answer: St. George / "God Save the Queen" (or "King") / pound.

U.S. GEOGRAPHY
Which states are nicknamed the "Cowboy State," the "Nutmeg State," and the "First State"?
Answer: Wyoming / Connecticut / Delaware.

HISTORY
Which king and queen of which country provided Christopher Columbus with ships to sail across the Atlantic Ocean?
Answer: King Ferdinand / Queen Isabella / Spain.

LITERATURE
In which folk tale does a human being marry an animal, whose life does the woman save by agreeing to live with the animal, and what does the animal become after the woman's love removes the curse?
Answer: *Beauty and the Beast* / her father's / a handsome prince.

ENTERTAINMENT
In which Disney films are the song lines, "Heigh-ho, heigh-ho, / It's home from work we go," "I saw a garden walk, a banana stalk," and "Take the straight and narrow path"?
Answer: *Snow White and the Seven Dwarfs* / *Dumbo* / *Pinocchio*.

SPORTS AND GAMES
In baseball, which 2 players are called the "battery," what is the "pasture," and what is the "dish"?
Answer: Pitcher and catcher / outfield / home plate.

SCIENCE AND NATURE
Identify the following animals: the only mammal that can fly, the world's longest living vertebrate animal, and the world's largest meat-eating animal that lives on land.
Answer: Bat / tortoise / Alaskan brown bear (accept Kodiak bear).

WORLD GEOGRAPHY

Which 2 countries combined to form the country of Tanzania in 1964, and what is its capital?

Answer: Tanganyika / Zanzibar / Dar es Salaam (accept Dodoma).

LEADERS & GOVERNMENT

Identify the 2 U.S. Presidents whose surnames begin with the letter *G* and the one besides Gerald Ford whose surname begins with the letter *F*.

Answer: Ulysses S. Grant / James Garfield / Millard Fillmore.

MUSIC & RHYMES

Complete the rhyme: "Monday's child is fair of _____, / Tuesday's child is full of _____, / Wednesday's child is full of _____."

Answer: "face" / "grace" / "woe."

LANGUAGE

Complete each of the following: "Don't count your _____ before they're hatched," "Don't judge a _____ by its cover," and "Don't put the _____ before the horse."

Answer: "chickens" / "book" / "cart."

ARTS, RELIGION, & CULTURE

Complete the following song lines: "It came upon the midnight _____, / That glorious song of old. / From _____ bending near the earth / To touch their _____ of gold."

Answer: "clear" / "angels" / "harps."

POTPOURRI

Give the number of wives of Henry VIII, the number of known planets that orbit the sun in our solar system, and the number of mythological Fates.

Answer: 6 / 9 / 3.

U.S. GEOGRAPHY

Which states are nicknamed the "Peach State," the "Aloha State," and the "Gem State"?

Answer: Georgia / Hawaii / Idaho.

HISTORY

In which month on which date in which year is Christopher Columbus credited with the discovery of the New World?

Answer: October / 12 / 1492.

LITERATURE

In the story of Snow White, which woman desires a child with "skin as white as snow," and which words complete the description with, "lips as red as _____, and hair as black as _____"?

Answer: Queen / "blood" / "ebony."

ENTERTAINMENT

Whom does the Queen send to kill Snow White in the Disney film, what is he to bring back in the casket she gives him, and what does he actually put in the casket?

Answer: Huntsman (accept Humbert) / Snow White's heart / a pig's heart.

SPORTS AND GAMES

In feet, what is the height of a regulation basketball goal or hoop, what is the height of a regulation soccer goal, and what is the distance between each base in baseball?

Answer: 10 feet / 8 feet / 90 feet.

SCIENCE AND NATURE

Identify the world's smallest dog; the world's smallest bird; and the fastest flying small bird, one capable of traveling over 100 miles per hour for short distances in level flight.

Answer: Chihuahua / hummingbird / swift.

WORLD GEOGRAPHY

Which continents include the following countries: Ghana and Guinea; Jamaica and Trinidad & Tobago; and Suriname and Guyana?

Answer: Africa / North America / South America.

LEADERS & GOVERNMENT

Identify the 3 U.S. Presidents whose surnames begin with the letter *R*.

Answer: Theodore Roosevelt / Franklin Roosevelt / Ronald Reagan.

MUSIC & RHYMES

Complete the rhyme: "Thursday's child has far to _____, / Friday's child is loving and _____, / Saturday's child works hard for his _____."

Answer: "go" / "giving" / "living" ["But a child that's born on the Sabbath day / Is fair (bonny) and wise (blithe) and good and gay"].

LANGUAGE

Complete each of the following: "Don't look a gift horse in the _____," "Don't put all your eggs in one _____," and "Don't take any wooden _____."

Answer: "mouth" / "basket" / "nickels."

ARTS, RELIGION, & CULTURE

Complete these lines from the song: "Oh, when the saints go _____ in, / . . . Oh, _____, I want to be in that _____."

Answer: "marching" / "Lord" / "number."

POTPOURRI

On which days are April Fools's Day, Halloween, and Armistice Day?

Answer: April 1 / October 31 / November 11.

U.S. GEOGRAPHY

Which states are nicknamed the "Land of Lincoln," the "Hoosier State," and the "Hawkeye State"?

Answer: Illinois / Indiana / Iowa.

HISTORY

Identify the 3 ships of Christopher Columbus on his first voyage to the New World.

Answer: *Niña / Pinta / Santa María.*

LITERATURE

In a Eugene Field poem, who are the 3 fishermen who "one night / Sailed off in a wooden shoe . . . on a river of crystal light into a sea of dew"?

Answer: Wynken / Blynken / Nod.

ENTERTAINMENT

Which words complete the song titles "Some Day My _____ Will Come" and "With a Smile and a _____," and which Disney film features these songs?

Answer: "Prince" / "Song" / *Snow White and the Seven Dwarfs*.

SPORTS AND GAMES

In checkers, what is the word for making one's piece a king; and in chess, which color moves first and what is the word for the inextricable trap of the opponent's king?

Answer: Crowning / white (or light-colored) / checkmate.

SCIENCE AND NATURE

What is the basic unit of all life, what is the essential living matter of this basic unit of life, and what is the name for the structure near the center containing hereditary material?

Answer: Cell / protoplasm / nucleus (accept nucleolus).

WORLD GEOGRAPHY

In which countries are Mandalay, Tipperary, and Timbuktu?

Answer: Burma (or Myanmar) / Ireland / Mali.

LEADERS & GOVERNMENT

Name the Presidents who succeeded to office upon the deaths of William H. Harrison, Zachary Taylor, and Abraham Lincoln.

Answer: John Tyler / Millard Fillmore / Andrew Johnson.

MUSIC & RHYMES

Identify the following from the song "On the Good Ship Lollipop": the shop "where bonbons play," the bay where there's "the sunny beach," and the bowl that does "a tootsie roll."

Answer: "candy shop" / "Peppermint Bay" / "sugar bowl."

LANGUAGE

Complete each of the following: "When it rains, it _____," "The _____ said the better," and "It takes two to _____."

Answer: "pours" ("It never rains but it pours") / "least" (or "less") / "tango."

ARTS, RELIGION, & CULTURE

Complete the song lines: "You're a _____ old flag / You're a high-_____ flag, / And forever in peace, may you _____."

Answer: "grand" / "flying" / "wave."

POTPOURRI

Which words complete the children's defensive statement against insults, "_____ and _____ may break my bones, but _____ will never hurt me"?

Answer: "sticks" / "stones" / "words" (or "names").

U.S. GEOGRAPHY
Which states are nicknamed the "Sunflower State," the "Bluegrass State," and the "Pelican State"?
Answer: Kansas / Kentucky / Louisiana.

HISTORY
What was the nationality of Christopher Columbus, in which city was he born, and how many voyages did he make to the New World?
Answer: Italian / Genoa / 4.

LITERATURE
Which author from which country wrote the story "The Ugly Duckling," and which kind of animal does this duckling become?
Answer: Hans Christian Andersen / Denmark / a lovely white swan.

ENTERTAINMENT
In which kind of a mine do the 7 dwarfs work in the film *Snow White and the Seven Dwarfs*, in which type of coffin is Snow White placed, and which dwarf is dressed in oversized clothing and has very large ears?
Answer: Diamond mine / glass coffin / Dopey.

SPORTS AND GAMES
Which 2 American League teammates for which baseball team combined for the most home runs in a single season at 115 in 1961?
Answer: Mickey Mantle / Roger Maris / New York Yankees.

SCIENCE AND NATURE
Identify the master gland in the body, the "chemical messengers" that help an organism to function in a coordinated manner, and the meaning of GH, which regulates the growth of children and adolescents.
Answer: Pituitary / hormones / growth hormone.

WORLD GEOGRAPHY

Name the smallest country in area in Central America, name its capital, and identify the body of water on which it is located.

Answer: El Salvador / San Salvador / Pacific Ocean.

LEADERS & GOVERNMENT

Name the Presidents who succeeded to office upon the deaths of James A. Garfield, William McKinley, and Warren G. Harding.

Answer: Chester A. Arthur / Theodore Roosevelt / Calvin Coolidge.

MUSIC & RHYMES

Which words complete the song lines: "Mairzy doats and _____ doats and liddle _____ divey, / A _____ divey too, wouldn't you?"

Answer: "dozy" / "lamzy" / "kiddley."

LANGUAGE

Complete each of the following: "It's better to give than to _____," "It's better late than _____," and "It's always darkest before the _____."

Answer: "receive" / "never" / "dawn."

ARTS, RELIGION, & CULTURE

Complete these song lines: "This train is bound for _____, this train, / . . . don't carry nothin' but the _____ and the _____."

Answer: "glory" / "righteous" / "holy."

POTPOURRI

Which inventor was the "Wizard of Menlo Park," in which state is this city, and which word complete his observation, "_____ is one percent inspiration and ninety-nine percent perspiration"?

Answer: Thomas Edison / New Jersey / Genius.

U.S. GEOGRAPHY
Which states are nicknamed the "Pine Tree State," the "Star-Spangled Banner State," and the "Bay State"?
Answer: Maine / Maryland / Massachusetts.

HISTORY
Which explorers were called the "Admiral of the Ocean Sea," the "Terror of the Spanish Main," and the "Father of New France"?
Answer: Christopher Columbus / Sir Francis Drake / Samuel de Champlain.

LITERATURE
What is the name of the wooden puppet whose nose grows longer each time he tells a lie, which old man carves him, and what is the nationality of this story's author, Carlo Collodi?
Answer: Pinocchio / Geppetto / Italian (also named Carlo Lorenzini).

ENTERTAINMENT
Doc, Dopey, Sleepy, and Sneezy are 4 of Snow White's 7 dwarfs. Name the other 3.
Answer: Bashful / Grumpy / Happy.

SPORTS AND GAMES
How long are the following regulation professional games or matches: outdoor soccer, ice hockey, and basketball?
Answer: 90 minutes / 60 minutes / 48 minutes.

SCIENCE AND NATURE
Which basic unit of matter forms the building blocks of the chemical elements, what is the center of this unit of matter, and what is the smallest physical unit of an element or compound?
Answer: Atom / nucleus / molecule.

WORLD GEOGRAPHY

On which continent is Mount Kosciusko the highest peak, and which extinct volcano in which country is Africa's highest mountain?

Answer: Australia / Mount Kilimanjaro (Mount Kibo is the highest point) / Tanzania.

LEADERS & GOVERNMENT

Which Presidents took office when Franklin Roosevelt and John Kennedy died, and who became President when Richard Nixon resigned?

Answer: Harry S Truman / Lyndon Johnson / Gerald Ford.

MUSIC & RHYMES

Complete these song lines: "The Camptown _____ sing this song, / The Camptown racetrack's _____ miles _____. / Doo-dah, doo-dah!"

Answer: "ladies" / "five" / "long."

LANGUAGE

According to the sayings, what is the "best teacher," what is the "spice of life," and where "does charity begin"?

Answer: Experience / variety / at home.

ARTS, RELIGION, & CULTURE

Complete the following song lines: "O little town of Bethlehem, / How still we see thee _____! / Above thy deep and dreamless _____ / The silent _____ go by."

Answer: "lie" / "sleep" / "stars."

POTPOURRI

How many Muses are there in Greek mythology, what is the advertised number of Heinz varieties, and how many walking legs does a scorpion have?

Answer: 9 / 57 / 8.

U.S. GEOGRAPHY

Which states are nicknamed the "Automobile State," the "Gopher State," and the "Magnolia State"?

Answer: Michigan / Minnesota / Mississippi.

HISTORY

Which European was the first to sail across the Pacific Ocean and was the commander of the first expedition that sailed around the world, what was his nationality, and which ship completed the trip?

Answer: Ferdinand Magellan / Portuguese / *Victoria*.

LITERATURE

Which legendary outlaw of medieval England takes money from the rich and gives to the poor, in which forest does this "outlaw" live, and who is his beloved?

Answer: Robin Hood / Sherwood Forest / Maid Marian.

ENTERTAINMENT

Which Disney film features the song "Whistle While You Work," what does the person singing the song use to clean the room, and, according to the song, what kind of a tune is one supposed to hum?

Answer: *Snow White and the Seven Dwarfs* / a broom / "a merry tune."

SPORTS AND GAMES

In which sports are the following terms used: *statue of liberty play*; *match play* or *medal play*; and *power play*, when a team has a man advantage?

Answer: Football / golf / ice hockey.

SCIENCE AND NATURE

Identify the 3 basic types of particles in an atom.

Answer: Protons / neutrons / electrons.

WORLD GEOGRAPHY

What is the official language of most South American countries, and what are the official languages of Guyana and Suriname?

Answer: Spanish / English / Dutch.

LEADERS & GOVERNMENT

Name 3 of the 4 U.S. Presidents who have been assassinated.

Answer: Abraham Lincoln / James A. Garfield / William McKinley / John F. Kennedy.

MUSIC & RHYMES

Complete these lines from the "Camptown Races" song: "Goin' to run all _____, / Goin' to run all _____. / I'll bet my money on a _____ nag; / Somebody bet on the bay."

Answer: "night" / "day" / "bobtail."

LANGUAGE

Which animal traditionally "never forgets," which one "has his day," and which ones "come home to roost"?

Answer: Elephant / dog / chickens.

ARTS, RELIGION, & CULTURE

Which words complete the song title "He's Got the Whole _____ in His Hands" and its line "He's got you and me, _____, in His hands," and which words describe the "baby in His hands"?

Answer: "World" / "brother" / "itty (little) bitty."

POTPOURRI

On which continents can Bigfoot, the Loch Ness Monster, and the Abominable Snowman allegedly be found?

Answer: North America / Europe / Asia.

U.S. GEOGRAPHY

Which states are nicknamed the "Show Me State," the "Big Sky State," and the "Cornhusker State"?

Answer: Missouri / Montana / Nebraska.

HISTORY

Which explorer from which country led the first European expedition to reach the Mississippi River in 1541, and off the coast of which present-day U.S. state did he land in 1539?

Answer: Hernando De Soto / Spain / Florida.

LITERATURE

Which line follows the queen's words, "Mirror mirror on the wall," in which story is this line, and who arrives to save the heroine and then marries her?

Answer: "Who is the fairest one of all?" / "Snow White and the Seven Dwarfs" / the Prince.

ENTERTAINMENT

What kind of suit does Disney's Donald Duck wear, what is the name of his girlfriend, and what is the relationship of Gus Goose to Donald Duck?

Answer: Sailor suit / Daisy Duck / his cousin.

SPORTS AND GAMES

What are the names of the NFL teams in Baltimore, Jacksonville, and San Diego?

Answer: Ravens / Jaguars / Chargers.

SCIENCE AND NATURE

What are the 3 basic pieces of information given for each of the chemical elements on the periodic table?

Answer: Atomic number / chemical symbol / atomic weight or mass number (the atomic name and number of electrons in each shell are also given).

WORLD GEOGRAPHY

Which 3 European countries are known as the "Low Countries"?

Answer: Belgium / Netherlands (or Holland) / Luxembourg.

LEADERS & GOVERNMENT

Which U.S. Presidents are known as "Old Zach," "Handsome Frank," and "Mischievous Andy"?

Answer: Zachary Taylor / Franklin Pierce / Andrew Jackson.

MUSIC & RHYMES

Which words complete the song lines: "In a cavern, in a _____, / Excavating for a mine, / Dwelt a miner, _____, / And his daughter _____"?

Answer: "canyon" / "forty-niner" / "Clementine."

LANGUAGE

According to the sayings, what "will never come to pass when dew is on the grass," what is the "mother of invention," and who "fiddled while Rome burned"?

Answer: Rain / necessity / Nero.

ARTS, RELIGION, & CULTURE

Complete these song lines: "We shall _____ some _____, / Oh, deep in my _____ I do believe / . . . We'll walk hand in hand."

Answer: "overcome" / "day" / "heart."

POTPOURRI

Name 3 of the 4 *H*'s in the 4-H Club.

Answer: Head / Heart / Hands / Health.

U.S. GEOGRAPHY

Which states are nicknamed the "Silver State," the "Granite State," and the "Garden State"?

Answer: Nevada / New Hampshire / New Jersey.

HISTORY

Who was the first Englishman to sail around the world (from 1577-1580), during the reign of which queen did he do so, and what was the name of his ship which completed the voyage?

Answer: Sir Francis Drake / Queen Elizabeth I / *Golden Hind* (formerly the *Pelican*).

LITERATURE

Give the name of the poem, the author, and the work in which the following lines are found: " 'Twas brillig, and the slithy toves / Did gyre and gimble in the wabe."

Answer: "Jabberwocky" / Lewis Carroll / *Through the Looking Glass*.

ENTERTAINMENT

What are the names of the 3 nephews of Donald Duck?

Answer: Huey / Dewey / Louie.

SPORTS AND GAMES

Which 3 *Monopoly* properties are green?

Answer: Pacific / North Carolina / Pennsylvania avenues.

SCIENCE AND NATURE

Identify the E, the m, and the c^2 in Albert Einstein's equation $E = mc^2$.

Answer: Energy / mass / the square of the velocity of light.

WORLD GEOGRAPHY
Identify the 2 independent African countries whose names begin with the letter *Z* and the one that became known as the Democratic Republic of the Congo.
Answer: Zambia / Zimbabwe / Zaire.

LEADERS & GOVERNMENT
What is the official title of the head of a city government in the U.S., in which city did Fiorella La Guardia and Ed Koch hold this post, and in which one did Richard Daley and Jane Byrne serve?
Answer: Mayor / New York / Chicago.

MUSIC & RHYMES
Which words complete the chorus of "Clementine": "Oh my darling, / Oh, my darling Clementine, / You are _____ and _____ forever, / _____ sorry, Clementine"?
Answer: "lost" / "gone" / "Dreadful."

LANGUAGE
According to the sayings, what is "always greener on the other side," which animal "doesn't change its spots," and what is "mightier than the sword"?
Answer: Grass / leopard / pen.

ARTS, RELIGION, & CULTURE
Complete the following song lines: "Hark!, the herald angels sing, / Glory to the newborn _____! / Peace on _____ and mercy mild, / God and _____ reconciled."
Answer: "King" / "earth" / "sinners."

POTPOURRI
Complete the Post Office pledge: "Neither snow, nor rain, nor _____, nor gloom of _____ stays these couriers from the swift completion of their appointed _____."
Answer: "heat" / "night" / "rounds."

U.S. GEOGRAPHY

In which states are the major cities of Birmingham and Mobile; Tucson and Mesa; and Aurora and Pueblo?

Answer: Alabama / Arizona / Colorado.

HISTORY

Which explorer from which country became the first known European to reach the Hawaiian Islands, and what did he name these islands?

Answer: James Cook / England / Sandwich Islands.

LITERATURE

Which words complete the Lewis Carroll poem, "'Beware the _____, my son! / The jaws that bite, the claws that catch! / Beware the _____ bird, and shun / The frumious _____!'"

Answer: "Jabberwock" / "Jubjub" / "Bandersnatch" (from "Jabberwocky").

ENTERTAINMENT

The popular Disney character Mickey Mouse was originally named Mortimer Mouse. What are the names of his girlfriend, his dog, and his silly friend?

Answer: Minnie Mouse / Pluto / Goofy.

SPORTS AND GAMES

How many players are in the starting lineup for each team at the beginning of a major league baseball game, an NBA basketball game, and an outdoor match in professional soccer?

Answer: 9 / 5 / 11.

SCIENCE AND NATURE

Give the common names for the 3 movable little bones of the middle ear that are linked together and connect the eardrum to the middle ear.

Answer: Hammer / anvil / stirrup.

WORLD GEOGRAPHY

Identify the 3 largest independent countries of North America in area.

Answer: Canada / United States / Mexico (listed in decreasing order of size).

LEADERS & GOVERNMENT

Which U.S. Presidents are known as "King Andrew the First," "King Martin the First," and "King Richard"?

Answer: Andrew Jackson / Martin Van Buren / Richard Nixon.

MUSIC & RHYMES

Match the Broadway musicals *Camelot*, *Oklahoma*, and *South Pacific* with these songs: "The Surrey with the Fringe on Top," "Bali Ha'i," and "Guenevere."

Answer: *Oklahoma* / *South Pacific* / *Camelot*.

LANGUAGE

Which animals complete the expressions: "To let the _____ out of the bag," "To keep the _____ from the door," and "To beat (flog) a dead _____"?

Answer: "cat" / "wolf" / "horse."

ARTS, RELIGION, & CULTURE

Complete these song lines: "Were you there when they _____ my Lord? / . . . Sometimes it causes me to _____, / . . . Were you there when they _____ Him to the Cross?"

Answer: "crucified" / "tremble" / "nailed."

POTPOURRI

Identify the pen name that means "a depth of 2 fathoms," give this author's real name, and tell how many feet are in 2 fathoms.

Answer: Mark Twain / Samuel Clemens / 12 feet.

U.S. GEOGRAPHY

In which states are the major cities of Anchorage and Fairbanks; Grand Rapids and Ann Arbor; and Long Beach and Oakland?

Answer: Alaska / Michigan / California.

HISTORY

How many legendary cities of Cibola were there, and which explorer from which country went searching for them in the American Southwest?

Answer: 7 / Francisco de Coronado / Spain.

LITERATURE

Give the names of Dr. Seuss's Turtle, Elephant, and Big-Hearted Moose.

Answer: Yertle the Turtle / Horton the Elephant / Thidwick the Big-Hearted Moose.

ENTERTAINMENT

In the song "Zip-A-Dee-Doo-Dah" in a Disney film, which kind of a bird sits on a shoulder, what is "headin' our way," and which word rhymes with "actch'll"?

Answer: Bluebird / sunshine / "satisfactch'll."

SPORTS AND GAMES

How many players are in the starting lineup for each team at the beginning of an NFL game, a Canadian football game, and a college lacrosse match?

Answer: 11 / 12 / 10 (accept 12 for women's lacrosse).

SCIENCE AND NATURE

Which "Father of Astronomy" first proposed that all planets revolve around the sun, which astronomer first used a telescope, and which scientist first stated the theory of relativity?

Answer: Nicholas Copernicus / Galileo / Albert Einstein.

WORLD GEOGRAPHY

Which chain of mountains is the world's longest above sea level, on which continent is it located, and from which cape, the southernmost on this continent, do these mountains extend?

Answer: Andes Mountains / South America / Cape Horn.

LEADERS & GOVERNMENT

Who was the first U.S. President to be impeached, which body voted to impeach him, and which one tried him, coming within one vote of convicting him?

Answer: Andrew Johnson / House of Representatives / Senate.

MUSIC & RHYMES

In the song, what is the name of the "magic dragon" who "lived by the sea," and in which "mist" in which "land" did he "frolick"?

Answer: Puff / "in the autumn mist" / Honah-Lee.

LANGUAGE

Which words complete these sayings: "Before one can say Jack _____," "In two shakes of a _____'s tail," and "At the drop of a _____"?

Answer: "Robinson" / "lamb" / "hat."

ARTS, RELIGION, & CULTURE

Which words complete these lines: "God bless _____, / Land that I _____, / Stand beside her and guide her / Thru the night with a light from _____"?

Answer: "America" / "love" / "above."

POTPOURRI

What is the meaning of the initialism NAACP, which 1857 Supreme Court decision declared that no black could claim U.S. citizenship, and which song is the national anthem of the U.S. Civil Rights movement?

Answer: National Association for the Advancement of Colored People / Dred Scott decision / "We Shall Overcome."

U.S. GEOGRAPHY

In which states are the major cities of Bridgeport and New Haven; Fort Smith and North Little Rock; and Pearl City and Kailua?

Answer: Connecticut / Arkansas / Hawaii.

HISTORY

Identify the 2 French explorers who discovered the Upper Mississippi River in 1673, and identify the river whose mouth they reached in the South before turning back.

Answer: Louis Joliet (Jolliet) / Jacques Marquette / Arkansas River.

LITERATURE

Complete the titles of these Dr. Seuss books: *And to Think That I Saw It on _____ Street* and *The _____ Hats of Bartolomew _____.*

Answer: *Mulberry* / *500* / *Cubbins.*

ENTERTAINMENT

Which Disney film features the song "Zip-A-Dee-Doo-Dah," which old man sings the song, and which word completes the line, "What a _____ day!"

Answer: *Song of the South* / Uncle Remus / "wonderful."

SPORTS AND GAMES

In the song "I'm Talkin' Baseball," which players are "Willie, Mickey, and the Duke"?

Answer: Willie Mays / Mickey Mantle / Duke Snider.

SCIENCE AND NATURE

Who said, "Give me somewhere to stand, and I will move the earth," to which device was he referring in his statement, and what was his nationality?

Answer: Archimedes / lever / Greek.

WORLD GEOGRAPHY

Name 3 of what most oceanographers consider the world's 4 oceans.

Answer: Pacific, Atlantic, Indian, and Arctic (some oceanographers believe that there are just the Pacific, the Atlantic, and the Indian—and that all other bodies of water are part of these 3; others consider there to be 5 oceans, adding the Antarctic as a separate body).

LEADERS & GOVERNMENT

Of which countries did Fidel Castro, Peter the Great, and Charles de Gaulle become the leaders?

Answer: Cuba / Russia / France.

MUSIC & RHYMES

In the song about the "magic dragon," what was the last name of "Little Jackie" who "loved that rascal" the magic dragon, and what 2 things did he bring him along with "other fancy stuff"?

Answer: (Little Jackie) Paper / "strings" / "and sealing wax."

LANGUAGE

Which letters of the alphabet complete these sayings: "To dot one's _____'s and to cross one's _____'s," and "To mind one's _____'s and q's"?

Answer: "i" / "t" / "p."

ARTS, RELIGION, & CULTURE

In the song "Here Comes Santa Claus," "right down" which lane is he coming, and which reindeer complete the line, "_____ and _____ and his reindeer are pulling on the reins"?

Answer: Santa Claus Lane / "Vixen" / "Blitzen."

POTPOURRI

Which wild horse in the West is named from the Spanish for "wild," which lizard that changes its colors is named from the Greek for "ground lion," and which dog is named from the French for "earth dog"?

Answer: Bronco (or bronc) / chameleon / terrier.

U.S. GEOGRAPHY

In which states are the major cities of Wilmington and Newark; Macon and Savannah; and Pocatello and Lewiston?

Answer: Delaware / Georgia / Idaho.

HISTORY

Which 2 men led the expedition of 1804-1806 sent to explore the U.S. to the Pacific Ocean, and which President was responsible for organizing this expedition?

Answer: Meriwether Lewis / William Clark / Thomas Jefferson.

LITERATURE

Complete the titles of these Dr. Seuss books: *One Fish, Two Fish _____ Fish, Blue Fish*; _____ *Hears a Who!*; and *You're Only Old*_____.

Answer: ***Red / Horton / Once.***

ENTERTAINMENT

Complete the missing words of the following Mouseketeer song: "M-I-C. See you _____ _____. K-E-Y. Why? Because we _____ you. M-O-U-S-E."

Answer: "real" / "soon" / "like" (or "love").

SPORTS AND GAMES

Which athlete from which country in which decade became the first man to run a mile in less than 4 minutes, doing so in 3 minutes 59.4 seconds?

Answer: Roger Bannister / Britain / 1950s (in 1954).

SCIENCE AND NATURE

Identify the creatures whose names mean "hundred-legged" and "thousand-legged," and identify the word for the pair of jointed feelers on their heads.

Answer: Centipedes / millipedes / antennae.

WORLD GEOGRAPHY

What is the world's longest river, on which continent is it located, and into which body of water does it empty?

Answer: Nile River / Africa / Mediterranean Sea.

LEADERS & GOVERNMENT

Of which countries did Chiang Kai-shek, Henry VII (or Henry Tudor), and Francisco Franco become the leaders?

Answer: China (or Taiwan, to which he moved the Nationalist Chinese government in 1949) / England / Spain.

MUSIC & RHYMES

In the song from *The Wizard of Oz*, which words complete these lines: "Ding-_____, the witch is _____! / Which old witch? / The _____ witch"?

Answer: "dong" / "dead" / "wicked."

LANGUAGE

According to the sayings, which bird catches the worm, which straw breaks the camel's back, and how many wrongs don't make a right?

Answer: Early bird / last straw / two wrongs.

ARTS, RELIGION, & CULTURE

Which words complete these song lines: "We are _____ Jacob's _____, / . . . Soldiers of the _____. / Ev'ry round goes higher, higher"?

Answer: "climbing" / "ladder" / "cross."

POTPOURRI

Which black American folk hero died competing with a sledge hammer, against which machine was he competing, and which railroad known as the C&O built the Big Bend Tunnel alluded to in this folk tale?

Answer: John Henry / steam drill / Chesapeake & Ohio.

U.S. GEOGRAPHY

In which states are the major cities of Cedar Rapids and Davenport; St. Petersburg and Pensacola; and Lexington and Owensboro?

Answer: Iowa / Florida / Kentucky.

HISTORY

Near which major city did the Lewis and Clark expedition set out to find a land route to the Pacific, up which river did they journey, and which Indian woman led them across the Rockies?

Answer: St. Louis / Missouri River / Sacajawea.

LITERATURE

Complete these titles: James Fenimore Cooper's *The Last of the* _____, Jules Verne's *Around the World in* _____ *Days*, and Nathaniel Hawthorne's *The House of the* _____ *Gables*.

Answer: *Mohicans* / *Eighty* / *Seven*.

ENTERTAINMENT

In "The Mickey Mouse Club March" song, which word completes, "Who's the _____ of the club / That's made for you and me," which name is said after Mickey's, and what must be held forever high?

Answer: "leader" / "Donald Duck" / "banner."

SPORTS AND GAMES

The revolver, the rope, and the wrench are 3 of the 6 murder weapons in the game of *Clue*. Name the other 3.

Answer: Candlestick / knife / lead pipe.

SCIENCE AND NATURE

Give the formulas for the area of a rectangle, the area of a square of side s, and the area of a circle.

Answer: Area = length x width ($A = l \times w$ or $A = lw$) / Area = side x side ($A = s \times s$ or $A = s^2$) / Area = *pi* r^2.

WORLD GEOGRAPHY

Identify the world's 2nd longest river, the continent on which it is located, and the body of water into which it empties.

Answer: Amazon River / South America / Atlantic Ocean.

LEADERS & GOVERNMENT

Of which countries did Ivan the Terrible, Gamal Abdel Nasser, and Napoleon III become the leaders?

Answer: Russia / Egypt / France.

MUSIC & RHYMES

Which words complete the song lines: "All around the _____'s bench, / The monkey chased the weasel. / The monkey thought 'twas all in _____, / _____! goes the weasel"?

Answer: "cobbler's" / "fun" / "Pop."

LANGUAGE

Complete each of the following: "Where there's a will, there's a _____," "Where there's life, there's _____," and "Where there's smoke, there's _____."

Answer: "way" / "hope" / "fire."

ARTS, RELIGION, & CULTURE

Which words complete these lines from "God Bless America": "From the mountains to the _____ / To the oceans white with _____ / . . . My home, _____ home"?

Answer: "prairies" / "foam" / "sweet."

POTPOURRI

Give the translation of France's motto, *Liberté*, *Égalité*, and *Fraternité*.

Answer: Liberty / Equality / Fraternity.

U.S. GEOGRAPHY

In which states are the major cities of Rockford and Peoria; Wichita and Overland Park; and Shreveport and Lafayette?

Answer: Illinois / Kansas / Louisiana.

HISTORY

Which explorer's name completes, "Dr. _____, I presume?"; who spoke that greeting in 1871 when he encountered the missing explorer; and on which continent did they meet?

Answer: "Livingstone" / Henry Morton Stanley / Africa.

LITERATURE

Which kind of an animal is Curious George, on which continent was he living when captured, and what color is the hat of the nice man who wanted to take him home to a zoo?

Answer: Monkey / Africa / yellow.

ENTERTAINMENT

Identify the following in the *Star Wars* films: the princess and youngest person to hold a seat in the Galactic Senate, the mighty wookiee from the planet Kashyyyk, and the Jedi Knight living on Tatooine who gives Luke his father's lightsaber.

Answer: Princess Leia (Organa) / Chewbacca / Obi-Wan Kenobi.

SPORTS AND GAMES

Identify 3 of the 4 corner squares in the game of *Monopoly*.

Answer: GO / In Jail (Just Visiting) / Free Parking / Go To Jail.

SCIENCE AND NATURE

Give the names for "the incoming or rising tide" and "the outgoing or falling tide," and give the word for the pull on the earth exerted by the sun and the moon.

Answer: Flood tide / ebb tide / gravitation.

WORLD GEOGRAPHY

Which country gave the Statue of Liberty to the U.S. to honor freedom and democracy, and on which island in which harbor is this statue?

Answer: France / Liberty Island / New York Harbor.

LEADERS & GOVERNMENT

Of which countries did Emperor Hirohito, V.I. Lenin, and Indira Gandhi become the leaders?

Answer: Japan / Soviet Union (accept Russia) / India.

MUSIC & RHYMES

In the song "This Land is Your Land," from which state to which island and from the redwood forest to which waters is "This land . . . made for you and me"?

Answer: "California" / "New York island" / "Gulf Stream waters."

LANGUAGE

Complete the following: "You can't fit a square _____ in a round hole," "You can't have your _____ and eat it too," and "You can't teach an old _____ new tricks."

Answer: "peg" / "cake" / "dog."

ARTS, RELIGION, & CULTURE

Complete these song lines: "Onward, Christian _____, marching as to _____, / With the _____ of Jesus going on before."

Answer: "soldiers" / "war" / "cross."

POTPOURRI

Name the American legendary lumberjack of superhuman strength with a large blue ox; name this ox; and identify the cowboy who, according to legend, dug the Rio Grande.

Answer: Paul Bunyan / Babe / Pecos Bill.

U.S. GEOGRAPHY
In which states are the major cities of Portland, Lewiston, and Bangor; Fort Wayne and Gary; and Minneapolis and Duluth?
Answer: Maine / Indiana / Minnesota.

HISTORY
Across which ocean did Norwegian explorer Thor Heyerdahl sail in 1947 from Peru to Polynesia, what was the name of his boat, and of which type of wood was this craft made?
Answer: Pacific Ocean / *Kon-Tiki* / balsa wood.

LITERATURE
Which fairy tale character enters the home of the bears, what does she find cooling on the table, and how many bears live in the house?
Answer: Goldilocks / porridge / 3.

ENTERTAINMENT
Despite the weather, who delivers the baby animals at the beginning of the Disney film *Dumbo*, where does Dumbo's mother work, and what is unusually big about her baby?
Answer: Mr. (Messenger) Stork / at the circus / his ears.

SPORTS AND GAMES
Mr. Green, Miss Scarlet, and Mrs. White are 3 of the 6 characters in the game of *Clue*. Name the other 3.
Answer: Colonel Mustard / Mrs. Peacock / Professor Plum.

SCIENCE AND NATURE
Name the 3 main parts into which the body of an insect is divided.
Answer: Head / thorax (or trunk) / abdomen (or metasoma).

WORLD GEOGRAPHY
What is the capital of Canada, and what are the 2 official languages of this country?
Answer: Ottawa / English / French.

LEADERS & GOVERNMENT
Of which countries did Benito Mussolini, Chou En-lai, and Joseph Stalin become the leaders?
Answer: Italy / China / Soviet Union (accept Russia).

MUSIC & RHYMES
In the song "Alouette," which words complete: "Oh Alouette, _____ Alouette; / Alouette, je t'y _____," and what is an *alouette*?
Answer: "gentille" / "plumerai" / lark (accept a bird).

LANGUAGE
Which words complete: "To blow hot and _____," "To rain cats and _____," and "To give a lick and a _____"?
Answer: "cold" / "dogs" / "promise."

ARTS, RELIGION, & CULTURE
Complete these lines from the poem "The New Colossus" written for the Statue of Liberty: "Give me your _____, your _____, / Your huddled _____ yearning to breathe free."
Answer: "tired" / "poor" / "masses."

POTPOURRI
Give the Wild West words for "a town abandoned after a gold strike" and for "a cemetery where gunfighters were buried," and name the scene of a famous gunfight between the Earps and the Clantons.
Answer: Ghost town / boot hill / O.K. Corral.

U.S. GEOGRAPHY

In which states are the major cities of Baltimore and Rockville; Fargo and Grand Forks; and Milwaukee and Green Bay?

Answer: Maryland / North Dakota / Wisconsin.

HISTORY

Which chieftain from which country discovered and colonized Greenland about A.D. 985, and which of his sons discovered North America about A.D. 1000, landing in an area he called Vinland?

Answer: Eric the Red / Norway / Leif Ericson.

LITERATURE

Identify the British author of *Kim*, the American author of *Deenie* and *Superfudge*, and the Scottish author of *The Master of Ballantrae*.

Answer: Rudyard Kipling / Judy Blume / Robert Louis Stevenson.

ENTERTAINMENT

Identify the following in the *Star Wars* films: the repellent crime lord living in Mos Eisley, the troops who are first-strike units for the Imperial Star Fleet and the Imperial Army, and the small furry creatures living in the forest of Endor.

Answer: Jabba the Hutt / Imperial Stormtroopers / Ewoks.

SPORTS AND GAMES

Which boxers are known by the nicknames "The Brown Bomber," "The Louisville Lip," and "Jack the Giant Killer"?

Answer: Joe Louis / Muhammad Ali (Cassius Clay) / Jack Dempsey.

SCIENCE AND NATURE

What is the name for the imaginary line along the 180th meridian marking the spot where a new calendar day begins, in which ocean is it located, and how many hours apart are the time zones on each side?

Answer: International Date Line (accept Date Line) / Pacific Ocean / 24 hours.

WORLD GEOGRAPHY

In which countries are Sydney and Brisbane; Salzburg and Innsbruck; and Ghent and Antwerp?

Answer: Australia / Austria / Belgium.

LEADERS & GOVERNMENT

Of which countries did Kemal Ataturk, Winston Churchill, and Menachem Begin become the leaders?

Answer: Turkey / England (accept Great Britain) / Israel.

MUSIC & RHYMES

In the rhyme, which queen "made some tarts," when did she make them, and who "stole the tarts and took them clean away"?

Answer: Queen of Hearts / "All on a summer's day" / Knave of Hearts.

LANGUAGE

Which words complete: "Lock, stock, and _____," "Tom, Dick, and _____," and "To swallow (a tale) hook, line, and _____"?

Answer: "barrel" / "Harry" / "sinker."

ARTS, RELIGION, & CULTURE

Complete these song lines: "What Child is this—who, laid to rest / On _____'s lap, is _____? / Whom _____ greet with anthems sweet while shepherds watch are keeping?"

Answer: "Mary" / "sleeping" / "Angels."

POTPOURRI

What was the nationality of the princess who became Catherine II of Russia, what was her well-known nickname, and what is the feminine form of *czar*?

Answer: German (born in present-day Poland) / "the Great" / czarina.

U.S. GEOGRAPHY

In which states are the major cities of Kansas City and Independence; Norfolk and Arlington; and Newark and Paterson?

Answer: Missouri / Virginia / New Jersey.

HISTORY

Which European explorer for which country discovered the Pacific Ocean in 1513, and what name did he give to this body of water?

Answer: Vasco de Balboa / Spain / South Sea.

LITERATURE

Complete the title of Scott O'Dell's *Island of the _____ Dolphins*, Mark Twain's *Life on the* _____, and Farley Mowat's *Never Cry* _____.

Answer: *Blue / Mississippi / Wolf.*

ENTERTAINMENT

After Dumbo wrecks the circus in the film *Dumbo*, how is he punished, what kind of elephants does he see when he gets drunk, and where do he and Timothy sleep off their drunkenness?

Answer: He is made a clown / pink elephants / in a tree.

SPORTS AND GAMES

In the game of *Clue*, how many rooms are there, which 2 begin with the letter *B*, and which 2 begin with the letter *L*?

Answer: 9 / Ballroom and Billiard Room / Library and Lounge (the others are the Hall, the Dining Room, the Kitchen, the Conservatory, and the Study).

SCIENCE AND NATURE

Which words from the Greek for "sailor of the stars" and "sailor of the universe" designate American and Soviet spacemen, and which vehicle, represented by the abbreviation LM, was used with the Apollo program?

Answer: Astronaut / cosmonaut / lunar module.

WORLD GEOGRAPHY

In which countries are Ho Chi Minh City and Da Nang; Liverpool and Birmingham; and Shanghai and Canton?

Answer: Vietnam / England / China.

LEADERS & GOVERNMENT

Of which countries did Nikita Khrushchev, Anwar Sadat, and the Ayatollah Ruhollah Khomeini become the leaders?

Answer: Soviet Union (accept Russia) / Egypt / Iran.

MUSIC & RHYMES

In the song "Tomorrow" from *Annie*, what will come out tomorrow, and which words complete, "Jus' thinking about tomorrow / Clears away the _____ and the _____"?

Answer: "the sun" / "cobwebs" / "sorrow."

LANGUAGE

Which words complete the following: "Two _____ are better than one," "To put two and _____ together," and "Two _____ in a pod"?

Answer: "heads" / "two" / "peas."

ARTS, RELIGION, & CULTURE

Which words complete the song lines: "_____ ba _____, my Lord, / Someone's _____, Lord"?

Answer: "Kum" / "yah" (or "ya") / "crying" (accept "praying" or "singing").

POTPOURRI

Name the western U.S. state that was the first to give women the right to vote, identify the failed amendment known as the ERA, and identify one of the 2 *E*'s in the name of the commission known as the EEOC.

Answer: Wyoming / Equal Rights Amendment / Equal or Employment (Opportunity Commission).

U.S. GEOGRAPHY
In which states are the major cities of Omaha and Grand Island; Billings and Great Falls; and Manchester and Nashua?
Answer: Nebraska / Montana / New Hampshire.

HISTORY
Which traveler from which country served Kublai Khan for 17 years from about 1275 to 1292, and in which country did Kublai Khan live?
Answer: Marco Polo / Italy / China.

LITERATURE
Who is the English author of *A Child's Garden of Verses*, and in one of his poems, what is it "that goes in and out with me," and from where to where is he "very, very like me"?
Answer: Robert Louis Stevenson / "(little) shadow" / "from the heels up to the head."

ENTERTAINMENT
Identify the following in the *Star Wars* films: the subtitle of 1999's prequel *Episode I*, the 9-year boy who is to become Darth Vader, and the elected queen of Naboo who is to become his wife.
Answer: *The Phantom Menace* / Anakin Skywalker / Queen Amidala.

SPORTS AND GAMES
In which cities were the Silverdome, the Superdome, and the Kingdome built?
Answer: Pontiac / New Orleans / Seattle.

SCIENCE AND NATURE
Name the "Father of Geometry," the "Father of Medicine," and the "Father of Bacteriology."
Answer: Euclid / Hippocrates / Louis Pasteur.

WORLD GEOGRAPHY

In which countries are Marseille and Toulouse; Leipzig and Dresden; and Hull and Saskatoon?

Answer: France / Germany / Canada.

LEADERS & GOVERNMENT

Of which ancient lands did Ptolemy, Cyrus the Great, and Nero become the leaders?

Answer: Egypt / Persia / Rome.

MUSIC & RHYMES

In the rhyme about "Little Jack Horner," where was he sitting, what was he eating, and what did he say when he "stuck in his thumb / And pulled out a plum"?

Answer: "In a corner" / "Eating his Christmas pie" / "What a good boy am I!"

LANGUAGE

Complete the following: "Too many _____ spoil the broth," "Too many _____ in the fire," and "Many hands make _____ work."

Answer: "cooks" / "irons" / "light."

ARTS, RELIGION, & CULTURE

Complete these song lines: "Rock of _____, cleft for me! / Let me hide myself in Thee; / Let the _____ and the _____; / From Thy wounded side which flowed, / Be of sin the double cure."

Answer: "Ages" / "water" / "blood."

POTPOURRI

Which thief and murderer from which state along with his older brother Frank robbed banks and trains, and who allegedly killed him in 1882?

Answer: Jesse James / Missouri / Robert Ford.

U.S. GEOGRAPHY

In which states are the major cities of Buffalo and Rochester; Las Vegas and Reno; and Cleveland and Cincinnati?

Answer: New York / Nevada / Ohio.

HISTORY

Which country invaded which country on June 25, 1950, and what is the name of the war that began on this day and ended on July 27, 1953?

Answer: North Korea / South Korea / Korean War.

LITERATURE

Which word completes, "Curiouser and curiouser! now I'm opening out like the largest _____ that ever was! Good-by feet!," and which character in which fictional work says the above?

Answer: "telescope" / Alice / *Alice's Adventures in Wonderland*.

ENTERTAINMENT

Which Disney film features the song "Give a Little Whistle," who sings the song, and which word completes, "And always let your _____ be your guide"?

Answer: *Pinocchio* / Jiminy Cricket / "conscience."

SPORTS AND GAMES

In which cities were the Astrodome, the Hoosierdome, and the Metrodome (Hubert H. Humphrey Metrodome) built?

Answer: Houston / Indianapolis / Minneapolis.

SCIENCE AND NATURE

Give the Roman numerals for 64, 599, and 1988.

Answer: LXIV / DXCIX / MCMLXXXVIII.

WORLD GEOGRAPHY
In which countries are Calcutta and Bombay; Tel Aviv and Haifa; and Milan and Bologna?
Answer: India / Israel / Italy.

LEADERS & GOVERNMENT
Which word completes, "But, in a larger sense, we cannot dedicate, we cannot consecrate, we cannot _____ this ground," and which U.S. President in which speech made this statement?
Answer: "hallow" / Abraham Lincoln / the Gettysburg Address.

MUSIC & RHYMES
Which words complete the rhyme: "Humpty Dumpty sat on a wall; / Humpty Dumpty had a great _____," and which 2 groups "Couldn't put Humpty Dumpty together again"?
Answer: "fall" / "All the king's horses" / "and all the king's men."

LANGUAGE
Complete the following: "There's more than one way to skin a _____," "There's no fool like an _____ fool," and "There's no place like _____."
Answer: "cat" / "old" / "home."

ARTS, RELIGION, & CULTURE
Complete these song lines: "Nearer, my _____, to Thee, / Nearer to Thee, / E'en tho' it be a _____ / That raiseth me, / Still all my _____ shall be / . . . Nearer to Thee."
Answer: "God" / "cross" / "song."

POTPOURRI
Which ancient manuscripts were found in caves near the Dead Sea, which stone serves as the key to hieroglyphics, and who flew a kite during a storm in 1752 to prove that lightning is electricity?
Answer: Dead Sea scrolls / Rosetta Stone / Benjamin Franklin.

U.S. GEOGRAPHY

In which states are the major cities of Albuquerque and Las Cruces; Worcester and Springfield; and Casper and Laramie?

Answer: New Mexico / Massachusetts / Wyoming.

HISTORY

Who was the U.S. President when the Korean War began, which American was the commander of the U.N. forces from 1950-1951, and which country intervened in this war in late 1950?

Answer: Harry S Truman / General Douglas MacArthur / People's Republic of China.

LITERATURE

Name the lion and the witch in *The Lion, the Witch and the Wardrobe*, and then name the author of this work.

Answer: Aslan / the White Witch, called the Queen of Narnia / C.S. Lewis.

ENTERTAINMENT

Which character is the narrator in the Disney film *Pinocchio*, into the house of which woodcarver does he enter, and who in the film is called "Little Wooden Head"?

Answer: Jiminy Cricket / Geppetto / Pinocchio.

SPORTS AND GAMES

How many career home runs did Babe Ruth hit, and which player for which team broke his record in 1974?

Answer: 714 / Henry (Hank) Aaron (he ended his career with 755) / Atlanta Braves.

SCIENCE AND NATURE

Which chemicals taste sour and react with some metals, which color do they turn litmus paper, and which ones taste bitter and feel slippery?

Answer: Acids / red / bases (they turn litmus paper blue).

WORLD GEOGRAPHY

In which countries are Yokohama and Osaka; Guadalajara and Monterrey; and Casablanca and Marrakech?

Answer: Japan / Mexico / Morocco.

LEADERS & GOVERNMENT

Name the first 3 U.S. Vice Presidents.

Answer: John Adams / Thomas Jefferson / Aaron Burr.

MUSIC & RHYMES

Which words complete the following: "Rock-a-bye, baby, / On the _____. / When the wind blows, / The cradle will _____. / When the _____ breaks, / The cradle will fall"?

Answer: "treetop" / "rock" / "bough" ("And down will come baby, / Cradle and all").

LANGUAGE

Complete the following: "There are lots of _____ in the sea," "There is a time to be born and a time to _____," and "There is no new thing under the _____."

Answer: "fish" / "die" / "sun."

ARTS, RELIGION, & CULTURE

Which words complete these song lines: "Jesus loves the _____ children, / All the children of the _____; / Red and yellow, black and white, / They are precious in His _____"?

Answer: "little" / "world" / "sight."

POTPOURRI

In which city do the Rockettes perform at Radio City Music Hall, and which states host the All-American Soap Box Derby at Akron and the Little League World Series finals at Williamsport?

Answer: New York / Ohio / Pennsylvania.

U.S. GEOGRAPHY

In which states are the major cities of Portland and Eugene; Charlotte and Greensboro; and Warwick and Cranston?

Answer: Oregon / North Carolina / Rhode Island.

HISTORY

Which 5th-century leader of which nomadic group is known as the "Scourge of God," and in which country at Orléans was he stopped and forced to retreat in 450?

Answer: Attila / Huns / Gaul (accept France).

LITERATURE

Give the first names of the 2 sons of Fenton and Laura Hardy featured in a series of books, and then name their home town where they lived on the corner of High and Elm.

Answer: Frank (Hardy) / Joe (Hardy) / Bayport.

ENTERTAINMENT

Which Disney film features the song "When You Wish Upon a Star"; what comes true when you wish upon a star; and which word completes the line, "No request is too _____"?

Answer: *Pinocchio* / "your dreams" / "extreme."

SPORTS AND GAMES

Which male golfers are known by the nicknames "Bantam Ben" and "Slammin' Sam," and which female golfer and all-round athlete is known as "Babe"?

Answer: Ben Hogan / Sam Snead / Mildred Didrikson (Zaharias).

SCIENCE AND NATURE

Which ancient Chinese medical treatment inserts which sharp objects into the body, and, according to Chinese philosophy, which 2 principal forces of nature are balanced by this technique?

Answer: Acupuncture / needles / yin and yang.

WORLD GEOGRAPHY

In which countries are Haarlem and Rotterdam; Christchurch and Auckland; and Krakow and Gdansk?

Answer: The Netherlands (or Holland) / New Zealand / Poland.

LEADERS & GOVERNMENT

Name the first woman who was the wife of one U.S. President and mother of another, and then name these 2 Presidents.

Answer: Abigail Adams / John Adams / John Quincy Adams.

MUSIC & RHYMES

Complete the song lines: "Frère Jacques, / Frère Jacques, / _____-vous, / _____ les _____, / Din din don, / Din din don."

Answer: "Dormez" / "Sonnez" / "matines."

LANGUAGE

Complete the following: "Practice makes _____," "Practice what you _____," and "_____ makes the world go round."

Answer: "perfect" / "preach" / "Love."

ARTS, RELIGION, & CULTURE

Which words complete these lines: "Jesus loves me! this I know, / For the _____ tells me so; / Little _____ to Him belong; / They are weak, but He is _____"?

Answer: "Bible" / "ones" / "strong."

POTPOURRI

Which Civil War Confederate general was known as "Marse Robert," which American WWI general was called "Black Jack," and which American WWII general was nicknamed "Old Blood and Guts"?

Answer: Robert E. Lee / John Joseph Pershing / George S. Patton Jr.

U.S. GEOGRAPHY

In which states are the major cities of Charleston and Greenville; Erie and Allentown; and Memphis and Knoxville?

Answer: South Carolina / Pennsylvania / Tennessee.

HISTORY

Which Carolingian king of the Franks is called "Charles the Great," which empire is he sometimes considered to have founded in 800, and in which city was he crowned emperor by Pope Leo III?

Answer: Charlemagne / Holy Roman Empire (others say 962 under Otto I) / Rome.

LITERATURE

In a poem in Lewis Carroll's *Through the Looking Glass*, which pair "Were walking close at hand," and which word completes, "O _____, come and walk with us!"

Answer: The Walrus / the Carpenter / "oysters."

ENTERTAINMENT

What are the names of Geppetto's goldfish and black kitten in the Disney film *Pinocchio*, and what is the name of the film's evil puppeteer who keeps Pinocchio locked up in a bird cage?

Answer: Cleo / Figaro / Stromboli.

SPORTS AND GAMES

Which basketball players are known by the nicknames "Doctor J," "Magic," and "Wilt the Stilt"?

Answer: Julius Erving / Earvin Johnson / Wilt Chamberlain.

SCIENCE AND NATURE

Which hormone secreted by which gland causes the body to change to be more efficient for "fight or flight," and which word named after Luigi Galvani means "stimulated as if by electric shock"?

Answer: Adrenaline (accept epinephrine) / adrenal gland / galvanic (or galvanized).

WORLD GEOGRAPHY

In which countries are Mecca and Medina; Zurich and Geneva; and Barcelona and Seville?

Answer: Saudi Arabia / Switzerland / Spain.

LEADERS & GOVERNMENT

Besides Madison, Monroe, and Carter, which other 3 U.S. Presidents were named "James"?

Answer: Polk / Buchanan / Garfield.

MUSIC & RHYMES

Complete the following rhyme: "Little _____ has lost her _____ / And doesn't know where to find them. / Leave them alone and they'll come home, / Wagging their _____ behind them."

Answer: "Bo-peep" / "sheep" / "tails."

LANGUAGE

Complete the following sayings: "One good _____ deserves another," "One rotten (or bad) _____ spoils the (whole) barrel," and "An ounce of _____ is worth a pound of cure."

Answer: "turn" / "apple" / "prevention."

ARTS, RELIGION, & CULTURE

Which words complete these lines from "Adeste, Fideles": "O come, all ye _____, / Joyful and _____, / O come ye, O come ye to _____"?

Answer: "faithful" / "triumphant" / "Bethlehem."

POTPOURRI

Identify the U.S. service academies located in Maryland, Colorado, and West Point, New York.

Answer: Naval Academy / Air Force Academy / Military Academy.

U.S. GEOGRAPHY
In which states are the major cities of El Paso and Fort Worth; Sioux Falls and Rapid City; and Seattle and Spokane?
Answer: Texas / South Dakota / Washington.

HISTORY
Which Mongol leader created one of history's largest land empires in the 13th century, on which continent did he do so, and in which country did he conquer the Chin empire from about 1213-1215?
Answer: Genghis (Jenghiz) Kahn / Asia / China.

LITERATURE
What kind of an animal is Babar in Brunhoff's series of stories, who becomes his queen, and what is the name of the city that he builds?
Answer: An elephant / Celeste (accept his cousin) / Celesteville.

ENTERTAINMENT
Identify the following in the *Star Wars* films: Darth Sidious' loyal apprentice, the elder Jedi Knight who mentors Obi-Wan Kenobi and discovers Anakin Skywalker's special powers, and the exiled member of the Gungan race indebted to this Jedi Knight.
Answer: Darth Maul / Qui-Gon Jinn / Jar Jar Binks.

SPORTS AND GAMES
Identify the 3 red properties in *Monopoly*.
Answer: Kentucky Avenue / Indiana Avenue / Illinois Avenue.

SCIENCE AND NATURE
In which exercise method does a person increase the supply and use of oxygen; in which one does a person run at a relaxed, moderate pace; and in which one does a person push against an immovable object?
Answer: Aerobics / jogging / isometrics.

WORLD GEOGRAPHY

In which countries are Sapporo and Kyoto; Tijuana and Acapulco; and Tangier and Fez?

Answer: Japan / Mexico / Morocco.

LEADERS & GOVERNMENT

Identify the 3 U.S. Presidents besides John Adams and John Quincy Adams with the first name John. One of them has a middle name of Calvin.

Answer: John Tyler / John Calvin Coolidge / John F. Kennedy.

MUSIC & RHYMES

Which words complete the rhyme: "Twinkle, twinkle, little _____, / How I wonder what you are! / Up above the _____ so high, / Like a _____ in the sky"?

Answer: "star" / "world" / "diamond."

LANGUAGE

According to the sayings, what should one not "throw out with the bath water," where should one not "shout fire," and where should one not "wash dirty linen"?

Answer: "the baby" / "in a crowded theater" / "in public."

ARTS, RELIGION, & CULTURE

Which words complete Matthew 19:24: "It is easier for a _____ to go through the eye of a _____, than for a rich man to enter the _____ of God"?

Answer: "camel" / "needle" / "kingdom."

POTPOURRI

How many signs of the Zodiac are there, what is the term for a person who tells fortunes by studying the stars, and what chart reports these predictions?

Answer: 12 / astrologer / horoscope (accept birth chart).

U.S. GEOGRAPHY

In which states are the major cities of Burlington and Rutland; Provo and Ogden; and Huntington and Wheeling?

Answer: Vermont / Utah / West Virginia.

HISTORY

Which war did the U.S. fight in 1898, which U.S. ship was blown up in the Havana harbor on February 15, and which battle on July 1 established Theodore Roosevelt's "Rough Rider" reputation?

Answer: Spanish-American War / *Maine* / San Juan Hill (accept Battle of Santiago or Kettle Hill).

LITERATURE

Which word completes the title of Mary Elizabeth Mapes Dodge's book *Hans* _____, in which country is it set, and which word completes the book's subtitle *The Silver* _____?

Answer: *Brinker* / Holland / *Skates*.

ENTERTAINMENT

In the Disney film *Pinocchio*, which 2 scheming animals convince Pinocchio to become an actor, and what are their names?

Answer: A fox and a cat / Honest John (or J. Worthington Foulfellow) / Gideon.

SPORTS AND GAMES

Which sport is "The Sport of Kings," which one is "The Grand Old Game," and which one is "The King of Autumn Sports"?

Answer: Horse racing / baseball / football.

SCIENCE AND NATURE

Identify the colors of an emerald, a ruby, and a sapphire.

Answer: Green / red / blue.

WORLD GEOGRAPHY

In which countries are Graz and Linz; Melbourne and Perth; and Nottingham, Manchester, and Leeds?

Answer: Austria / Australia / England.

LEADERS & GOVERNMENT

Identify 3 of the 4 U.S. Presidents with the first name William.

Answer: William H. Harrison / William McKinley / William H. Taft / William J. Clinton.

MUSIC & RHYMES

Which words complete "The Muppet Show Theme": "It's time to play the music;" "light the lights;" "put on _____;" "dress up _____;" and "raise the _____"?

Answer: "makeup" / "right" / "curtain."

LANGUAGE

Complete these sayings: "A rolling stone gathers no _____," "A stitch in time saves _____," and "Time flies when you're having _____."

Answer: "moss" / "nine" / "fun."

ARTS, RELIGION, & CULTURE

Which words from the Bible's King James Version complete the proverbs from Matthew: "Ye cannot serve God and _____," "Ask and it shall be _____," and "Seek and ye shall _________"?

Answer: "mammon" / "given" / "find."

POTPOURRI

Which Greek carried a lantern in daytime to look for an honest man, to whom did God speak from a burning bush, and which Indian leader, the "great soul," spun thread and cloth for his own garments?

Answer: Diogenes / Moses / Mahatma Gandhi.

U.S. GEOGRAPHY

Which capital cities are nicknamed the "Capital of the Confederacy," the "City of Three Capitols," and the "Mile High City"?

Answer: Richmond (accept Montgomery) / Little Rock / Denver.

HISTORY

With which country did the U.S. fight the War of 1812, who was the U.S. President at the time, and which U.S. city did the enemy burn on August 24, 1814?

Answer: Great Britain / James Madison / Washington, D.C.

LITERATURE

Which character in which work by which author is known for saying "Bah, Humbug"?

Answer: Ebenezer Scrooge / *A Christmas Carol* / Charles Dickens.

ENTERTAINMENT

In which country is the 1998 Disney film *Mulan* set, across what barrier does Shan-Yu lead his invading army, and what name designates the warlike invaders he leads?

Answer: China / Great Wall / Huns.

SPORTS AND GAMES

Which positions are numbered 2, 4, and 8 in baseball's scoring system?

Answer: Catcher / second base / center field.

SCIENCE AND NATURE

Identify the largest organ of the human body, and then identify its outermost layer and its middle layer.

Answer: Skin / epidermis / dermis.

WORLD GEOGRAPHY

In which division of Great Britain are Glasgow and Aberdeen, and in which countries are Cork, Limerick, and Kilkenny, and Wiesbaden, Hamburg, and Stuttgart?

Answer: Scotland / Ireland / Germany.

LEADERS & GOVERNMENT

Identify the 2 Presidents with the first name Andrew and the only one known by his first name Thomas.

Answer: Andrew Jackson / Andrew Johnson / Thomas Jefferson.

MUSIC & RHYMES

Complete these song lines: "Home, home on the range, / Where the _____ and the _____ play, / Where seldom is heard a _____ word, / And the skies are not cloudy all day."

Answer: "deer" / "antelope" / "discouraging."

LANGUAGE

Which words complete these sayings: "Don't bite the _____ that feeds you," "Don't cross that _____ till you come to it," and "Don't cut off your _____ to spite your face"?

Answer: "hand" / "bridge" / "nose."

ARTS, RELIGION, & CULTURE

Complete each of the following from Matthew: "The spirit is willing, but the flesh is _____," "No man can serve two _____," and "An eye for an eye, and a tooth for a _____."

Answer: "weak" / "masters" / "tooth."

POTPOURRI

Which American in which year in which location said, "That's one small step for (a) man, one giant leap for mankind"?

Answer: Neil Armstrong / 1969 / on the moon.

U.S. GEOGRAPHY

Which capital cities are nicknamed the "Insurance Capital of the World," the "First City of the First State," and the "Big Peach"?

Answer: Hartford / Dover / Atlanta.

HISTORY

In which year was a peace treaty signed at Ghent ending the War of 1812, and which battle won by which American commander, later a U.S. President, was fought the following year on January 8?

Answer: 1814 (Treaty of Ghent) / Battle of New Orleans / Andrew Jackson.

LITERATURE

Complete the following titles by John Steinbeck: *Of Mice and* _____ and *The Grapes of* _____, and then identify the animal in his *Travels with Charley*.

Answer: *Men* / *Wrath* / dog (or pet poodle).

ENTERTAINMENT

Into which animals are all the bad boys changed in the Disney film *Pinocchio*; which animal, the "Terror of the Deep," swallows Geppetto; and what is this animal's name?

Answer: Donkeys (jackasses) / a whale / Monstro.

SPORTS AND GAMES

Which positions are numbered 3, 6, and 9 in baseball's scoring system?

Answer: First base / shortstop / right field.

SCIENCE AND NATURE

Besides the mouth and the stomach, identify the 3 main parts of the long tube called the alimentary canal, the main part of the digestive system.

Answer: Esophagus / small intestine / large intestine.

WORLD GEOGRAPHY

In which foreign countries are Vancouver and Windsor; Alexandria and Port Said; and Lyon and Nice?

Answer: Canada / Egypt / France.

LEADERS & GOVERNMENT

Give the political party of each of the following: Franklin Roosevelt, Harry Truman, and Dwight Eisenhower.

Answer: Democrat / Democrat / Republican.

MUSIC & RHYMES

Which words complete the lines from "Jack and the Beanstalk": "Fee-fi-fo-fum! / I smell the blood of an _____ / Be he alive, or be he _____, / I'll grind his _____ to make my bread"?

Answer: "Englishman" / "dead" / "bones."

LANGUAGE

Which words complete the phrases: "To rest on one's _____," "To be the _____ of one's eye," and "To bring down the _____"?

Answer: "laurels" (accept "oars") / "apple" / "house."

ARTS, RELIGION, & CULTURE

Which words complete these Biblical verses: "The wages of sin is _____," "A soft answer turneth away _____," and "Man cannot live by bread _____"?

Answer: "death" / "wrath" / "alone."

POTPOURRI

According to superstition, on which side of the bed should one not arise in the morning, where should one not open an umbrella, and on which day should one not risk any new enterprise?

Answer: Wrong side (accept left side) / in a building / Friday the 13th.

U.S. GEOGRAPHY
Which capital cities are nicknamed the "Crossroads of the Pacific," the "Home of Abraham Lincoln," and the "Hoosier Capital"?
Answer: Honolulu / Springfield / Indianapolis.

HISTORY
At which campground in which state did which leader of the Continental Army spend a harsh winter with his 11,000 troops in 1777-1778?
Answer: Valley Forge / Pennsylvania / George Washington.

LITERATURE
Which words complete the line, "second to the _____ and then straight on till _____" in the play *Peter Pan*, and what is the name of Peter Pan's fairyland?
Answer: "right" / "morning" / Never Land (accept Never-Never Land).

ENTERTAINMENT
In which type of box does Jiminy Cricket sleep in Geppetto's house in the Disney film *Pinocchio*, which object does he carry in his hand, and which shiny object does the Fairy award him?
Answer: A match box / an umbrella / a gold medallion.

SPORTS AND GAMES
Which positions are numbered 1, 5, and 7 in baseball's scoring system?
Answer: Pitcher / third base / left field.

SCIENCE AND NATURE
What are the words used to designate a group of lions, a group of ants, and a group of elephants?
Answer: Pride / colony / herd.

WORLD GEOGRAPHY

In which countries are Montreal and Hamilton; Munich and Frankfurt; and Turin and Genoa?

Answer: Canada / Germany / Italy.

LEADERS & GOVERNMENT

Give the political party of each of the following: John Kennedy, Lyndon Johnson, and Richard Nixon.

Answer: Democrat / Democrat / Republican.

MUSIC & RHYMES

In the nursery rhyme, who killed Cock Robin, which weapon did he use, and who saw Cock Robin die with his "little eye"?

Answer: The sparrow / bow and arrow / the fly.

LANGUAGE

Which words complete these phrases: "To be like a _____ in a china shop," "To have two _____ feet," and "To make a mountain out of a _____"?

Answer: "bull" / "left" / "molehill."

ARTS, RELIGION, & CULTURE

Which words complete, "Do unto _____ as you would have them do unto _____," and what "colorful" name is given to this Biblical principle?

Answer: "others" / "you" / Golden Rule.

POTPOURRI

Which speedy little cartoon animal travels in a cyclonic fashion, which type of animal does he love to chase and eat, and which country owns the island where this fierce animal lives in real life?

Answer: Tasmanian Devil / rabbit / Australia.

U.S. GEOGRAPHY
Which capital cities are nicknamed the "Center of the Nation," the "Bluegrass Capital," and the "Home of the U.S. Naval Academy"?
Answer: Topeka / Frankfort / Annapolis.

HISTORY
Which theologian in which country started the Protestant Reformation in the 16th century, and which major branch of Protestantism is named after him?
Answer: Martin Luther / Germany / Lutheranism.

LITERATURE
Name the 3 children of the Darling family whom Peter Pan persuades to go with him to the fairyland he calls home.
Answer: Wendy / John / Michael.

ENTERTAINMENT
Which Disney films feature the songs "I've Got No Strings," "The Bare Necessities," and Stravinsky's ballet *Rite of Spring*?
Answer: *Pinnochio / The Jungle Book / Fantasia.*

SPORTS AND GAMES
Which boxers are known by the nicknames "Gentleman Jim," "Smokin' Joe," and "The Great John L."?
Answer: James J. Corbett / Joe Frazier / John L. Sullivan.

SCIENCE AND NATURE
Which parts of the body are studied in cardiology, audiology, and odontology?
Answer: Heart / ears (hearing) / teeth.

WORLD GEOGRAPHY

Name 3 of the 4 continents bordering the Indian Ocean.

Answer: Africa / Asia / Australia / Antarctica.

LEADERS & GOVERNMENT

Give the political party of each of the following: Gerald Ford, James Carter, and Ronald Reagan.

Answer: Republican / Democrat / Republican.

MUSIC & RHYMES

Complete the rhyme: "Peter, Peter Pumpkin-_____, / Had a _____ and couldn't keep her, / He put her in a pumpkin _____, / And there he kept her very well."

Answer: "Eater" / "wife" / "shell."

LANGUAGE

Complete each of the following triplets: "Blood, sweat, and _____"; "Cool, calm, and _____"; and "Hop, skip, and a _____."

Answer: "tears" / "collected" / "jump."

ARTS, RELIGION, & CULTURE

Complete these song lines: "So I'll cherish the old rugged _____ / Till my trophies at last I lay _____. / . . . And exchange it some day for a _____."

Answer: "cross" / "down" / "crown."

POTPOURRI

What are the better known names of a U.S. President born Leslie Lynch King Jr., a magician born Erich Weiss, and a writer born Theodor Seuss Geisel?

Answer: Gerald R. Ford / Houdini / Dr. Seuss.

U.S. GEOGRAPHY

Which capital cities are nicknamed the "Cradle of the American Revolution," the "Saintly City," and "Last Chance Gulch"?

Answer: Boston / St. Paul (accept Salt Lake City) / Helena.

HISTORY

Which 15th-century goldsmith in which country is credited with the development of printing from movable type, and what was the first book ever produced mechanically?

Answer: Johann Gutenberg / Germany / (Gutenberg) Bible.

LITERATURE

Name the villainous captain of the pirate ship in James Barrie's *Peter Pan*, name his ship, and then name the animal that swallows a clock and kills this captain.

Answer: Captain James Hook / *Jolly Roger* / crocodile.

ENTERTAINMENT

Which Disney films feature the songs "Honor to Us All," "Zero to Hero," and "A Guy Like You"?

Answer: *Mulan* / *Hercules* / *The Hunchback of Notre Dame*.

SPORTS AND GAMES

Which baseball players are known by the nicknames "Stan the Man," "Joltin Joe," and the "the Pride of the Yankees"?

Answer: Stan Musial / Joe DiMaggio / Lou Gehrig.

SCIENCE AND NATURE

Which parts of the body are studied in craniology, osteology, and ophthalmology?

Answer: Skull / bones / eyes.

WORLD GEOGRAPHY
In which country are Windsor Castle and Stonehenge; in which one are Banff National Park and Niagara Falls; and which one has the Great Barrier Reef on its northeast coast?
Answer: England / Canada / Australia.

LEADERS & GOVERNMENT
Give the political party of each of the following: George Washington, Andrew Jackson, and Abraham Lincoln.
Answer: Federalist / Democrat (accept Democrat-Republican) / Republican.

MUSIC & RHYMES
Complete the nursery rhyme: "Hey diddle diddle / The _____ and the _____, / The _____ jumped over the moon."
Answer: "cat" / "fiddle" / "cow."

LANGUAGE
According to the sayings, what kind of a "lining is every cloud supposed to have," what is the "root of all evil," and what does a "person not have enough of to come in out of the rain"?
Answer: Silver / (love of) money / intelligence (accept sense).

ARTS, RELIGION, & CULTURE
What 3 vows do Roman Catholic priests and nuns profess when they join the order?
Answer: Poverty / chastity / obedience.

POTPOURRI
Which Indian girl was known as Matoaka and Lady Rebecca and later as Mrs. John Rolfe, and of which tribes were Geronimo and Sitting Bull the leaders?
Answer: Pocahontas / Apache / (Hunkpapa Teton) Sioux.

U.S. GEOGRAPHY

Which capital cities are nicknamed the "Cornhusker Capital," the "Oldest and Quaintest City in the U.S.," and the "Capital of Soonerland"?

Answer: Lincoln / Santa Fe / Oklahoma City.

HISTORY

Which term from the French for "rebirth" describes the 14th-16th century European movement that revived ancient values and styles, in which country did it start, and which period preceded it?

Answer: Renaissance / Italy / Middle Ages.

LITERATURE

Who is Peter Pan's fairy friend with a fading light; what is the name of the family dog; and who is the Indian maiden, daughter of the chief of the Piccaninnies, whom Peter rescues?

Answer: Tinker Bell / Nana / Tiger Lily.

ENTERTAINMENT

Name the 3 Good Fairies in the Disney film *Sleeping Beauty*.

Answer: Mistress Flora / Mistress Fauna / Mistress Merryweather.

SPORTS AND GAMES

Identify 3 of the 4 track events in the decathlon.

Answer: 100-meter run / 400-meter run / 1500-meter run / 110-meter hurdles.

SCIENCE AND NATURE

What is studied in ecology, entomology, and dermatology?

Answer: Environment / insects / skin.

WORLD GEOGRAPHY
In which countries are the Gobi Desert and the Forbidden City; the Bay of Pigs and the Guantánamo U.S. Naval Base; and the Little Mermaid Statue and Tivoli Amusement Park?
Answer: China / Cuba / Denmark.

LEADERS & GOVERNMENT
Give the political party of each of the following: Theodore Roosevelt, Woodrow Wilson, and Herbert Hoover.
Answer: Republican / Democrat / Republican.

MUSIC & RHYMES
Which words complete the rhyme which begins with the words "Hey diddle diddle": "The little _____ laughed / To see such sport / And the _____ ran away with the _____"?
Answer: "dog" / "dish" / "spoon."

LANGUAGE
Which words complete the sayings: "Get a _____ of one's own medicine," "Get a _____ in edgewise," and "Get off on the _____ foot"?
Answer: "dose" (accept "taste") / "word" / "right" (accept "wrong").

ARTS, RELIGION, & CULTURE
Which word completes this statement from Luke, "_____, forgive them; for they know not what they do," who made this statement, and at which Biblical site?
Answer: "Father" / Jesus / Calvary (or Golgotha).

POTPOURRI
On which avenue is the White House, on which street does the prime minister of Great Britain live, and on which avenue does the president of France live?
Answer: (1600) Pennsylvania Avenue / (10) Downing Street / Les Champs Elysées.

U.S. GEOGRAPHY

Which capital cities are nicknamed the "Roger Williams City," the "Gateway to the Black Hills," and the "Music City, U.S.A."?

Answer: Providence / Pierre / Nashville.

HISTORY

What is the word for the Christian military expeditions to recapture which area from which religious group between the 11th and 14th centuries?

Answer: Crusades / Holy Land / Muslims (or Moslems).

LITERATURE

Into which German city does the Pied Piper come, what kind of animals does he lead into the river and drown, and whom does he lead away to a cave where they disappear forever?

Answer: Hamelin / rats / children.

ENTERTAINMENT

Whom does Mulan need to impress to make a good match in marriage in the Disney film *Mulan*, whose place does she take in the army, and what name does she take as a soldier?

Answer: Matchmaker / her father's / Ping.

SPORTS AND GAMES

Which 2 major league baseball teams moved from which Eastern state to California in 1958?

Answer: San Francisco Giants / Los Angeles Dodgers / New York (formerly the New York Giants and the Brooklyn Dodgers).

SCIENCE AND NATURE

How many cells does an amoeba have, what is the meaning of pseudopodia, the means by which amoebas move, and what does an amoeba do when it encounters food?

Answer: One / "false feet" / it surrounds it (before engulfing it; called phagocytosis).

WORLD GEOGRAPHY

In which countries are the Library at Alexandria and the Aswan Dam; the Eiffel Tower and Montmartre; and the Black Forest and the Cologne Cathedral?

Answer: Egypt / France / Germany.

LEADERS & GOVERNMENT

According to legend, which U.S. President said he could not tell a lie, to whom did he make this statement, and which type of tree did he say he chopped down?

Answer: George Washington / his father / cherry tree.

MUSIC & RHYMES

Complete the rhyme: "One a penny, two a penny, hot cross _____; / If you have no _____, give them to your _____."

Answer: "buns" / "daughters" / "sons."

LANGUAGE

Which words complete the following: "Give him enough _____ and he'll hang himself," "Give him an inch and he'll take a _____," and "Give someone the _____ shoulder"?

Answer: "rope" / "mile" / "cold."

ARTS, RELIGION, & CULTURE

In which Christmas ballet by which Russian composer do all the toys come alive, and which fairy leads the Waltz of the Flowers?

Answer: *The Nutcracker* / Peter Tchaikovsky / Sugar Plum Fairy.

POTPOURRI

What is the meaning of the acronym UFO, in which Atlantic Ocean triangle have many ships allegedly disappeared, and which Pacific Ocean island is the site of huge stone statues of unknown origin?

Answer: Unidentified Flying Object / Bermuda Triangle (accept Devil's Triangle) / Easter Island.

U.S. GEOGRAPHY

Which capital cities are nicknamed the "Mormon Capital," the "Capital of the Green Mountain State," and the "Capital City of the Evergreen State"?

Answer: Salt Lake City / Montpelier / Olympia.

HISTORY

Of which country was Cleopatra (VII) the queen, whom did she marry in 36 B.C., and by which animal did she allow herself to be bitten, thus killing herself?

Answer: Egypt / Mark Antony / asp (accept cobra).

LITERATURE

Which 2 animals are "fighting for the crown" in Lewis Carroll's *Through the Looking Glass*, and whom do these animals call "The Monster"?

Answer: The Lion / the Unicorn / Alice.

ENTERTAINMENT

In the Disney film, Sleeping Beauty is cursed to die before she reaches which birthday, on which part of a spinning wheel does she prick her finger, and which wicked fairy curses her?

Answer: 16th birthday / spindle / Mistress Maleficent.

SPORTS AND GAMES

How many innings are there in a regular complete major league baseball game, how many outs are in each inning, and in which inning is there a "stretch"?

Answer: 9 / 6 (3 for each team) / 7th.

SCIENCE AND NATURE

Give the words for "an animal doctor," for "a person who mounts animal skins," and for "a map maker."

Answer: Veterinarian / taxidermist / cartographer (accept topographer).

WORLD GEOGRAPHY

In which countries are Mount Olympus and the Acropolis; the Taj Mahal and the Ganges River; and the River Shannon and the beautiful lakes of Killarney?

Answer: Greece / India / Ireland.

LEADERS & GOVERNMENT

Which U.S. President served the longest term of office, how many times was he elected, and which President served the shortest term?

Answer: Franklin Roosevelt / 4 / William H. Harrison (31 days).

MUSIC & RHYMES

Which words complete the rhyme: "A dillar, a _____, / A ten o'clock _____, / What makes you come so soon? / You used to come at ten o'clock, / And now you come at _____"?

Answer: "dollar" / "scholar" / "noon."

LANGUAGE

Which words complete these sayings: "To lock the barn door after the _____ has gone," "Strike while the _____ is hot," and "The pot calls the kettle _____"?

Answer: "horse" / "iron" / "black."

ARTS, RELIGION, & CULTURE

Complete the following: "Many are called, but few are _____," "Cleanliness is next to _____," and "To err is human, to forgive _____."

Answer: "chosen" / "godliness" / "divine."

POTPOURRI

How many days are ordinarily in a year, how many days are in a leap year, and how often does a leap year usually occur?

Answer: 365 / 366 / every 4 years (except for some century years).

U.S. GEOGRAPHY

Which Alabama cities are nicknamed the "Pittsburgh of the South," and the "Queen City of the Gulf," and which Alaska city is the "Largest City in the Largest State"?

Answer: Birmingham / Mobile / Anchorage.

HISTORY

Which American naval commanders said: "Don't give up the ship" and "We have met the enemy and they are ours"; and which U.S. President said, "It was involuntary. They sank my boat"?

Answer: James Lawrence / Oliver Hazard Perry / John Kennedy.

LITERATURE

Which German-Jewish girl wrote a diary during her 2 years in hiding during WWII, in which city did she hide, and what name did she give to her diary?

Answer: Anne Frank / Amsterdam (The Netherlands) / "Kitty."

ENTERTAINMENT

In the Disney film *Mulan*, what kind of creature is named Mushu, what kind of animal is named Khan, and what kind of insect is named Cri-Kee?

Answer: Dragon / horse / cricket.

SPORTS AND GAMES

How many minutes and how many periods are in a regulation NFL game, and what "gruesome" name is given to the overtime period?

Answer: 60 / 4 / "sudden death."

SCIENCE AND NATURE

Which ancient form of chemistry tried to change base metals into gold, which metal is called quicksilver, and which spring was fabled to have waters that restored health and youth?

Answer: Alchemy (accept transmutation) / mercury / Fountain of Youth.

WORLD GEOGRAPHY

In which countries are the Wailing Wall and the Negev Desert; St. Mark's Square and St. Peter's Basilica; and the Seikan Tunnel and the Imperial Palace?

Answer: Israel / Italy / Japan.

LEADERS & GOVERNMENT

Which U.S. President was the first to get stuck in a bathtub, which one was the first to be attacked by a bunny, and which one was the first to work with Bonzo the chimpanzee?

Answer: William H. Taft / Jimmy Carter / Ronald Reagan.

MUSIC & RHYMES

Which words complete the rhyme: "One flew _____, one flew _____, / One flew over the _____'s nest"?

Answer: "east" / "west" / "cuckoo."

LANGUAGE

Which words complete the sayings: "Spare the _____ and spoil the _____" and "Speech is _____; silence is gold"?

Answer: "rod" / "child" / "silver."

ARTS, RELIGION, & CULTURE

Which 3 words complete the phrase based on Ecclesiastes 8:15: "_____, _____, and be _____ for tomorrow we die"?

Answer: "Eat" / "drink" / "merry."

POTPOURRI

How many strings does a ukulele have, in which U.S. state was this instrument developed from a small guitar, and what is the spelling of the word *ukulele*?

Answer: 4 / Hawaii / U-K-U-L-E-L-E.

U.S. GEOGRAPHY

Which Arizona city is nicknamed "The Old Pueblo," which California city is the "Big Orange," and which Montana city is the "City That is a Mile High and a Mile Deep"?

Answer: Tucson / Los Angeles / Butte.

HISTORY

After which one of the 2 legendary founders of Rome was the city named, and on which hill above which river was the city founded about 753 B.C.?

Answer: Romulus / Palatine Hill / Tiber River.

LITERATURE

What are the names of the land of tiny people and the land of giants in the satirical *Gulliver's Travels*, and who wrote this work?

Answer: Lilliput / Brobdingnag / Jonathan Swift.

ENTERTAINMENT

Name the sea witch banished from the sea god's palace in Disney's *The Little Mermaid*, name her 2 pet eels, and identify what the Little Mermaid must give up to become human for 3 days.

Answer: Ursula / Flotsam and Jetsam / her voice.

SPORTS AND GAMES

Identify the 3 events in the Ironman Triathlon.

Answer: Swimming / bicycling / marathon run.

SCIENCE AND NATURE

How many feet are in a yard, how many feet are in a mile, and how many yards are in a mile?

Answer: 3 / 5,280 / 1,760.

WORLD GEOGRAPHY
In which countries are the Aztec ruins and Chapultepec Park; Kruger National Park and the Johannesburg gold mines; and Lake Baikal and Mount Elbrus, Europe's highest point?
Answer: Mexico / South Africa / Russia.

LEADERS & GOVERNMENT
In which month does the inauguration of the U.S. President take place, in which month was it formerly held, and which person traditionally administers the oath of office?
Answer: January (20) / March (4) / Chief Justice of the United States.

MUSIC & RHYMES
Which words complete the rhyme: "What are little boys made of? / _____ and _____, and _____ dogs' tails; / That's what little boys are made of"?
Answer: "snips" (accept "snaps") / "snails" / "puppy."

LANGUAGE
Complete the sayings: "No news is _____ news," "You're never too _____ to learn," and "To have no more idea than the man in the _____."
Answer: "good" / "old" / "moon."

ARTS, RELIGION, & CULTURE
Name the colors of 3 of the 4 horses of the Bible's Four Horsemen of the Apocalypse.
Answer: White / red / black / pale (accept ashen).

POTPOURRI
Traditionally, which phenomenon has gold at the end of its path, which mythological king turned whatever he touched into gold, and which "golden" gift is usually given to retiring employees?
Answer: Rainbow / Midas / gold watch.

U.S. GEOGRAPHY

Which California city is nicknamed the "City by the Golden Gate," which Delaware city is the "Chemical Capital of the World," and which Illinois city is the "City of the Big Shoulders"?

Answer: San Francisco / Wilmington / Chicago.

HISTORY

How many Punic Wars were fought between 264 and 146 B.C., and between which 2 cities were these wars fought?

Answer: 3 / Rome / Carthage.

LITERATURE

According to Edward Lear's verse, which 2 animals "went to sea / In a beautiful pea-green boat," and what did they take to sea along with "plenty of money"?

Answer: "Owl" / "Pussycat" / "some honey" (in "The Owl and the Pussycat").

ENTERTAINMENT

Identify the frog who hosts *The Muppet Show*, the pig who is in love with him, and the bear with the peaked head and tiny hat who wants to be a comedian.

Answer: Kermit the Frog / Miss Piggy / Fozzie Bear.

SPORTS AND GAMES

Who broke Ty Cobb's record of 4,191 career hits, of which team did he become the manager in 1984, and which word completes his nickname "Charlie _____"?

Answer: Pete Rose / Cincinnati Reds / "Hustle."

SCIENCE AND NATURE

How many inches are in a foot, how many inches are in a yard, and which unit in the metric system equals 39.37 inches?

Answer: 12 / 36 / metre (meter).

WORLD GEOGRAPHY
In which countries are the El Escorial palace and The Alhambra; Oxford and Cambridge universities; and the CN Tower and the Calgary Stampede?
Answer: Spain / England / Canada.

LEADERS & GOVERNMENT
Which U.S. Presidents are associated with the slogans "Square Deal," "New Deal," and "Great Society"?
Answer: Theodore Roosevelt / Franklin Roosevelt / Lyndon Johnson.

MUSIC & RHYMES
Which words complete the rhyme: "What are little girls made of? / _____ and _____, and everything _____; / That's what little girls are made of"?
Answer: "Sugar" / "spice" / "nice."

LANGUAGE
Identify the word with the same, or nearly the same, meaning as another; the one opposite in meaning to another; and the one with the same pronunciation as another, but with a different meaning.
Answer: Synonym / antonym / homonym (or homophone).

ARTS, RELIGION, & CULTURE
Give the English translation of 3 of the 4 parts of the letters I.N.R.I. that were placed on the cross of Christ.
Answer: Jesus / (of) Nazareth / King / (of the) Jews.

POTPOURRI
Traditionally, which song is sung to close New Year's Eve, which "kiss" is given before gangsters murder a victim, and what is the Catholic rite administered to a person at the hour of death?
Answer: "Auld Lang Syne" / kiss of death / Anointing of the Sick (formerly called Extreme Unction; accept last rites).

U.S. GEOGRAPHY

Which Kansas city is nicknamed the "Cow Capital," which Kentucky city is the "Home of the Kentucky Derby," and which Louisiana city is the "City of Jazz"?

Answer: Wichita / Louisville / New Orleans.

HISTORY

Which great Carthaginian general in the Second Punic War attacked Italy, which mountains did he cross with soldiers and elephants to enter Italy, and which battle did he win in 216 B.C.?

Answer: Hannibal / Alps / Battle of Cannae.

LITERATURE

Who is the author of *Alice's Adventures in Wonderland*, what is its sequel, and which subject did this author teach at Oxford?

Answer: Lewis Carroll (Charles Lutwidge Dodgson) / *Through the Looking Glass* / mathematics.

ENTERTAINMENT

What is the surname of Beaver on TV's *Leave It To Beaver*, what is his real first name in the show, and what is his brother's name?

Answer: Cleaver / Theodore / Wally.

SPORTS AND GAMES

In which cities were Madison Square Garden, The Omni, and the Joe Louis Sports Arena built?

Answer: New York / Atlanta / Detroit.

SCIENCE AND NATURE

Who invented a stove in 1740 that was named after him, for which astronomer is the comet that appears about every 76 years named, and for which scientist is the process of using heat to kill germs named?

Answer: Benjamin Franklin / Edmund Halley / Louis Pasteur (pasteurization is the process).

WORLD GEOGRAPHY

In which countries are the Rhône River and Grenoble; the Parthenon and the Temple of Apollo in Corinth; and the Po Valley and La Scala Opera House?

Answer: France / Greece / Italy.

LEADERS & GOVERNMENT

Identify the U.S. Presidents whose homes were Mount Vernon, Monticello, and Montpelier.

Answer: George Washington / Thomas Jefferson / James Madison.

MUSIC & RHYMES

Which words complete the rhyme: "Solomon Grundy, / _____ on a Monday, / _____ on Tuesday, / _____ on Wednesday"?

Answer: "Born" / "Christened" / "Married."

LANGUAGE

What are the 2 voices of verbs in English grammar, and in which voice is the sentence, "The novel was written by John"?

Answer: Active voice / passive voice / passive voice.

ARTS, RELIGION, & CULTURE

Which 2 Biblical cities destroyed by God are figuratively regarded as centers of vice and immorality, and which word completes their means of destruction by "a rain of brimstone and _____"?

Answer: Sodom / Gomorrah / "fire."

POTPOURRI

Of which Asian country did Corazon Aquino become the leader, in which body of water is it located, and how is this country's name spelled?

Answer: Philippines / Pacific Ocean / P-H-I-L-I-P-P-I-N-E-S.

U.S. GEOGRAPHY

Which Pennsylvania city is nicknamed the "City of Brotherly Love," which Michigan city is the "Motor City," and which Missouri city is the "Gateway Arch City"?

Answer: Philadelphia / Detroit / St. Louis.

HISTORY

During which war did Joan of Arc fight, against which country's forces did she do so, and which country's forces did she lead into battle?

Answer: Hundred Years' War / English / French.

LITERATURE

Which sheriff is Robin Hood's foe, who is the biggest in Robin Hood's Band of Merry Men, and who is the group's plump religious member?

Answer: Sheriff of Nottingham / Little John / Friar Tuck.

ENTERTAINMENT

Name these *Muppet Show* regulars: the character who always tries to open the show with a trumpet fanfare, the shaggy piano-playing dog, and the drummer in the band.

Answer: Gonzo / Rowlf / Animal.

SPORTS AND GAMES

What are the names of the National Hockey League teams in Calgary, Edmonton, and Los Angeles?

Answer: Flames / Oilers / Kings.

SCIENCE AND NATURE

What is 11 times 11, what is 1/2 times 1/2, and what is 312 divided by 12?

Answer: 121 / 1/4 / 26.

WORLD GEOGRAPHY

What is the capital of China, what is this country's basic monetary unit, and what is its longest river?

Answer: Peking (Beijing) / yuan / Yangtze River (accept the Chang).

LEADERS & GOVERNMENT

Identify the U.S. Presidents whose retreats were the Gettysburg Farm, San Clemente, and Rancho del Cielo.

Answer: Dwight Eisenhower / Richard Nixon / Ronald Reagan.

MUSIC & RHYMES

Which words complete the rhyme about Solomon Grundy: "Took _____ on a Thursday, / Worse on Friday, / _____ on Saturday, / _____ on Sunday: / This is the end / Of Solomon Grundy"?

Answer: "ill" / "Died" / "Buried."

LANGUAGE

What are the French, Italian, and German words for "goodbye," each one literally meaning "to see again"?

Answer: *Au revoir* / *arrivederci* / *auf Wiedersehen*.

ARTS, RELIGION, & CULTURE

Complete the description of the way to heaven given in Matthew 7:14: "_____ is the gate, and _____ is the way, which leadeth unto _____, and few there be that find it."

Answer: "strait" (accept "narrow") / "narrow" (accept "hard") / "life."

POTPOURRI

Which phrases with the word "old" identify the following: the European artists of the 13th to 16th century; the personification of winter; and the superstitious belief passed around by gossipy women?

Answer: Old Masters / Old Man Winter / old wives' tale.

U.S. GEOGRAPHY

Which Nevada cities are nicknamed the "City of Little Wedding Churches" and the "Biggest Little City in the World," and which New Mexico city is the "Hot Air Balloon Capital of the World"?

Answer: Las Vegas / Reno / Albuquerque.

HISTORY

How did Joan of Arc die on May 30, 1431; with what offense was she charged; and in canonizing her in 1920, what did the Roman Catholic Church declare her to be?

Answer: She was burned at the stake / witchcraft (accept being a heretic) / a saint.

LITERATURE

Name the coon dog of a poor black sharecropper and his family in a William Armstrong novel; the dog who accompanies Sally, Dick, and Jane in a series of primers; and the gigantic "fiend dog" in an Arthur Conan Doyle tale.

Answer: Sounder / Spot / Hound of the Baskervilles.

ENTERTAINMENT

Identify the large bird on *Sesame Street*, its color, and the bird that is its distant relative.

Answer: Big Bird / yellow / Little Bird.

SPORTS AND GAMES

What are the names of the National Hockey League teams in Atlanta, Anaheim, and Chicago?

Answer: Thrashers / Mighty Ducks / Blackhawks.

SCIENCE AND NATURE

How many decigrams, centigrams, and milligrams are there in a gram?

Answer: 10 / 100 / 1000.

WORLD GEOGRAPHY

What is India's official language, what is its basic monetary unit, and what is its capital?

Answer: Hindi / rupee / New Delhi.

LEADERS & GOVERNMENT

Name the U.S. government body that has 2 legislative chambers, and name these 2 chambers.

Answer: Congress / Senate / House of Representatives.

MUSIC & RHYMES

In the rhyme, who "picked a peck of" peppers, what kind of "peppers" did he pick, and what is the phrase for "a sequence of words difficult to pronounce, usually because of alliteration"?

Answer: Peter Piper / pickled peppers / tongue twister.

LANGUAGE

Give the English translation of the French phrases *Vive la France*, *par avion*, and *c'est la vie*.

Answer: Long live France / by airmail (by airplane) / that's life.

ARTS, RELIGION, & CULTURE

Whose wife in the Bible was turned into a pillar of salt, what disobedient action prompted such punishment, and from which city was she escaping when she disobeyed God?

Answer: Lot's wife / she looked back / Sodom.

POTPOURRI

Name the occupations of Frank Lloyd Wright, Billy Graham, and Ernest Hemingway.

Answer: Architect / evangelist (or minister or preacher) / writer.

U.S. GEOGRAPHY

Which New York city is nicknamed the "Queen City of the Great Lakes," which Ohio city is the "Queen City of the Ohio River," and which Missouri city is the "Queen City of the Mississippi"?

Answer: Buffalo / Cincinnati / St. Louis.

HISTORY

What is the popular name for the bubonic plague that ravaged Asia and Europe between 1334 and 1351, and which insects that lived on which animals spread this disease?

Answer: Black Death (Plague) / fleas / rodents (rats).

LITERATURE

What kind of animal is Michael Bond's Paddington, and with which family in which country does he live?

Answer: Bear / Brown family / England.

ENTERTAINMENT

Identify the large elephant-like character seen only by Big Bird on *Sesame Street*, give this character's color, and identify its baby sister.

Answer: Snuffleupagus / brown / Alice Snuffleupagus.

SPORTS AND GAMES

What are the names of the National Hockey League teams in Detroit, Dallas, and St. Louis?

Answer: Red Wings / Stars / Blues.

SCIENCE AND NATURE

What time of day does each day begin, and what are the Latin phrases for a.m. and p.m.?

Answer: Midnight / ante meridiem / post meridiem.

WORLD GEOGRAPHY

What is Brazil's official language, what is its largest city by population, and what is its capital?

Answer: Portuguese / São Paulo / Brasília.

LEADERS & GOVERNMENT

What is the highest court in the U.S., how many justices currently sit on it, and what is the term used for the presiding judge of this court?

Answer: Supreme Court / 9 / Chief Justice of the United States.

MUSIC & RHYMES

In the rhyme "Baa, baa, black sheep," for which 3 people are the 3 "bags full" of wool intended?

Answer: "my master" / "my dame" / "and one for the little boy—Who lives down the lane."

LANGUAGE

Which American names are traditionally synonymous with "a mathematical genius" or "very brilliant person"; "a notorious robber"; and "a powerful home run hitter"?

Answer: An Einstein / a Jesse James / a Babe Ruth.

ARTS, RELIGION, & CULTURE

On the first, second, and third days of Christmas in the rhyme and song, what did "My true love send to me"?

Answer: "A partridge in a pear tree" / "Two turtle doves" / "Three French hens."

POTPOURRI

Which word for "divine wind" identifies pilots who flew suicide missions to blow up American ships, which country's pilots engaged in such actions, and during which war did they fly?

Answer: Kamikaze / Japan's / World War II.

U.S. GEOGRAPHY

Which Pennsylvania cities are nicknamed the "Birthplace of American Liberty" and the "Birmingham of America," and which Texas city is the "Big D"?

Answer: Philadelphia / Pittsburgh / Dallas.

HISTORY

Which leader of which country broke with the Roman Catholic Church with the Act of Supremacy of 1534, and which wife had he divorced in 1533 because she had not borne him a male child?

Answer: Henry VIII / England / Catherine of Aragon.

LITERATURE

In Eugene Field's poem "The Duel," what kind of dog and what kind of cat sat "side by side" and had "a terrible spat," and which kind of clock or which kind of plate related this fight?

Answer: Gingham dog / calico cat / Dutch clock or Chinese plate.

ENTERTAINMENT

Give the name of Bert's favorite pigeon, Oscar's pet worm, and Ernie's favorite companion who is the subject of Ernie's favorite song on *Sesame Street.*

Answer: Bernice / Slimey / Rubber Duckie.

SPORTS AND GAMES

What are the names of the Toronto, New Jersey, and Philadelphia NHL teams?

Answer: Maple Leafs / Devils / Flyers.

SCIENCE AND NATURE

Give the latitude at the equator, at the North Pole, and at the South Pole.

Answer: 0 degrees / 90 degrees / 90 degrees.

WORLD GEOGRAPHY

What is Japan's highest mountain, what is its basic monetary unit, and what is its capital?

Answer: Mount Fuji (Fujiyama) / yen / Tokyo.

LEADERS & GOVERNMENT

Name 3 of the following 4: the 2 main U.S. political parties and the symbols of these parties.

Answer: Democratic / Republican / donkey / elephant.

MUSIC & RHYMES

Complete the rhyme: "Mary, Mary, quite contrary, / How does your garden grow? / With _____ bells and cockle_____, / And pretty _____ all in a row."

Answer: "silver" / "shells" / "maids" (or "And marigolds all in a row").

LANGUAGE

Give the words for "the story of a person's life written by another," "the story of a person's life, written by oneself," and "a list of the books or articles used by an author."

Answer: Biography / autobiography / bibliography.

ARTS, RELIGION, & CULTURE

On the fourth, fifth, and sixth days of Christmas in the rhyme and song, what did "My true love send to me"?

Answer: "Four colly (calling) birds" / "Five gold(en) rings" / "Six geese a-laying."

POTPOURRI

According to legend, which water bird sings beautifully just before it dies, how many lives does a cat have, and which animals march to the sea and drown themselves every few years?

Answer: Swan / 9 lives / lemmings.

U.S. GEOGRAPHY

Which Illinois city was called the "Hog Butcher for the World," which Kentucky city is known as the "Capital of the Horse World," and which Nevada city is the "City Without Clocks"?

Answer: Chicago / Lexington / Las Vegas.

HISTORY

Which U.S. Civil War leaders said: "No terms except an unconditional and immediate surrender can be accepted"; "I can't spare this man, he fights"; and "War is Hell"?

Answer: Ulysses S. Grant / Abraham Lincoln / William Tecumseh Sherman.

LITERATURE

Who is the author of *Twenty-Thousand Leagues Under the Sea*, what is the name of the submarine in the novel, and who is the mysterious commander of this ship?

Answer: Jules Verne / *Nautilus* / Captain Nemo.

ENTERTAINMENT

On *Sesame Street*, what is the color of Oscar's fur, where does he live, and what color is the Cookie Monster?

Answer: Green / in a garbage can / blue.

SPORTS AND GAMES

What are the names of the Pittsburgh, Washington, and Boston NHL teams?

Answer: Penguins / Capitals / Bruins.

SCIENCE AND NATURE

Give the words for the distance around a circle, the widest distance across a circle, and one half the distance across a circle.

Answer: Circumference / diameter / radius.

WORLD GEOGRAPHY

What is Mexico's official language, what is its basic monetary unit, and what is its capital?

Answer: Spanish / peso / Mexico City.

LEADERS & GOVERNMENT

On which holiday on which date does the U.S. celebrate its birthday, and in which year was the United States of America formed?

Answer: Independence Day / July 4 / 1776.

MUSIC & RHYMES

Name the 3 who "all jumped out of a rotten potato" in the nursery rhyme, "Rub-a-dub-dub, / Three men in a tub."

Answer: Butcher / baker / candlestick-maker.

LANGUAGE

What are the 3 moods (modes) of modern English verbs?

Answer: Indicative / imperative / subjunctive.

ARTS, RELIGION, & CULTURE

On the 7th, 8th, and 9th days of Christmas in a song, the true love sent "swans a-swimming," "maids a-milking," and "ladies dancing." What does he send on the 10th, 11th, and 12th days of Christmas?

Answer: "lords a-leaping" / "pipers piping" / "drummers drumming" (no order required as versions vary).

POTPOURRI

Which month of the year identifies "an auxiliary verb used to convey possibility," which one identifies "a large beetle," and which one is a verb?

Answer: May / June / March.

U.S. GEOGRAPHY

In which 3 states is the Yellowstone National Park located?

Answer: Wyoming / Idaho / Montana.

HISTORY

Between which 2 countries did Pope Alexander VI divide up the world in 1493 to prevent disputes over newly discovered lands, and what was the name of the papal line dividing it?

Answer: Spain / Portugal / Line of Demarcation.

LITERATURE

Identify the American author who wrote about a fictional frog in Calaveras County, name the frog, and name the state where Calaveras County is located.

Answer: Mark Twain (Samuel Langhorne Clemens) / Dan'l Webster / California.

ENTERTAINMENT

Which words complete these song titles in the 1965 film *The Sound of Music*: "Do, Re, _____," "My Favorite _____," and "Sixteen, Going on _____"?

Answer: "Mi" / "Things" / "Seventeen."

SPORTS AND GAMES

Which New York Yankee baseball player is known as the "Iron Horse," which record of 2,130 did he set, and which Baltimore Oriole broke his record in 1995?

Answer: Lou Gehrig / consecutive games played / Cal Ripken (he played in 2,632 consecutive games).

SCIENCE AND NATURE

What is the name of the line used as the basis for measuring time zones for the world; through which borough of London, England, does it pass; and at how many degrees longitude is it?

Answer: Greenwich meridian (or prime meridian) / Greenwich / 0 degrees.

WORLD GEOGRAPHY

What was Italy's basic monetary unit before the Euro, what is the religion of most of its people, and what is its capital?

Answer: Lira / Roman Catholicism / Rome.

LEADERS & GOVERNMENT

In which city was the U.S. Declaration of Independence signed, who was the President of the Second Continental Congress at the time of the signing, and what is the first word of this document?

Answer: Philadelphia / John Hancock / "When."

MUSIC & RHYMES

Complete the rhyme: "Ladybug, ladybug, fly away _____, / Your _____ is on fire, and your _____ will burn" (or "are all gone").

Answer: "home" / "house" / "children."

LANGUAGE

In which case is the subject of an infinitive, in which case is the predicate nominative, and in which case is the noun or pronoun before a gerund?

Answer: Objective / nominative / possessive.

ARTS, RELIGION, & CULTURE

Which 3 frightful mythological sisters could allegedly turn one to stone, which one of them was mortal, and which animals did they have for hair?

Answer: Gorgons / Medusa / snakes.

POTPOURRI

Which 2 animals are associated with the stock market's rising and falling, and who invented the stock ticker, the teletype machine that records purchases and sales of stock?

Answer: Bulls / bears / Thomas Edison.

U.S. GEOGRAPHY

Identify the 3 longest rivers in the U.S.

Answer: Mississippi / Missouri / the Rio Grande.

HISTORY

Which king of which country is known as the "Sun King," and which term is used to refer to his allegedly God-given right to rule?

Answer: Louis XIV / France / Divine right of kings.

LITERATURE

In Katherine Paterson's *Bridge to Terabithia*, in which city is Jesse when Leslie dies, how does she die after the rope breaks and she hits her head, and what kind of animal is Prince Terrien?

Answer: Washington, D.C. / she drowns / a dog.

ENTERTAINMENT

Complete the phrase about Superman, "Faster than a _____ bullet! More powerful than a _____! Able to leap tall buildings at a single _____."

Answer: "speeding" / "locomotive" / "bound."

SPORTS AND GAMES

What are the names of the 2 National Hockey League teams with the names New York, and what is the name of the team in Colorado?

Answer: Islanders / Rangers / Avalanche.

SCIENCE AND NATURE

What word is used to designate the time periods at which day and night are the same length, and in which 2 months do these days occur?

Answer: Equinox / March (20 or 21) / September (22 or 23).

WORLD GEOGRAPHY

What was Germany's basic monetary unit before the Euro, what is its only major river flowing eastward from the Black Forest, and what was the capital of West Germany before reunification?

Answer: (Deutsche) mark / Danube River / Bonn.

LEADERS & GOVERNMENT

Name the lawmaking body of Great Britain, and name its 2 houses.

Answer: Parliament / House of Lords / House of Commons.

MUSIC & RHYMES

Complete the rhyme: "Here comes a _____ to light you to bed, / Here comes a _____ to chop off your _____."

Answer: "candle" / "chopper" / "head."

LANGUAGE

Name the 3 parts of speech besides noun, pronoun, adjective, verb, and adverb.

Answer: Conjunction / preposition / interjection.

ARTS, RELIGION, & CULTURE

In which country was Buddhism founded in the 6th and 5th centuries B.C., who founded this religion, and what is his better known name?

Answer: India / Siddhartha Gautama / Buddha.

POTPOURRI

Give the word for a person who took the law into his own hands in the Western U.S., and name both the chief law-enforcement officer of a county and the band of men he enlisted to help keep the peace.

Answer: Vigilante / sheriff / posse (accept deputies).

U.S. GEOGRAPHY

In which states are the Boll Weevil Monument and Muscle Shoals; the Aleutian Islands and Prudhoe Bay; and El Capitan and the Mojave Desert?

Answer: Alabama / Alaska / California.

HISTORY

In which country is the Palace of Versailles, which king built it, and which war was ended by the treaty signed in this palace's Hall of Mirrors?

Answer: France / Louis XIV / World War I.

LITERATURE

Who is the author of the Nancy Drew series of books, how old is Nancy Drew, and in which city does she live with her widowed father Carson Drew?

Answer: Carolyn Keene / 18 years old / River Heights.

ENTERTAINMENT

Complete the saying, "Superman, who can change the course of mighty _____, bend _____ in his bare hands, and . . . fights a never-ending battle for truth, justice, and the _____ way!"

Answer: "rivers" / "steel" / "American."

SPORTS AND GAMES

In which country was the game of ice hockey first played, and what are the names of the National Hockey League teams in Vancouver and Ottawa?

Answer: Canada / Canucks / Senators.

SCIENCE AND NATURE

Which word is used to designate the shortest or longest day of the year, and in which months do these days occur?

Answer: Solstice / June (21 or 22) / December (21 or 22).

WORLD GEOGRAPHY

What was France's basic monetary unit before the Euro, what is its national anthem, and what is its capital?

Answer: Franc / "La Marseillaise" / Paris.

LEADERS & GOVERNMENT

In which city in which hall in which year was the U.S. Constitution signed?

Answer: Philadelphia / Independence Hall / 1787.

MUSIC & RHYMES

Complete the rhyme: "Cock a doodle _____! / My dame has lost her _____; / My master's lost his fiddle _____, / And knows not what to do."

Answer: "doo" / "shoe" / "stick."

LANGUAGE

Give the 3 ways in which a pronoun agrees with its antecedent.

Answer: In person / number / gender.

ARTS, RELIGION, & CULTURE

What is the symbol of Judaism and of Israel, and which 2 religions grew out of Judaism?

Answer: Star of David (in Hebrew, the *Magen David*, meaning the Shield of David) / Christianity / Islam.

POTPOURRI

Which automobile was named after a U.S. President, which one was named after the founder of Detroit, and which one was named after a chief of the Ottawa tribe?

Answer: Lincoln / Cadillac / Pontiac.

U.S. GEOGRAPHY

In which states are the Saguaro National Monument and the Painted Desert; the Crater of Diamonds Mine and Hot Springs; and Aspen and Vail ski resorts?

Answer: Arizona / Arkansas / Colorado.

HISTORY

Of which country was Napoleon the leader, and at which battle in which country was he defeated on June 18, 1815?

Answer: France / Waterloo / Belgium.

LITERATURE

Complete the following Judy Blume titles: *Tales of a _____ Grade Nothing*, *Freckle _____*, and *It's Not the End of the _____*.

Answer: *Fourth / Juice / World.*

ENTERTAINMENT

Which masked comic strip character is known as "The Ghost Who Walks," on which continent does he seek justice, and what is the name of the cave in which he keeps his large treasure?

Answer: The Phantom / Africa / Skull Cave.

SPORTS AND GAMES

How many balls result in a walk in baseball, how many strikes result in a strikeout, and what is the game's term for 2 outs being made on the same play?

Answer: 4 / 3 / double play.

SCIENCE AND NATURE

Which imaginary line divides a globe into northern and southern hemispheres, which one divides a globe into western and eastern hemispheres, and which one is located at 66 degrees 30 minutes North?

Answer: Equator / prime meridian (accept Greenwich meridian) / Arctic Circle.

WORLD GEOGRAPHY

Which countries are known as the "Land Down Under," the "Land of the Rising Sun," and the "Land of the Gaucho"?

Answer: Australia (accept New Zealand) / Japan / Argentina (accept Uruguay).

LEADERS & GOVERNMENT

Name the 3 requirements a person must meet according to the U.S. Constitution to become a senator.

Answer: At least 30 years of age / a citizen for at least 9 years / an inhabitant of the state from which elected.

MUSIC & RHYMES

Which nursery rhyme character was "a merry old soul," and which words complete the lines: "He called for his _____, / And he called for his _____, / And he called for his fiddlers three"?

Answer: Old King Cole / "pipe" / "bowl."

LANGUAGE

Which words complete the expressions: "Like mother, like, _____," "So far, so _____," and "Like father, like _____"?

Answer: "daughter" / "good" / "son."

ARTS, RELIGION, & CULTURE

In which building do Jews worship on the Sabbath, what is the ceremony in which a Jewish boy at 13 is recognized as an adult, and what is the name for the first 5 books of the Hebrew Bible?

Answer: Synagogue / Bar Mitzvah / Torah (accept Pentateuch or the Five Books of Moses).

POTPOURRI

Identify the knee-length pleated skirt worn by Scottish men; the long robe with short, wide sleeves and a sash worn by Japanese women; and the long, loose, colorful garment worn by Hawaiian women.

Answer: Kilt / kimono / muumuu.

U.S. GEOGRAPHY
In which states are Bethany Beach and Rehoboth Beach; the Cypress Gardens and Daytona Beach; and Callaway Gardens and the Franklin D. Roosevelt Memorial near Warm Springs?
Answer: Delaware / Florida / Georgia.

HISTORY
In which country was *The Communist Manifesto* published in 1848, and which 2 Germans wrote it?
Answer: England / Karl Marx / Friedrich Engels.

LITERATURE
Which word completes Esther Forbes' title _____ *Tremain*, during which war is this work set, and which part of the boy's body is crippled?
Answer: *Johnny* / American Revolutionary War / his hand.

ENTERTAINMENT
Which Disney films feature the songs "I Just Can't Wait to Be King," "Belle," and "Prince Ali"?
Answer: *The Lion King* / *Beauty and the Beast* / *Aladdin*.

SPORTS AND GAMES
What are the names of the Buffalo, Carolina, and Montreal NHL teams?
Answer: Sabres / Hurricanes / Canadiens.

SCIENCE AND NATURE
Identify the first disease conquered by vaccination, the one characterized by inflammation of the lung, and the one sometimes called *scarlatina*.
Answer: Smallpox / pneumonia / scarlet fever.

WORLD GEOGRAPHY

What is France's highest peak, what is the English translation of its name, and in which mountain system is it located?

Answer: Mt. Blanc / "White Mountain" / Alps.

LEADERS & GOVERNMENT

What is the term of office of a U.S. senator, how often are elections for the U.S. Senate held, and how many senators represent each state?

Answer: 6 years / every 2 years / 2.

MUSIC & RHYMES

Which words complete the rhyme: "Jack _____ could eat no fat, / His wife could eat no _____; / And so betwixt them both, / They licked the _____ clean"?

Answer: Sprat / "lean" / "platter."

LANGUAGE

What are the 3 degrees of comparison for both adjectives and adverbs?

Answer: Positive / comparative / superlative.

ARTS, RELIGION, & CULTURE

Who is the founder of Judaism, what name means the "anointed one" and designates the promised and expected deliverer of the Jews, and what is the name for the collection of Jewish civil and religious law?

Answer: Abraham / Messiah / Talmud.

POTPOURRI

Which countries' airlines are known as El Al, KLM, and Aeroflot?

Answer: Israel / The Netherlands (or Holland) / Russia.

U.S. GEOGRAPHY

In which states are the USS *Arizona* monument and Waikiki Beach; Hells Canyon and Sun Valley; and the Abraham Lincoln home and gravesite and the Joseph Smith home?

Answer: Hawaii / Idaho / Illinois.

HISTORY

Which terms identify the mounted warrior of the Middle Ages who served a king, the young man who was an armor-bearer to this warrior, and the boy at a lord's castle who learned to hunt and to ride.

Answer: Knight / squire / page.

LITERATURE

Which kind of animal is Stuart Little in a work of the same name by E.B. White, which kind of animal named Snowbell doesn't like him, and which kind of animal is Margale, his best friend?

Answer: Mouse / cat / bird.

ENTERTAINMENT

Name the 3 Stooges.

Answer: Larry (Fine) / Moe (Howard) / Curly (Howard; accept Shemp Howard, another brother who replaced Curly—Joe Besser then replaced Shemp).

SPORTS AND GAMES

Which words complete the sayings derived from the sport of baseball: "He was born with _____ strikes against him," "He's way off _____ on that," and "He was safe by a _____"?

Answer: "two" / "base" / "mile."

SCIENCE AND NATURE

What part of the body is referred to as grey matter, what is the colored part of the human eye called, and what is the term for a person with white skin, whitish hair, and pink eyes?

Answer: The brain / iris / albino.

WORLD GEOGRAPHY
What was the official language of the Soviet Union, what was its basic monetary unit, and which animal was used in cartoons to depict this country?
Answer: Russian / ruble / bear.

LEADERS & GOVERNMENT
What is the term of office of a U.S. representative, how many times may a representative be reelected, and what determines the number of representatives for each state?
Answer: 2 years / unlimited / population.

MUSIC & RHYMES
Which words complete the song lines: "Bye, baby bunting / _____'s gone a _____, / To get a little _____ skin, / To wrap his baby bunting in"?
Answer: "Daddy" / "hunting" / "rabbit."

LANGUAGE
Identify the parts of speech for these words: *woman*, *into*, and *ouch!*
Answer: Noun / preposition / interjection.

ARTS, RELIGION, & CULTURE
Complete the common expressions: "There, but for the grace of _____, go I," "Idle hands are the _____'s workshop," and "To move _____ and earth."
Answer: "God" / "devil" / "heaven."

POTPOURRI
Complete Benjamin Franklin's statements: "Nothing is certain but _____ and _____," and "Eat to live, and not live to _____."
Answer: "death" / "taxes" / "eat."

U.S. GEOGRAPHY

In which states are the Hoosier National Forest and Wyandotte Cave; the Herbert Hoover birthplace and the Amana Colonies near Cedar Rapids; and Dodge City and Fort Leavenworth?

Answer: Indiana / Iowa / Kansas.

HISTORY

In which city in which theatre was President Lincoln assassinated, and who killed him?

Answer: Washington, D.C. / Ford's Theatre / John Wilkes Booth.

LITERATURE

What kind of animal is the fictional Rikki-Tikki-Tavi, which author created him, and which kind of animal named Nag does he attack to save Teddy?

Answer: Mongoose / Rudyard Kipling / cobra.

ENTERTAINMENT

Zeppo and Gummo are the stage names of 3 of the 5 Marx Bothers. Name the other 3.

Answer: Chico / Harpo / Groucho.

SPORTS AND GAMES

How many men or checkers does each player have in Backgammon, what is the name for the center division on the board, and what are the 24-spear-shaped divisions called?

Answer: 15 / bar / points.

SCIENCE AND NATURE

Give the words for "the hardening of the arteries"; "the science of the stars, planets, and all other heavenly bodies"; and the insects long but mistakenly known as "white ants."

Answer: Arteriosclerosis / astronomy / termites.

WORLD GEOGRAPHY

The *U* in the name of the country formerly known as the U.S.S.R. stands for "Union." Give the meaning of the other 3 letters.

Answer: (Union of) Soviet / Socialist / Republics.

LEADERS & GOVERNMENT

Who was the first Chief Justice of the U.S. Supreme Court, who nominated him, and which President nominated William Rehnquist as Chief Justice?

Answer: John Jay / George Washington / Ronald Reagan.

MUSIC & RHYMES

Complete the song lines: "Oh, ye'll tak' the _____ road an' I'll tak' the _____ road, / An' I'll be in _____ afore ye; / But me and my true love will never meet again."

Answer: "high" / "low" / "Scotland" ("On the bonnie, bonnie banks o' Loch Lomond").

LANGUAGE

Identify the parts of speech for these words: *and*, *gives*, and *herself*.

Answer: Conjunction / verb / pronoun.

ARTS, RELIGION, & CULTURE

In the song with the line, "You better watch out; you better not cry," who is "comin' to town," what is he "making," and how often is he "checking it"?

Answer: Santa Claus / a list / twice.

POTPOURRI

What are the "middle" phrases for "the period from 476-1450"; "the U.S. area bounded by the Rockies, Missouri, Ohio, and Kansas"; and the states of New York, New Jersey, and Pennsylvania?

Answer: Middle Ages / Middle West (accept Midwest) / Middle Atlantic States.

U.S. GEOGRAPHY

In which states are the Bluegrass Region and Mammoth Cave; the Bayou Country and Acadiana; and Bar Harbor and Quoddy Head?

Answer: Kentucky / Louisiana / Maine.

HISTORY

In which city in which year was President Kennedy assassinated, and who killed him?

Answer: Dallas / 1963 / Lee Harvey Oswald.

LITERATURE

Which fairy tale character's name literally means "little cinder girl," and which family members abuse her and make her work hard before she falls in love with a Prince at a ball?

Answer: Cinderella / her stepmother / her stepsisters.

ENTERTAINMENT

Identify *Sesame Street*'s "world's greatest detective"; the black little-boy muppet; and the sheep, a blonde acting teacher with violet eyeshadow and an East European accent.

Answer: Sherlock Hemlock / Roosevelt Franklin / Meryl Sheep.

SPORTS AND GAMES

In chess, which piece is the most powerful, which one can move only one space at a time in any direction, and which one moves in an L-shaped direction?

Answer: Queen / king / knight (or horse).

SCIENCE AND NATURE

Who was the first American in space, who was the first American in orbit, and who was the first American woman to go into space?

Answer: Alan Shepard / John Glenn / Sally Ride.

WORLD GEOGRAPHY

What is the capital of Austria, on which river is this capital, and what is this country's official language?

Answer: Vienna / Danube River / German.

LEADERS & GOVERNMENT

Which U.S. Presidents said: "Ask not what your country can do for you; ask what you can do for your country"; "Speak softly and carry a big stick"; and "I am not a crook"?

Answer: John Kennedy / Theodore Roosevelt / Richard Nixon.

MUSIC & RHYMES

A mixed voice choir contains men and women arranged S.A.T.B. Name 3 of the 4 voice ranges for which these initials stand.

Answer: Soprano / alto / tenor / bass.

LANGUAGE

As what 3 parts of speech may infinitives be used?

Answer: As noun / adjective / adverb.

ARTS, RELIGION, & CULTURE

In the song, what Snow Man with coal for his eyes was "a jolly, happy soul," what kind of pipe did he have, and what did he have for a nose?

Answer: Frosty the Snow Man / corncob pipe / button nose.

POTPOURRI

Proverbially, how many winks does one get if a nap is taken, to which thoughts does a young man's fancy lightly turn in the spring, and where does a person have a skeleton if he's hiding a secret?

Answer: 40 / to thoughts of love / in the closet.

U.S. GEOGRAPHY

In which states are Catoctin Mountain and Ocean City; Harvard University and Martha's Vineyard; and the Hiawatha National Forest and the Mackinac Bridge?

Answer: Maryland / Massachusetts / Michigan.

HISTORY

Which "unsinkable" ocean liner sank in which year on the night of April 14-15, and what did it hit that caused it to sink?

Answer: *Titanic* / 1912 / iceberg.

LITERATURE

Which Grimm brothers' character is a deformed dwarf, what does he help the miller's beautiful daughter spin into gold, and what does she promise to give him after she becomes the queen?

Answer: Rumpelstiltskin / straw (or hay) / her first child.

ENTERTAINMENT

Identify Edgar Rice Burroughs' fictional character called "Lord of the Jungle," the continent on which he was raised, and the group of animals that raised him.

Answer: Tarzan / Africa / apes.

SPORTS AND GAMES

In chess, which playing pieces are designated by the letters *P* and *N*, and what is the meaning of the letter *x* in chess notation?

Answer: Pawn / knight / captures.

SCIENCE AND NATURE

How many bands of color are there in a rainbow, how many sides do most snowflakes have, and how many faces does a cube have?

Answer: 7 / 6 / 6.

WORLD GEOGRAPHY

What are the 2 capitals of Bolivia, and what is this country's official language?

Answer: La Paz / Sucre / Spanish (accept Aymara and Quechua).

LEADERS & GOVERNMENT

Who was the first Jewish justice of the U.S. Supreme Court, who was the first black justice, and who was the first woman justice?

Answer: Louis Brandeis / Thurgood Marshall / Sandra Day O'Connor.

MUSIC & RHYMES

Complete the song lines: "Au clair de la _____, / Mon ami _____, / Prête-moi ta _____ / Pour écrire un mot."

Answer: "lune" / "Pierrot" / "plume."

LANGUAGE

Which words complete the expressions: "Forgive and _____," "Few and _____ between," and "Touch and _____"?

Answer: "forget" / "far" / "go."

ARTS, RELIGION, & CULTURE

Complete the biblically-derived phrases: "To fall by the _____," "To sell one's _____ for a mess of pottage," and "To worship the _____ calf."

Answer: "wayside" / "birthright" / "golden."

POTPOURRI

Proverbially, what is the weaker sex, what is thicker than water, and which part of the body do vampires bite?

Answer: Female / blood / neck.

U.S. GEOGRAPHY

In which states are the Mesabi Range and a statue of Paul Bunyan; Elvis Presley's birthplace and Vicksburg; and the house where Jesse James was killed and the Harry S Truman Library?

Answer: Minnesota / Mississippi / Missouri.

HISTORY

Identify the home country of the large passenger ship sunk on May 7, 1915; the name of the ship; and the country whose submarine sank it.

Answer: Britain / *Lusitania* / Germany.

LITERATURE

Identify the Grimm brothers' character whose name is another name for rampion, a flower used in salads; the person to whom the couple give their child in exchange for the rampion; and the location where this child is locked away.

Answer: Rapunzel / a witch / in a tower.

ENTERTAINMENT

What is the better known name of the fictional John Clayton whose father was Lord Greystoke, an Englishman; who was this character's mate; and who is their only son in most movie versions?

Answer: Tarzan / Jane / Boy.

SPORTS AND GAMES

In which sports did Gordie Howe, Rocky Marciano, and Lee Trevino become famous?

Answer: Ice hockey / boxing / golf.

SCIENCE AND NATURE

Give, in lowest terms, the common fractions for 50%, 80%, and 125%.

Answer: 1/2; 4/5; 5/4 (accept 1 1/4).

WORLD GEOGRAPHY

What is the national anthem of Canada, and what are the country's 2 national symbols?

Answer: "O Canada" / beaver / maple leaf.

LEADERS & GOVERNMENT

Which U.S. Presidents said: "The business of America is business"; "We have nothing to fear but fear itself"; and "I am a Ford, not a Lincoln"?

Answer: Calvin Coolidge / Franklin Roosevelt / Gerald Ford.

MUSIC & RHYMES

Which words complete the nursery rhyme: "Little Tommy _____ / Sings for his _____; / What shall he eat? / White bread and _____"?

Answer: "Tucker" / "supper" / "butter."

LANGUAGE

Give the first and last letters of the Greek alphabet; give the name for the letter *Z* in Canada and Great Britain; and identify the only major language that does not have an alphabetical system of writing.

Answer: Alpha and Omega / Zed (accept izzard) / Chinese.

ARTS, RELIGION, & CULTURE

Name the 3 main orders of classical Greek architecture.

Answer: Doric / Ionic / Corinthian.

POTPOURRI

What is the most frequently used word in conversational English, what is the most frequently used one in written English, and what word beginning with *F* is the longest in the Oxford English Dictionary?

Answer: I / the / floccinaucinihilipilification (meaning "the action of estimating as worthless").

U.S. GEOGRAPHY

In which states are the John F. Kennedy Space Center and Tamiami Trail; Napa Valley and Squaw Valley; and the Little White House and Jekyll Island?

Answer: Florida / California / Georgia.

HISTORY

For which country were Julius and Ethel Rosenberg considered to be working when they were executed in June 1953, for which reason were they executed, and in which state did the execution take place in Sing Sing prison?

Answer: Soviet Union (Russia) / espionage (or spying) / New York.

LITERATURE

Which Grimm brothers' character is given a little red velvet cloak, who gives it to her, and which wicked animal does this little girl meet in the wood?

Answer: Red Riding Hood / her grandmother / a wolf.

ENTERTAINMENT

Identify Donald Duck's uncle who is the world's richest duck, name the city in which he lives, and identify the group of boys who constantly harass him.

Answer: Scrooge McDuck / Duckburg / Beagle Boys.

SPORTS AND GAMES

In which sports did Mario Andretti, Johnny Unitas, and Oscar Robertson become famous?

Answer: Auto racing / football / basketball.

SCIENCE AND NATURE

How many ounces are there in a cup, how many cups are in a pint, and how many pints are in a quart?

Answer: 8 / 2 / 2.

WORLD GEOGRAPHY
What is the capital of Cuba, what is its official language, and in which sea is this island located?
Answer: Havana / Spanish / Caribbean Sea.

LEADERS & GOVERNMENT
Into which 3 branches does the U.S. Constitution separate the work of the government?
Answer: Legislative / judicial / executive.

MUSIC & RHYMES
Which terms designate "a group of singers trained to sing together in a church," "a music club at an American university," and "a group of 4 male singers who sing harmony without accompaniment"?
Answer: Choir / Glee Club / Barbershop quartet.

LANGUAGE
How many letters are in the English and Greek alphabets, respectively, and what alphabet, named after St. Cyril, is used in the writing of some Slavic languages such as Russian?
Answer: 26 / 24 / Cyrillic (the Russian alphabet, called the Cyrillic alphabet, has 32 letters).

ARTS, RELIGION, & CULTURE
Which religion, known for its caste system, calls its sacred writing the Veda; in which country is it the major religion; and which word is used to designate this religion's belief in rebirth?
Answer: Hinduism / India / reincarnation.

POTPOURRI
Which cereal is "the breakfast of champions," through which book are you asked to "let your fingers do the walking," and which chicken did Col. Harland Sanders say is, "Finger lickin' good"?
Answer: Wheaties / *Yellow Pages* / Kentucky Fried Chicken.

U.S. GEOGRAPHY

In which states are the U.S. Gold Bullion Depository and the Natural Bridge; the Bighorn Canyon and the Lewis and Clark national forests; and Buffalo Bill's Home and Chimney Rock?

Answer: Kentucky / Montana / Nebraska.

HISTORY

Which words complete Julius Caesar's statements: "All Gaul is divided into _____ parts," "The die is _____," and "I came, I saw, I _____"?

Answer: "three" / "cast" / "conquered."

LITERATURE

Which Grimm brothers' characters are abandoned in the woods by the woodcutter and his wife, whose house do they find made of bread and roofed with cake, and how does this person die?

Answer: Hansel and Gretel / an old witch's / in the oven.

ENTERTAINMENT

Which fictional characters' real names are Bruce Wayne, Dick Grayson, and Peter Parker?

Answer: Batman / Robin / Spiderman.

SPORTS AND GAMES

In which sports did Sonja Henie, Nancy Lopez, and Chris Evert (Lloyd) become famous?

Answer: Ice skating / golf / tennis.

SCIENCE AND NATURE

How many pints are there in a gallon, how many quarts are there in a gallon, and how many pounds are there in a ton?

Answer: 8 / 4 / 2,000.

WORLD GEOGRAPHY
Name the 3 largest islands in the world according to area.
Answer: Greenland / New Guinea / Borneo (listed in decreasing order of size).

LEADERS & GOVERNMENT
What was the name for the agreement under which the original American colonies established a government of states in 1781, how many colonies were there, and which document replaced this one?
Answer: Articles of Confederation / 13 / the Constitution.

MUSIC & RHYMES
Which words complete the rhyme: "Seesaw, Margery _____, / Jacky shall have a new _____; / Jacky must have but a _____ a day, / Because he can work no faster"?
Answer: "Daw" / "master" / "penny."

LANGUAGE
Complete the expressions: "Don't cry over spilt _____," "Familiarity breeds _____," and "A good man is hard to _____."
Answer: "milk" / "contempt" / "find."

ARTS, RELIGION, & CULTURE
Who founded the Christian religion, what word meaning "good news" designates the 4 books that tell the story of His life, and which Roman governor condemned this person to death?
Answer: Jesus Christ / the Gospels / Pontius Pilate.

POTPOURRI
Complete the following 1897 editorial written to a little girl: "Yes, _____, there is a _____. He exists as certainly as _____ and generosity and devotion exist."
Answer: "Virginia" / "Santa Claus" / "love."

U.S. GEOGRAPHY

In which states are Lake Mead and Lake Tahoe; the "Old Man of the Mountain" formation and Dartmouth College; and Hilton Head Island and Myrtle Beach?

Answer: Nevada / New Hampshire / South Carolina.

HISTORY

Identify the American inventors of the mechanical mower-reaper, the cylinder lock, and bifocals.

Answer: Cyrus McCormick / Linus Yale / Ben Franklin.

LITERATURE

What is the title of a fairy tale about Princess Rosamond, how long do she and everyone in the castle sleep, and how does the prince awaken her and the whole court?

Answer: "Sleeping Beauty" / 100 years / with a kiss.

ENTERTAINMENT

Which fictional character's real name is Billy Batson, which one is known as Diana Prince, and which one's assumed name is Mr. Kit Walker?

Answer: Captain Marvel / Wonder Woman / The Phantom.

SPORTS AND GAMES

In which sports did Wilma Rudolph, Martina Navratilova, and Peggy Fleming become famous?

Answer: Track / tennis / ice skating.

SCIENCE AND NATURE

From which animals do venison, mutton, and bacon come?

Answer: Deer / sheep / pigs (hogs).

WORLD GEOGRAPHY

On which continents are the Sahara Desert, the Gobi Desert, and the Mojave Desert located?

Answer: Africa / Asia / North America.

LEADERS & GOVERNMENT

Which amendments to the U.S. Constitution protect the freedom of religion, provide due process of law, and provide that electors vote for one person as President and another as Vice President?

Answer: Amendment 1 / Amendments 5 or 14 / Amendment 12.

MUSIC & RHYMES

Complete the following nursery rhyme: "Sing a song of _____, / A pocket full of _____; / Four and _____ blackbirds / Baked in a pie."

Answer: "sixpence" / "rye" / "twenty."

LANGUAGE

Complete the sayings: "A little learning is a _____ thing," "A little _____ told me," and "Little pitchers have big _____."

Answer: "dangerous" / "bird" / "ears."

ARTS, RELIGION, & CULTURE

Identify the Christian doctrine that there are 3 Persons in one God and then name 2 of the 3 Persons.

Answer: Doctrine of the Trinity / Father / Son / Holy Spirit (or Holy Ghost).

POTPOURRI

On which American symbol of freedom in which city are the words, "Proclaim liberty throughout all the land unto all the inhabitants thereof," and from which work are these words taken?

Answer: Liberty Bell / Philadelphia / Bible (Leviticus 25:10).

U.S. GEOGRAPHY

In which states are the Atlantic City boardwalk and Thomas Edison State Park; the All-American Soap Box Derby site and the Great Serpent Mound; and Alamogordo and the Carlsbad Caverns?

Answer: New Jersey / Ohio / New Mexico.

HISTORY

Who patented the revolver in England in 1835, who developed packaged frozen foods in 1924, and who developed penicillin in 1928?

Answer: Samuel Colt / Clarence Birdseye / Alexander Fleming.

LITERATURE

Who is the author of *Kidnapped*, in which country is this novel set, and to which country is the young hero David Balfour being transported aboard a ship to be sold as a slave?

Answer: Robert Louis Stevenson / Scotland / America.

ENTERTAINMENT

In which Tennessee city is Opryland, "The Home of American Music"; which word completes "_____ Flags Over Texas"; and which type of ride in several Disney parks is named Space Mountain?

Answer: Nashville / Six / roller coaster.

SPORTS AND GAMES

In which sports did Kathy Whitworth, Billie Jean King, and Jackie Joyner-Kersee become famous?

Answer: Golf / tennis / track.

SCIENCE AND NATURE

Name the part of a fraction written above the fraction line, name the part written below the line, and give the name of a whole number accompanied by a fraction.

Answer: Numerator / denominator / mixed number.

WORLD GEOGRAPHY

Name the only 2 landlocked countries of South America, and identify the only South American country bordering both the Pacific and Atlantic oceans.

Answer: Bolivia / Paraguay / Colombia.

LEADERS & GOVERNMENT

Which amendments to the U.S. Constitution protect the freedom of speech and the press, provide for the direct election of senators, and limit the President to 2 terms of office?

Answer: Amendment 1 / Amendment 17 / Amendment 22.

MUSIC & RHYMES

In the rhyme "Sing a Song of Sixpence," while the "king was counting out his money," "who was "in the parlor / Eating bread and honey," who was "hanging out the clothes," and what "snipped off her nose"?

Answer: Queen / maid / blackbird.

LANGUAGE

Complete the expressions: "Live and let _____," "Live high off (on) the _____ ," and "Live from hand to _____."

Answer: "live" (accept "die") / "hog" / "mouth."

ARTS, RELIGION, & CULTURE

What name did Jesus give to the men chosen to preach the gospel after His death, how many were there, and who, according to tradition, became the first pope of the church in Rome?

Answer: Apostles (accept disciples) / 12 / Peter.

POTPOURRI

Friday is named for Frigg, the Norse goddess of love. Which days of the week are named for Tiu, or Tiw, the Norse god of war; for Thor, the Norse god of thunder; and for Woden, or Odin, the chief Norse god?

Answer: Tuesday / Thursday / Wednesday.

U.S. GEOGRAPHY

In which states are the Catskills and Lake Placid; the Green Mountain National Forest and the Mt. Snow ski area; and Lookout Mountain and the Parthenon?

Answer: New York / Vermont / Tennessee.

HISTORY

Who invented the telegraph, what set of signals did he develop for the telegraph, and which word completes his first message on May 24, 1844, to Congress, "What hath God _____!"

Answer: Samuel Morse / Morse Code / "wrought."

LITERATURE

In the fairy tale "Jack and the Beanstalk," what 3 things does Jack steal from the giant's kingdom?

Answer: Sack of gold / hen that lays golden eggs / magic harp.

ENTERTAINMENT

Give the stage names of the following actors: John _____, born Marion Morrison; Roy _____, born Leonard Slye; and Woody _____, born Allen Stewart Konigsberg.

Answer: Wayne / Rogers / Allen.

SPORTS AND GAMES

In which college athletic conferences do Georgia, Texas, and Boston College compete?

Answer: Southeastern (SEC) / Big 12 / Big East.

SCIENCE AND NATURE

Name the disease sometimes called "infantile paralysis," and name the 2 men who created vaccines to control this disease.

Answer: Polio (or poliomyelitis) / (Jonas E.) Salk / (Albert) Sabin.

WORLD GEOGRAPHY

Name the 3 largest Canadian provinces in area.

Answer: Quebec / Ontario / British Columbia (listed from largest to smallest).

LEADERS & GOVERNMENT

Which amendment to the U.S. Constitution prohibited the consumption of liquor, in which decade was it passed, and which amendment repealed this prohibition amendment?

Answer: Amendment 18 / 1910s (ratified in 1919) / Amendment 21 (in 1933).

MUSIC & RHYMES

Match the musicals *Grease*, *Hair*, and *Can-Can* with these songs: "Aquarius," "C'est Magnifique," and "Look at Me, I'm Sandra Dee."

Answer: *Hair / Can Can / Grease.*

LANGUAGE

What happened at work if your father received his "walking papers," what happened if your brother received a "call from Uncle Sam," and what happened if your neighbor "bought the farm"?

Answer: He was fired / he was drafted / he died.

ARTS, RELIGION, & CULTURE

On which day do Christians believe Christ rose from the dead, what is the word for this return to life, and on which day do they believe their souls will be reunited with their risen bodies?

Answer: Easter Sunday (or the third day after the Crucifixion) / Resurrection / Judgment Day.

POTPOURRI

Which poisonous spider may consume the male after mating, which "hooded" snake can squirt poison in its victim's eyes, and which poisonous Southeastern U.S. snake is called a *cottonmouth*?

Answer: Black widow spider / cobra (most, however, bite their victims with poisonous fangs) / water moccasin.

U.S. GEOGRAPHY

In which states are the Davy Crockett and Sam Houston national forests; Cape Lookout and Nags Head; and the Cascade Mountains and Mount Rainier?

Answer: Texas / North Carolina / Washington.

HISTORY

Which ancient Greek city-states, long-standing rivals, fought the Peloponnesian War from 431 to 404 B.C., and which one became the main power in Greece for the next 30 years?

Answer: Athens / Sparta / Sparta.

LITERATURE

Complete the title of Kate Douglas Wiggin's *Rebecca of _____ Farm*, Dr. Seuss's *The _____ Battle Book*, and Jack London's *White _____*.

Answer: ***Sunnybrook / Butter / Fang.***

ENTERTAINMENT

Give the stage names of the following actresses: Judy _____, born Frances Gumm; Marilyn _____, born Norma Jean Baker; and Sophia _____, born Sofia Scicolone.

Answer: Garland / Monroe / Loren.

SPORTS AND GAMES

In which college athletic conferences do Southern California, Brigham Young, and Ohio State compete?

Answer: Pacific-10 (Pac-10) / Mountain West / Big Ten.

SCIENCE AND NATURE

Which particle in an atom has a negative electric charge, which one has a positive electric charge, and which one has no electric charge?

Answer: Electron / proton / neutron.

WORLD GEOGRAPHY
Name the world's 3 largest nations in area after the disintegration of the Soviet Union.
Answer: Russia / Canada / China (listed from largest to smallest).

LEADERS & GOVERNMENT
Which amendments to the U.S. Constitution forbid Congress to establish a church, give Congress the power to collect taxes on income, and provide for presidential disability and succession?
Answer: Amendment 1 / Amendment 16 / Amendment 25.

MUSIC & RHYMES
Complete the rhyme: "Tom, Tom, the _____'s son, / Stole a pig, and away did run; / The pig was eat, and Tom was _____, / And Tom went _____ down the street."
Answer: "piper" / 'beat" / "howling" (accept "running" or "crying").

LANGUAGE
What happened if you received a "pink slip" in your pay envelope, what happened if you were "caught with your hand in the cookie jar," and what happened if you "bit the dust"?
Answer: You were fired / You were caught stealing / you died.

ARTS, RELIGION, & CULTURE
Which ceremony celebrates an individual's entrance into Christianity, which one represents the Last Supper, and what food and drink did Jesus share with His disciples at the final meal?
Answer: Baptism / Eucharist (accept Holy Communion) / bread and wine.

POTPOURRI
Name 3 of the 4 cardinal directions.
Answer: North / south / east / west.

U.S. GEOGRAPHY

In which states are Mt. Vernon and Skyline Drive; the Flagship *Niagara* in Erie and Allegheny National Forest; and Wounded Knee and the Crazy Horse Memorial?

Answer: Virginia / Pennsylvania / South Dakota.

HISTORY

Which French leaders are known as the "Maid of Orleans," the "Little Corporal," and "Le Grand Charles"?

Answer: Joan of Arc / Napoleon (Bonaparte) / Charles de Gaulle.

LITERATURE

Who wrote the story of "The Little Match Girl," how does she die, and on which day of the year does her death occur?

Answer: Hans Christian Andersen / freezes to death / New Year's Eve.

ENTERTAINMENT

Which flower does an enchantress offer the Prince in exchange for shelter in the Disney film *Beauty and the Beast*, into what does she transform him, and what does she give him to see the outside world?

Answer: (Red) rose / Beast / an enchanted or magic mirror.

SPORTS AND GAMES

In which college athletic conferences do Harvard, North Carolina, and Penn State compete?

Answer: Ivy League / Atlantic Coast (ACC) / Big Ten.

SCIENCE AND NATURE

Identify the 3 ways in which heat travels from a high temperature to a low temperature.

Answer: Conduction / convection / radiation.

WORLD GEOGRAPHY
Name the 3 largest South American countries in area.
Answer: Brazil / Argentina / Peru (listed from largest to smallest).

LEADERS & GOVERNMENT
Which amendments to the U.S. Constitution give women the right to vote, provide for suffrage in the District of Columbia, and provide for suffrage to 18-year-olds?
Answer: Amendment 19 / Amendment 23 / Amendment 26.

MUSIC & RHYMES
Complete the lines from the rhyme: "Here we go round the _____ bush, / . . . On a _____ and _____ morning."
Answer: "Mulberry" / "cold" / "frosty."

LANGUAGE
Complete the expressions: "To hit a man when he's _____," "To hit (someone) like a ton of _____," and "To hit one's _____ against a brick wall."
Answer: "down" / "bricks" / "head."

ARTS, RELIGION, & CULTURE
What kind of ship did the Biblical Noah build; for how many days and nights did it rain during the Deluge, or Great Flood; and how many people did he take aboard the ship?
Answer: Ark / 40 days and 40 nights / 7 (his wife, his 3 sons, and their wives).

POTPOURRI
Which courageous blind deaf-mute's story is told in the play and motion picture *The Miracle Worker*, in which state was she born in the town of Tuscumbia, and who was her first teacher?
Answer: Helen Keller / Alabama / Anne Sullivan.

U.S. GEOGRAPHY

In which states are the Badlands and the Red River Valley; the Creek Capitol building and the Will Rogers Memorial; and Crater Lake and Mount Hood?

Answer: North Dakota / Oklahoma / Oregon.

HISTORY

What was the nationality of Socrates, whom was he accused of corrupting, and which poison was he ordered to drink after being found guilty?

Answer: Greek / the youth (of Athens) / hemlock.

LITERATURE

Which fairy tale boy is "no bigger than a man's thumb"; which "mighty magician" grants the woman the wish for this size son; and after a large fish swallows the boy, which king makes him his dwarf?

Answer: Tom Thumb / Merlin / King Arthur.

ENTERTAINMENT

Give the stage names of the following: Stevie _____, born Stevland Morris; Crystal _____, born Brenda Gail Webb; and Elton _____, born Reginald Kenneth Dwight.

Answer: Wonder (also listed as being born Stevland Judkins) / Gayle / John.

SPORTS AND GAMES

Which golfer is known by the nickname "The Golden Bear," which baseball player is "The Yankee Clipper," and which ice hockey player is "The Great One"?

Answer: Jack Nicklaus / Joe DiMaggio / Wayne Gretzky.

SCIENCE AND NATURE

What are the specialties of a pediatrician, an obstetrician, and a gerontologist?

Answer: Children / pregnancy (and childbirth) / aging (and the elderly).

WORLD GEOGRAPHY

Name the 3 largest African countries in area.

Answer: Sudan / Algeria / Democratic Republic of the Congo (formerly Zaire; listed from largest to smallest).

LEADERS & GOVERNMENT

Which words complete the line from Lincoln's Gettysburg Address in which he referred to America's democracy as a government "_____ the people, _____ the people and _____ the people"?

Answer: "of" / "by" / "for."

MUSIC & RHYMES

Which words complete the rhyme: "Little Miss Muffet / Sat on a _____, / Eating some (her) _____ and _____"? A spider then came along and frightened her away.

Answer: "tuffet" / "curds" / "whey."

LANGUAGE

What is studied in the fields of *herpetology*, *entomology*, and *ichthyology*?

Answer: Reptiles (and amphibians) / insects / fish.

ARTS, RELIGION, & CULTURE

Which religion was preached by the Prophet Muhammad in the A.D. 600s, what name is given to this religion's followers, and which one god do they worship?

Answer: Islam / Muslims (or Moslems; accept Mohammedans) / Allah.

POTPOURRI

Which American sharpshooter was known as "Little Sure Shot," in whose Wild West show did she star for 16 years, and which word completes the musical comedy title *Annie Get Your* _____?

Answer: Annie Oakley / Buffalo Bill's / *Gun*.

U.S. GEOGRAPHY
In which states are the Dwight Eisenhower birthplace and the Lyndon B. Johnson Library; Promontory Point and the Bonneville Salt Flats; and St. John's Church and Kings Dominion?
Answer: Texas / Utah / Virginia.

HISTORY
In which country was the Battle of Marathon fought in 490 B.C., about how far did Pheidippides run to announce the victory, and which country's forces led by Darius were defeated?
Answer: Greece / about 25 miles (accept 26 miles) / Persia's.

LITERATURE
Identify the school for Witchcraft and Wizardry that Harry Potter attends, the track from which the train at London's King's Cross Station leaves for the school, and the soccer-like game with 7 players, 4 balls, and flying broomsticks he plays there.
Answer: Hogwarts / Platform 9 3/4 / Quidditch.

ENTERTAINMENT
Identify the following young actresses who were given special Oscars: 6-year-old Shirley _____ in 1934; 17-year-old Judy _____ in 1939; and 9-year-old Tatum _____ in 1974.
Answer: Temple / Garland / O'Neal.

SPORTS AND GAMES
Identify the American athletes who both won 4 Olympic gold medals in track and field, one in 1936 and the other in 1984, and then identify the city in which the 1936 Olympic Games were held.
Answer: Jesse Owens / Carl Lewis / Berlin (1984s were in Los Angeles).

SCIENCE AND NATURE
Which parts of the body are studied by a podiatrist, a neurologist, and an orthopedist?
Answer: Feet (and hands) / nervous system / bones (joints and muscles).

WORLD GEOGRAPHY

Name the 3 largest Asian countries in area after the disintegration of the Soviet Union.

Answer: Russia / China / India (listed from largest to smallest).

LEADERS & GOVERNMENT

Who represents the U.S. executive branch, and which bodies make up the legislative and judicial branches?

Answer: President / Congress / courts.

MUSIC & RHYMES

Complete the lines from the rhyme: "Lucy _____ lost her pocket, / Kitty _____ found it; / Not a penny was there in it, / Only a _____ round it."

Answer: "Locket" / "Fisher" / "ribbon" (accept "binding").

LANGUAGE

Un and *deux* are 1 and 2 in French. Give the French words for the numerals 3, 4, and 5.

Answer: *Trois* / *quatre* / *cinq*.

ARTS, RELIGION, & CULTURE

In which country is the holiest shrine of Islam, how many times a day must Moslems pray, and in which city is the Great Mosque toward which they must face?

Answer: Saudi Arabia / 5 times / Mecca.

POTPOURRI

In British English, what are "chips" in "fish and chips," what are you doing if you are riding "the tube," and what are you doing if you are "playing draughts"?

Answer: French fries / riding the subway / playing checkers.

U.S. GEOGRAPHY

In which Alabama cities are the Statue of the Roman god Vulcan; the U.S.S. *Alabama*; and the George C. Marshall Space Flight Center and the Redstone Arsenal?

Answer: Birmingham / Mobile / Huntsville.

HISTORY

Which leader of which country said following which war, "From Stettin in the Baltic to Trieste in the Adriatic, an iron curtain has descended across the continent"?

Answer: Winston Churchill / Britain / World War II.

LITERATURE

In an Aesop tale, which fruit is hanging on a trellis out of reach, which animal tries to jump to get some, and which word completes his statement, "I am sure they are _____ anyway"?

Answer: Grapes / fox / "sour."

ENTERTAINMENT

Which singer is buried in Graceland, and in which city in which state is this home?

Answer: Elvis Presley / Memphis / Tennessee.

SPORTS AND GAMES

In words and phrases from sports, which "dog" is expected to lose, behind which "ball" are you if you are at a disadvantage, and what kind of dice is your opponent using if you have no chance?

Answer: Underdog / behind the eight ball / loaded dice.

SCIENCE AND NATURE

How many stages of development does a butterfly go through, what is the common name for the larva stage, and which 13-letter word describes this process of development?

Answer: 4 (egg, larva, pupa, and adult) / caterpillar / metamorphosis.

WORLD GEOGRAPHY
Excluding Russia, name the 3 largest European countries in area.
Answer: France / Spain / Sweden (listed from largest to smallest).

LEADERS & GOVERNMENT
Identify the government system of the following as either presidential or parliamentary: Australia, Canada, and Mexico.
Answer: Parliamentary / parliamentary / presidential.

MUSIC & RHYMES
Which words complete the nursery rhyme: "Georgie Porgie, _____ and _____, / Kissed the girls and made them _____; / When the boys came out to play, / Georgie Porgie ran away?"
Answer: "Pudding" / "pie" / "cry."

LANGUAGE
Uno and *dos* are 1 and 2 in Spanish. Give the Spanish words for the numerals 3, 4, and 5.
Answer: *Tres / cuatro / cinco.*

ARTS, RELIGION, & CULTURE
In which book of the Bible is the story of the Red Sea's parting, who was commanded by God to lift a rod to part this sea, and which group was enabled to escape from Egypt by this sea's parting?
Answer: Exodus / Moses / Israelites.

POTPOURRI
Name 3 of the 4 months in the rhyme: "Thirty days hath _____, / _____, _____, and _____; / All the rest have thirty-one."
Answer: "September" / "April" / "June" / "November" ("Excepting February alone, / Which hath but twenty-eight, in fine, / Till leap year gives it twenty-nine").

U.S. GEOGRAPHY

In which California cities are the La Brea Tar Pits and Sunset Boulevard; the *Star of India* and the Cabrillo National Monument; and Alcatraz and Fisherman's Wharf?

Answer: Los Angeles / San Diego / San Francisco.

HISTORY

What are the native countries of the following foreign leaders who helped America during the Revolutionary War: Thaddeus Kosciusko, the Marquis de Lafayette, and Baron von Steuben?

Answer: Poland / France / Prussia.

LITERATURE

In an Aesop fable, which animal gets water by putting pebbles in the pitcher, and in another fable what is choking the wolf and which animal draws it out of his throat?

Answer: Crow / bone / crane.

ENTERTAINMENT

Complete the titles of the following Elvis Presley songs: "Hound _____," "Don't Be _____," and "Love Me _____."

Answer: "Dog" / "Cruel" / "Tender."

SPORTS AND GAMES

In which states are the National Baseball Hall of Fame in Cooperstown, the Naismith Memorial Basketball Hall of Fame in Springfield, and the National Football Hall of Fame in Canton?

Answer: New York / Massachusetts / Ohio.

SCIENCE AND NATURE

What is the world's largest living animal, what is the largest living land bird, and what is the largest living land animal?

Answer: Blue whale / ostrich / elephant.

WORLD GEOGRAPHY

Name the 3 largest continents in area.

Answer: Asia / Africa / North America (listed from largest to smallest).

LEADERS & GOVERNMENT

What is the word for "an advisory body to the U.S. President consisting of the heads of the major government departments," how many heads are in this body, and which one is not called "Secretary"?

Answer: Cabinet / 14 / the Attorney General.

MUSIC & RHYMES

Complete the following nursery rhyme: "1-2 buckle my shoe / 3-4 knock at the door / 5-6 pick up _____ / 7-8 lay them _____ / 9-10 a good (big) fat _____."

Answer: "sticks" / "straight" / "hen."

LANGUAGE

Eins and *zwei* are 1 and 2 in German. Give the German words for the numerals 3 to 5.

Answer: *Drei* / *vier* / *fünf*.

ARTS, RELIGION, & CULTURE

Complete the words to the gospel song: "Give me that old-time _____, / It's good _____ for me. / . . . It was good for _____ and Silas."

Answer: "religion" / "enough" / "Paul."

POTPOURRI

Which day of the week is usually described as *blue*, which color are bulls said to hate, and which color is the Bird of Happiness?

Answer: Monday / red / blue.

U.S. GEOGRAPHY
In or near which Florida cities are Coral Gables and Coconut Grove; The Dark Continent and Busch Gardens; and Sea World and EPCOT Center?
Answer: Miami / Tampa / Orlando.

HISTORY
Which Americans are remembered for saying: "I shall return," "Ich bin ein Berliner," and "I have a dream"?
Answer: General Douglas MacArthur / John F. Kennedy / Martin Luther King Jr.

LITERATURE
In one Aesop fable, which boy keeps calling "Wolf! Wolf!" until eventually the villagers don't come when he needs them; in another fable, which 2 mice visit each other; and which word completes the expression "a wolf in _____'s clothing" derived from his work?
Answer: Shepherd boy / Town Mouse and Country Mouse / sheep.

ENTERTAINMENT
Which actors are known as "The Little Tramp," "The King of Hollywood," and "The Great One"?
Answer: Charlie Chaplin / Clark Gable / Jackie Gleason.

SPORTS AND GAMES
In which Indiana city is the Motor Speedway Racing Hall of Fame, in which one is the College Football Hall of Fame located near the University of Notre Dame, and in which state is the International Swimming Hall of Fame located in Fort Lauderdale?
Answer: Indianapolis / South Bend / Florida.

SCIENCE AND NATURE
What are the names for the offspring of a tom and a puss, a dog and a bitch, and a stallion and a dam?
Answer: Kitten / pup (or puppy) / foal.

WORLD GEOGRAPHY

What are the basic monetary units of South Africa and Venezuela, and what was the basic unit of the Netherlands before the Euro?

Answer: Rand / Bolivar / Guilder.

LEADERS & GOVERNMENT

Of the U.S. Cabinet departments, which one begins with the letter *A*, which one begins with the letter *C*, and which one begins with the letter *V*?

Answer: Agriculture / Commerce / Veterans' Affairs.

MUSIC & RHYMES

Which words complete the wedding rhyme: "Something old, something _____, / Something _____, something _____, / And a lucky sixpence in her shoe"?

Answer: "new" / "borrowed" / "blue."

LANGUAGE

Give the words for "Thank you" in French, Spanish, and German.

Answer: *Merci* / *Gracias* / *Danke*.

ARTS, RELIGION, & CULTURE

Give the word for "a Jewish scholar, teacher, and spiritual leader"; give the word for "being fit to eat according to Jewish dietary laws"; and give the name for "a candelabrum used during Hanukkah."

Answer: Rabbi / kosher / menorah.

POTPOURRI

Which French leaders are known for saying: "I am the State," "Let them eat cake," and "How can anyone govern a country that has 246 kinds of cheese"?

Answer: Louis XIV / Marie Antoinette / Charles de Gaulle.

U.S. GEOGRAPHY

In or near which cities are the Loop and O'Hare International Airport; the Garden of the Gods and Pikes Peak; and William F. Cody's grave and the United States Mint?

Answer: Chicago / Colorado Springs / Denver.

HISTORY

Who was shot and killed by James Earl Ray in 1968, who was shot and killed by Sirhan Sirhan in 1968, and who was shot and wounded by Mehmet Ali Agca in 1981?

Answer: Martin Luther King Jr. / Robert Kennedy / Pope John Paul II.

LITERATURE

In an Aesop fable, which king of the beasts is caught by hunters, how do they catch this animal, and which animal frees him by gnawing away the hunters' ropes that bind him?

Answer: A lion / in a net / a mouse.

ENTERTAINMENT

Which actors are known by the nicknames "Bogie," "The Duke," and "Ol' Blue Eyes"?

Answer: Humphrey Bogart / John Wayne / Frank Sinatra.

SPORTS AND GAMES

In which states are the U.S. National Ski Hall of Fame in Ishpeming and the National Wrestling Hall of Fame in Stillwater, and in which city in Ontario is the Hockey Hall of Fame?

Answer: Michigan / Oklahoma / Toronto.

SCIENCE AND NATURE

What are the names for the offspring of a gander and a goose, a lion and a lioness, and a cock and a hen?

Answer: Gosling / cub / chick.

WORLD GEOGRAPHY

Of which country is Greenland a province, which country rules Corsica, and which one governs the Canary Islands?

Answer: Denmark / France / Spain.

LEADERS & GOVERNMENT

Of the U.S. Cabinet departments, which one besides Energy begins with the letter *E*, which one begins with the letter *I*, and which one begins with the letter *S*?

Answer: Education / Interior / State.

MUSIC & RHYMES

In the rhyme "The Farmer in the Dell," what does the farmer take, what does the child take, and what does the nurse take?

Answer: A wife / the nurse / the dog.

LANGUAGE

Give the words for "Good morning" or "Good day" in French, Spanish, and German.

Answer: *Bonjour* / *Buenos días* / *Guten Morgen*.

ARTS, RELIGION, & CULTURE

In the Bible, whose names are synonymous with "great wisdom," with "extreme age," and with "extreme patience"?

Answer: Solomon / Methuselah / Job.

POTPOURRI

Which animal allegedly brings bad luck if it deserts a ship before it sails, which animal supposedly can scare an elephant, and which animals traditionally play when the cat's away?

Answer: Rat / mouse / mice.

U.S. GEOGRAPHY

In which cities are Emory University and Centennial Olympic Park; Iolani Palace and Waikiki Beach; and the Sears Tower and Grant Park?

Answer: Atlanta / Honolulu / Chicago.

HISTORY

Which word completes the epitaph, "Free at last, free at last, thank God _____, I'm free at last," and on whose tombstone in which city are these words inscribed?

Answer: "Almighty" / Martin Luther King Jr.'s / Atlanta.

LITERATURE

In the fable about a slave and a lion, what is the name of the slave, which object does he remove from the lion's paw, and where does the lion later refuse to kill the slave in the presence of the king?

Answer: Androcles / thorn / in the arena.

ENTERTAINMENT

Which entertainers are known by the nicknames "Uncle Milty," "Old Ski Nose," and "Candy Man"?

Answer: Milton Berle / Bob Hope / Sammy Davis Jr.

SPORTS AND GAMES

Identify the line along which offensive and defensive teams face each other in American football, the minimum number of players on the offensive line, and the term for the zone between the 2 player lines.

Answer: Line of scrimmage / 7 / neutral zone.

SCIENCE AND NATURE

Identify the longest and strongest bone in the human body, the type of joint where the bone meets the hipbone, and the strong cords of tissue by which muscles are attached to the bones.

Answer: Femur (or thigh bone) / ball-and-socket joint / tendons (accept sinews).

WORLD GEOGRAPHY

Which countries control the Azores, Martinique, and Sicily?

Answer: Portugal / France / Italy.

LEADERS & GOVERNMENT

Who was the second U.S. President to be impeached, in which year was he acquitted of the charges against him, and with which intern did he admit improper conduct?

Answer: William Jefferson Clinton / 1999 / Monica Lewinsky.

MUSIC & RHYMES

In the rhyme "The Farmer in the Dell," what does the wife take, what does the cat take, and what stands alone?

Answer: The child / the rat / the cheese.

LANGUAGE

Give the words for both "Yes" and "No" in French, Spanish, and German.

Answer: Oui and Non / Sí and No / Ja and Nein.

ARTS, RELIGION, & CULTURE

Which of the 12 Disciples, or Apostles, refused to believe in the Resurrection of Jesus until he saw certain features on the risen Christ, which marks were they, and what expression refers to this disciple today?

Answer: Thomas (or Didymus) / the crucifixion wounds / "Doubting Thomas."

POTPOURRI

What are the 2 colors of the Red Cross flag, in which European country was the Red Cross founded in 1863, a country honored by this flag, and which woman founded the American Red Cross in 1881?

Answer: Red and white / Switzerland / Clara Barton.

U.S. GEOGRAPHY

In which cities are Churchill Downs and the home of George Rogers Clark; the French Quarter and Bourbon Street; and the National Aquarium and the U.S.S. *Constellation*?

Answer: Louisville / New Orleans / Baltimore.

HISTORY

Which document issued by which U.S. President declared that all slaves in the territory in rebellion against the Union would be freed on January 1, and in which year did it take effect?

Answer: Emancipation Proclamation / Abraham Lincoln / 1863.

LITERATURE

Which American author is known for her series of 9 "Little House" novels, and which words complete the titles *Little House in the Big* _____ and *Little House on the* _____?

Answer: Laura Ingalls Wilder / *Woods* / *Prairie*.

ENTERTAINMENT

What kinds of animals are Tom and Jerry in the cartoons, and what are the rhyming names of the 2 famous magpies in Terrytoon cartoons?

Answer: Cat / mouse / Heckle and Jeckle.

SPORTS AND GAMES

Give the nicknames of the college athletic teams at West Virginia, Wyoming, and Stanford.

Answer: Mountaineers / Cowboys / The Cardinal.

SCIENCE AND NATURE

Which vitamin is also called the "Sunshine Vitamin," which one is also known as ascorbic acid, and a deficiency of which vitamin causes night blindness?

Answer: Vitamin D / Vitamin C / Vitamin A.

WORLD GEOGRAPHY

Identify the Asian nations whose flags display the following: a cedar tree; 4 stars on a red background; and a red sun on a white background.

Answer: Lebanon / China / Japan.

LEADERS & GOVERNMENT

Which phrase refers to the system of shared powers among the 3 branches of the U.S. government, what is the term for the executive right to cancel a legislative decision, and which President used this power the most?

Answer: Checks and balances / veto / Franklin Roosevelt.

MUSIC & RHYMES

Complete the rhyme: "It's raining, it's _____ / The old man's a-_____ / Bumped his head on the side of the bed / And couldn't get up in the _____."

Answer: "pouring" / "snoring" / "morning."

LANGUAGE

Proverbially, which new household item sweeps clean, what never strikes twice in the same place, and from which animal's mouth does one get something from a reliable source?

Answer: Broom / lightning / horse's mouth.

ARTS, RELIGION, & CULTURE

Identify the song's title and complete the lines: "Come, they told me, (Pa-rum-pum-pum-pum) / A new born _____ to see; / Our finest _____ we bring, / To lay before the King, / So to honor him."

Answer: "The Little Drummer Boy" / "King" / "gifts."

POTPOURRI

Complete the typewriting test phrases: "The quick brown _____ jumps over the lazy dog" and "Now is the time for all good _____ to come to the aid of the _____."

Answer: "fox" / "men" / "party" (or "country").

U.S. GEOGRAPHY

In which cities are Breed's Hill and Bunker Hill; the Joe Louis Arena and the Renaissance Center; and the Mark Twain Cave and Tom Sawyer and Huckleberry Finn statues?

Answer: Boston / Detroit / Hannibal (Missouri).

HISTORY

Which color schoolhouse became symbolic of education in the U.S., which Greek educator established the Lyceum, and which Greek educator established the Academy?

Answer: Red schoolhouse / Aristotle / Plato.

LITERATURE

Complete these lines from a Robert Louis Stevenson poem: "I was the giant great and still / That sits upon the _____-hill, / And sees before him, dale and _____, / The pleasant land of _____."

Answer: "pillow" / "plain" / "counterpane" (from "The Land of Counterpane").

ENTERTAINMENT

On which planet was Superman born, what was his name at birth, and in which city in Illinois did he land after his planet was destroyed?

Answer: Krypton / Kal-El / Smallville.

SPORTS AND GAMES

In which sports are the cries "Tallyho," "Fore," and "Play Ball" heard?

Answer: Fox hunting / golf / baseball.

SCIENCE AND NATURE

Give the terms for the solid outer layer of the earth, for the portion of the earth between the solid outer layer and the inner layer, and for the inner layer of the earth?

Answer: Crust / mantle / core.

WORLD GEOGRAPHY

In which Italian cities are the Grand Canal, the Leaning Tower, and the Colosseum?

Answer: Venice / Pisa / Rome.

LEADERS & GOVERNMENT

Which U.S. Presidents served from 1789 to 1797, from 1861 to 1865, and from 1901 to 1909?

Answer: George Washington / Abraham Lincoln / Theodore Roosevelt.

MUSIC & RHYMES

Complete the rhyme: "This little pig went to _____; / This little pig stayed at _____; / This little pig had _____; / This little pig had none; / And this little pig cried, Wee, wee, wee; / I can't find my way home."

Answer: "market" / "home" / roast beef."

LANGUAGE

Complete each of the following proverbs: "Opportunity seldom knocks _____," " _____ comes but once a year," and "Time and _____ wait for no man."

Answer: "Twice" / "Christmas" / "tide."

ARTS, RELIGION, & CULTURE

Which of Jesus's disciples was called the "rock," how many times did he deny he knew Jesus, and in which city was a church built over his supposed burial place?

Answer: Peter / 3 / Vatican City (accept Rome).

POTPOURRI

Which words complete the legend of the "Three Wise Monkeys" carved over a door in Japan: "_____ no evil, _____ no evil, _____ no evil"?

Answer: "Hear" / "see" / "speak."

U.S. GEOGRAPHY
In which state is Lake Pontchartrain Causeway, the world's longest; in which one is the Golden Gate Bridge, the world's tallest; and in which one is the Royal Gorge Bridge, the world's highest?
Answer: Louisiana / California / Colorado.

HISTORY
Name 3 of the 4 wars the U.S. military engaged in during the 19th century.
Answer: War of 1812 / Mexican-American War / U.S. Civil War / Spanish-American War.

LITERATURE
In Hans Christian Andersen's "The Steadfast Tin Soldier," how many soldiers are there, from which "old tin" object were they cast, and what is the "steadfast soldier" missing?
Answer: 25 / spoon / a leg.

ENTERTAINMENT
Give the name of the Lone Ranger's "fiery horse with the speed of light," the name of his sidekick, and the name of his sidekick's horse.
Answer: Silver / Tonto / Scout (earlier, White Feller and Paint).

SPORTS AND GAMES
Which color card does a soccer referee use when ejecting a player from the game, which color is used for giving a warning, and what is the color of the light used in ice hockey to indicate a goal?
Answer: Red / yellow / red.

SCIENCE AND NATURE
Traditionally, which dogs rescue lost persons in the Swiss Alps, which ones ride on fire trucks, and which ones are used as police dogs?
Answer: Saint Bernards / Dalmatians / German shepherds.

WORLD GEOGRAPHY
Name the 3 largest of the Great Lakes in area.
Answer: Superior / Huron / Michigan (listed in order from largest to smallest).

LEADERS & GOVERNMENT
Which U.S. Presidents served from 1801 to 1809, from 1869 to 1877, and from 1913 to 1921?
Answer: Thomas Jefferson / Ulysses S. Grant / Woodrow Wilson.

MUSIC & RHYMES
Complete the rhyme: "Pat-a-cake, pat-a-cake, _____'s man, / Bake me a cake as fast as you can; / Pat it and prick it, and mark it with a _____, / And put it in the oven for _____ and me."
Answer: "Baker" / "B" (accept any letter that rhymes with "me") / "baby."

LANGUAGE
Which words complete the proverbs: "There is safety in _____," "Look before you _____," and "The end justifies the _____"?
Answer: "numbers" / "leap" / "means."

ARTS, RELIGION, & CULTURE
Which traditional meat, pie, and berry are served at a Thanksgiving Day dinner in the U.S.?
Answer: Turkey / pumpkin pie / cranberry.

POTPOURRI
Which organization began placing Bibles in hotel rooms in 1908, which restaurant-motel chain is known for its bright orange roofs, and which restaurant chain is known for its golden arches?
Answer: Gideons / Howard Johnson's / McDonalds.

U.S. GEOGRAPHY

In which cities are Stone Mountain and the Cyclorama; Fort McHenry and the Inner Harbor; and Grant's Tomb, Greenwich Village, and Rockefeller Center?

Answer: Atlanta / Baltimore / New York.

HISTORY

In which year and in which U.S. state was the first atomic bomb exploded, and on which Japanese city was the first such bomb dropped?

Answer: 1945 / New Mexico / Hiroshima.

LITERATURE

Identify the wizard world's supreme villain, murderer of Harry Potter's parents; the shape of the scar on Harry's forehead incurred when his parents were killed; and the name the wizard world gives to a mortal who has no magical power.

Answer: (Lord) Voldemort / Lightning-bolt-shaped / Muggle.

ENTERTAINMENT

On a Disney TV series, which character was the "King of the Wild Frontier," who was the "King of the River," and to which city did they race their riverboats?

Answer: Davy Crockett / Mike Fink / New Orleans.

SPORTS AND GAMES

Who was the first NFL player to gain more than 2,000 yards in a season, who was the first to score more than 100 touchdowns, and who was the first to rush for more than 16,000 yards?

Answer: O.J. Simpson / Jim Brown / Walter Payton.

SCIENCE AND NATURE

Which country's sailors were nicknamed "limeys" because they took barrels of limes on trips, which disease did citrus fruits prevent on these trips, and which vitamin prevents this disease?

Answer: Britain's / scurvy / Vitamin C.

WORLD GEOGRAPHY

Which continents include the following countries: Gabon and Gambia; Chile and the Falkland Islands; and Costa Rica and Cuba?

Answer: Africa / South America / North America.

LEADERS & GOVERNMENT

Which words complete the slogans: "One man, one _____," "As _____ goes, so goes the nation," and "America, love it or _____ it"?

Answer: "vote" / "Maine" / "leave."

MUSIC & RHYMES

Complete the rhyme: "Wee Willie _____ runs through the town, / Upstairs and downstairs in his _____, / . . . Are the children in their beds, for now its _____ o'clock."

Answer: "Winkie" / "nightgown" ("Rapping at the window, crying through the lock") / "eight."

LANGUAGE

Which words complete the sayings: "Nothing ventured, nothing _____," Out of sight, out of _____," and "First come, first _____"?

Answer: "gained" / "mind" / "served."

ARTS, RELIGION, & CULTURE

Which countries are traditionally associated with bagpipers, flamenco dancers, and Cossack dancers?

Answer: Scotland (accept Ireland) / Spain / Russia (accept Soviet Union).

POTPOURRI

Proverbially, with which neighboring family must one keep up to maintain social standing, how many corners of the earth are there, and what is the way to a man's heart?

Answer: Joneses / 4 / through his stomach.

U.S. GEOGRAPHY

In which cities are Faneuil Hall and the U.S.S. *Constitution*; Battery Park and the Empire State Building; and The Citadel and the USS *Yorktown*?

Answer: Boston / New York / Charleston (South Carolina).

HISTORY

Who was the U.S. President when 52 Americans were held hostage for 444 days from November 4, 1979, to January 20, 1981; in which country were they held; and who was the leader of that country?

Answer: Jimmy Carter / Iran / Ayatollah Ruhollah Khomeini.

LITERATURE

Which words complete the last line of Charles Dickens' *A Christmas Carol*, "And so as Tiny _____ observed, _____ Bless Us, Every _____"?

Answer: "Tim" / "God" / "One."

ENTERTAINMENT

What are the names of the Flintstones' pet dinosaur and their daughter, and what is the name of the Rubble's adopted son?

Answer: Dino / Pebbles / Bamm Bamm.

SPORTS AND GAMES

Which Massachusetts university played in the first football game in 1874, for which college team did Harold "Red" Grange play, and which college team won 47 straight games from 1953 to 1957?

Answer: Harvard / Illinois / Oklahoma.

SCIENCE AND NATURE

Which vitamin obtained from carrots is beneficial to the eyes, which vitamin helps prevents rickets, and what parts of the body are affected by rickets?

Answer: Vitamin A / Vitamin D / bones.

WORLD GEOGRAPHY

What is the world's highest mountain, and in which mountain range on which continent is it located?

Answer: Mount Everest / Himalayas / Asia.

LEADERS & GOVERNMENT

Which U.S. Presidents served from 1809 to 1817, from 1929 to 1933, and from 1953 to 1961?

Answer: James Madison / Herbert Hoover / Dwight Eisenhower.

MUSIC & RHYMES

In the rhyme, which bridge "is falling down, falling down, falling down," and which words complete the lines, "My fair _____" and "Take the key and _____ her up"?

Answer: London Bridge / "lady" / "lock."

LANGUAGE

According to the sayings, who die many times before their deaths, who cannot be choosers, and which animals could fly if they had wings?

Answer: Cowards / beggars / pigs.

ARTS, RELIGION, & CULTURE

What is the word used to designate the birth of Christ; in which city was He born; and what is the French word for the stable display that represents the birth of Jesus?

Answer: Nativity / Bethlehem / crèche.

POTPOURRI

Which fruit if eaten every day supposedly keeps the doctor away, what is supposed to be stranger than fiction, and what is considered to be the typical, wholesome American dessert?

Answer: Apple / truth (accept fact) / apple pie.

U.S. GEOGRAPHY

In which Texas cities are the Texas Commerce Tower and the Lyndon B. Johnson Space Center; the area called *Paseo del Rio* or the River Walk and the Tower of the Americas; and Dealey Plaza and Reunion Tower?

Answer: Houston / San Antonio / Dallas.

HISTORY

Identify the trained warriors in ancient Rome who fought others for entertainment of spectators, name their 3-pronged spear, and identify the largest theatre in ancient Rome where they fought.

Answer: Gladiators (retiarii) / trident / Colosseum (or Flavian Amphitheater).

LITERATURE

Which Dickens character asks the workhouse-master for more gruel, what name is given to the fictional monster Mary Shelley created, and which hunchbacked bellringer of Notre Dame did Victor Hugo create?

Answer: Oliver Twist / Frankenstein / Quasimodo.

ENTERTAINMENT

Give the names of Mr. and Mrs. Flintstone on *The Flintstones*, a cartoon set in the Stone Age, and give the surname of their neighbors, Barney and Betty.

Answer: Fred / Wilma / Rubble.

SPORTS AND GAMES

Which baseball positions are known by the abbreviations DH and PH, and what is an RBI?

Answer: Designated Hitter / Pinch Hitter / Run Batted In.

SCIENCE AND NATURE

Give the first 3 colors of the spectrum represented by the mnemonic device Roy G. Biv.

Answer: Red / orange / yellow (green, blue, indigo, and violet are the others).

WORLD GEOGRAPHY

On which continents are Mount Aconcagua, the Matterhorn, and Godwin Austen or K2?

Answer: South America / Europe / Asia.

LEADERS & GOVERNMENT

Which U.S. Presidents served from 1817 to 1825, from 1933 to 1945, and from 1961 to 1963?

Answer: James Monroe / Franklin Roosevelt / John Kennedy.

MUSIC & RHYMES

Complete the rhyme: "Can you make me a cambric shirt, / Parsley, _____, _____, and _____, / Without any seam or needlework? / And you shall be a true lover of mine."

Answer: "sage" / "rosemary" / "thyme."

LANGUAGE

According to the expressions, who never win or prosper, where doesn't money grow, and what shouldn't you do if you live in a glass house?

Answer: Cheaters (quitters) / on trees / throw stones.

ARTS, RELIGION, & CULTURE

In which city did the parents of Jesus live, and what were the names of His parents?

Answer: Nazareth / (Virgin) Mary / Joseph.

POTPOURRI

Which Frenchman invented a system of writing for the blind, which French oceanographer invented the aqualung, and which American invented the phonograph?

Answer: Louis Braille / Jacques-Yves Cousteau / Thomas Edison.

U.S. GEOGRAPHY

In which cities are Independence Hall and the Liberty Bell; Lincoln Center and Wall Street; and the Mormon Temple and the Seagull Monument?

Answer: Philadelphia / New York / Salt Lake City.

HISTORY

Identify the U.S. frigate known as "Old Ironsides," the war in which it earned its nickname, and the poet whose poem helped save the ship from destruction?

Answer: U.S.S. *Constitution* / War of 1812 / Oliver Wendell Holmes.

LITERATURE

How many doors are in the hole the soldier climbs into in Hans Christian Andersen's "The Tinder Box," which animals guard the money, and whom does the soldier marry at the end of the story?

Answer: 3 / dogs / the princess.

ENTERTAINMENT

In which states are Hershey Park and Dollywood, and in which one is Hollywood, the "motion-picture capital of the world"?

Answer: Pennsylvania / Tennessee (in Pigeon Forge) / California.

SPORTS AND GAMES

Which football players are known by the nicknames "The Galloping Ghost" and "The Fabulous Indian," and which football coach is called "the Bald Eagle of Notre Dame"?

Answer: Harold "Red" Grange / Jim Thorpe / Knute Rockne.

SCIENCE AND NATURE

What is the chemical formula for water, and how many atoms of each element make up a water molecule?

Answer: H_2O / 2 atoms of hydrogen / 1 atom of oxygen.

WORLD GEOGRAPHY

On which continents are Mount Kilimanjaro and Mount Rainier, and on which continent did a volcano erupt on the island of Krakatoa in 1883, causing one of the world's most violent explosions?

Answer: Africa / North America / Asia.

LEADERS & GOVERNMENT

Which U.S. Presidents served from 1797 to 1801, from 1945 to 1953, and from 1969 to 1974?

Answer: John Adams / Harry S Truman / Richard M. Nixon.

MUSIC & RHYMES

Complete the rhyme: "Mary had a little lamb, / Its _____ was _____ as _____; / And everywhere that Mary went / The lamb was sure to go."

Answer: "fleece" / 'white" / "snow."

LANGUAGE

Complete each of the following proverbs: "All's fair in love and _________," "Health is better than _____," and "All that glitters is not _____."

Answer: "war" / "wealth" / "gold."

ARTS, RELIGION, & CULTURE

Of Paul Cézanne, Pablo Picasso, and Claude Monet, which one is noted for his Blue Period, which one for his *Impression: Sunrise*, and which one is the "Father of Modern Art"?

Answer: Picasso / Monet / Cézanne.

POTPOURRI

Which color is worn by winners of the Masters Golf Championship, which one is symbolic of virginity, and which one describes a business being operated at a loss?

Answer: Green / white / red.

U.S. GEOGRAPHY

Name the 3 largest states according to area.

Answer: Alaska / Texas / California (listed from largest to smallest).

HISTORY

What name was given to the union of states that seceded from the United States in 1860-1861, how many states were there when they first organized, and how many states eventually joined?

Answer: The Confederate States of America / 6 / 11.

LITERATURE

In a Brothers Grimm story, who finish during the night what a shoemaker had cut out in the evening, what presents do the shoemaker and his wife give them, and how long do they work afterwards?

Answer: Elves / clothes / they never returned.

ENTERTAINMENT

Which entertaining basketball team did Abe Saperstein found in Chicago in 1926, which 3 colors are on their uniforms, and what is their theme song?

Answer: Harlem Globetrotters / red, white, and blue / "Sweet Georgia Brown."

SPORTS AND GAMES

What are the meanings of the baseball abbreviations ERA and LOB, and what does the letter *K* designate in baseball scoring?

Answer: Earned Run Average / Left On Base / Strike-out.

SCIENCE AND NATURE

Identify 3 of the world's 4 most valuable gems.

Answer: Diamond / ruby / emerald / sapphire.

WORLD GEOGRAPHY

What is the world's largest desert, what is the word for "a fertile place in the desert," and what is the word for "an optical illusion in a desert"?

Answer: Sahara Desert / oasis / mirage.

LEADERS & GOVERNMENT

Which U.S. Presidents served from 1829 to 1837, from 1963 to 1969, and from 1977 to 1981?

Answer: Andrew Jackson / Lyndon Johnson / Jimmy Carter.

MUSIC & RHYMES

Complete the rhyme: "Rich man, / poor man, / Beggar-man, / Thief, / _____, / _____, / _____."

Answer: "Doctor" / "Lawyer" / "Indian (or merchant) chief."

LANGUAGE

Proverbially, what kind of pot never boils, what can't you make out of a sow's ear, and which people tell no tales?

Answer: A watched pot / a silk purse / dead men.

ARTS, RELIGION, & CULTURE

Identify 3 of the 4 Gospels, or the first 4 books of the New Testament.

Answer: Matthew / Mark / Luke / John.

POTPOURRI

Which 2 countries collaborated to produce the world's first supersonic passenger plane, and what is the name of this plane?

Answer: France / England / Concorde.

U.S. GEOGRAPHY

Name the 3 smallest states according to area.

Answer: Rhode Island / Delaware / Connecticut (listed from smallest to largest).

HISTORY

How many Wonders of the Ancient World were there, in which city were the Hanging Gardens, and which king probably had the Hanging Gardens built?

Answer: 7 / Babylon / King Nebuchadnezzar.

LITERATURE

Which words complete the title of Robert O'Brien's novel *Mrs. _____ and the _____ of NIMH*, and which kind of animal is this mother of four?

Answer: *Frisby* / *Rats* / a mouse.

ENTERTAINMENT

Complete the names of 2 well known circus owners, P.T. _____ and James A. _____, and give the surname of the 5 brothers who bought out the other 2 to form history's most famous circus.

Answer: Barnum / Bailey / Ringling.

SPORTS AND GAMES

In 1947, who became the first black player in modern major league baseball, for which team did he play, and at which position did he gain fame from 1948 to 1952?

Answer: Jackie Robinson / Brooklyn Dodgers / second base.

SCIENCE AND NATURE

From which country do Valencia oranges come; which citrus fruit was named after Tangier, Morocco; and which 2 fruits were combined to form the tangelo?

Answer: Spain / tangerine / tangerine and grapefruit (accept mandarin orange or shaddock).

WORLD GEOGRAPHY

Identify the Brazilian city whose name literally means "River of January," the Argentinean city whose name means "Good Air," and the South American area whose name means the "Land of Fire."

Answer: Rio de Janeiro / Buenos Aires / Tierra del Fuego.

LEADERS & GOVERNMENT

Which 2 U.S. Presidents served from 1921 to 1923 and from 1974 to 1977, and which one served from 1885 to 1889 and from 1893 to 1897?

Answer: Warren G. Harding / Gerald R. Ford / Grover Cleveland.

MUSIC & RHYMES

Complete the rhyme: "Oh, where have you been, Billy _____? / Oh, where have you been, _____ Billy? / I have been to seek a _____; / She's the joy of my life."

Answer: "Boy" ("Billy Boy") / "charming" / "wife."

LANGUAGE

Proverbially, what does everyone talk about but no one does anything about, what should one make while the sun shines, and what part of the body is charged with not knowing what the left hand is doing?

Answer: The weather / hay / the right hand.

ARTS, RELIGION, & CULTURE

Which pie and which log are associated with Christmas, and under which evergreen sprig hung as a Christmas decoration do people traditionally kiss?

Answer: Mince pie (accept pumpkin) / yule log / mistletoe.

POTPOURRI

When does a somnambulist walk, what does a spelunker explore, and what does an equestrian ride?

Answer: When he is asleep / a cave / a horse.

U.S. GEOGRAPHY

Which country borders the U.S. on the north, which one borders it on the south, and which island in the Bering Strait is about 2 miles from the U.S.'s Little Diomede island?

Answer: Canada / Mexico / Big Diomede Island (belonging to Russia).

HISTORY

In which countries were these 3 Wonders of the Ancient World: the Mausoleum at Halicarnassus, the Colossus of Rhodes, and the Lighthouse at Alexandria?

Answer: Turkey / Greece / Egypt.

LITERATURE

Complete the titles in Tolkien's trilogy *The Lord of the Rings*: *The* _____ *of the Ring*, *The Two* _____, and *The* _____ *of the King*.

Answer: *Fellowship* / *Towers* / *Return*.

ENTERTAINMENT

What is the term for the largest tent in a circus, how many rings does a large circus use for simultaneous performances, and which animals are fitted with a saddle called a *howdah*?

Answer: Big top / 3 / elephants.

SPORTS AND GAMES

Which tennis player from which country won the men's singles title at the All-England Championships 5 straight times from 1976 to 1980, and what is the better known name for this tennis tournament?

Answer: Bjorn Borg / Sweden / Wimbledon.

SCIENCE AND NATURE

Which 2 heavenly bodies produce the Earth's tides, and which planet was long thought to have canals?

Answer: Sun / moon / Mars.

WORLD GEOGRAPHY

Which 3 countries besides Slovenia border Italy?

Answer: France / Switzerland / Austria.

LEADERS & GOVERNMENT

Which U.S. Presidents served from 1897 to 1901, from 1909 to 1913, and from 1923 to 1929?

Answer: William McKinley / William H. Taft / Calvin Coolidge.

MUSIC & RHYMES

Complete the song lines: "Are you sleeping, are you sleeping? _____ John, / Morning _____ are _____; / Ding, ding, dong."

Answer: "Brother" / "bells" / "ringing."

LANGUAGE

Which words complete the sayings: "A word to the wise is _____," "A miss is as good as a _____," and "A fool and his money are soon _____"?

Answer: "sufficient" ("enough") / "mile" / "parted."

ARTS, RELIGION, & CULTURE

In the Bible, who was given a coat of many colors by his father, and who were his parents?

Answer: Joseph / Jacob / Rachel.

POTPOURRI

In which year did Colorado, the "Centennial State," join the Union; how many feet above sea level is Denver, the "Mile High City"; and what color is designated by the Spanish word *colorado*?

Answer: 1876 / 5,280 / red.

U.S. GEOGRAPHY

Identify the only U.S. city not located in a U.S. state, and then identify the 2 men after whom this city is named.

Answer: Washington (D.C. or the District of Columbia) / George Washington / Christopher Columbus.

HISTORY

In which countries were the following 3 Wonders of the Ancient World built: the Pyramids, the Temple of Artemis at Ephesus, and the Statue of Zeus?

Answer: Egypt / Turkey (accept Greece where it was formerly) / Greece.

LITERATURE

Which words complete the title of Margery Williams' *The Velveteen _____ or How Toys Become _____*, and out of which object does the nursery magic Fairy come?

Answer: *Rabbit* / *Real* / a flower.

ENTERTAINMENT

As which types of circus performers did Emmett Kelly, Clyde Beatty, and the Wallendas gain fame?

Answer: Clown / wild animal trainer / high-wire aerial act.

SPORTS AND GAMES

Identify the boxers involved in the famous "long-count" fight in 1927, and name the one who delayed the referee's count by not going to a neutral corner.

Answer: Jack Dempsey / Gene Tunney / Dempsey.

SCIENCE AND NATURE

Name the 3 main classes of foods essential to the human body.

Answer: Carbohydrates / fats / proteins.

WORLD GEOGRAPHY

Which 3 countries border Vietnam?

Answer: China / Laos / Cambodia (Kampuchea).

LEADERS & GOVERNMENT

Of which countries did Golda Meir, Arthur Neville Chamberlain, and Colonel Muammar al-Qadhafi become the leaders?

Answer: Israel / Britain / Libya.

MUSIC & RHYMES

In the song, which words complete: "If a body meet a body / Comin' through the _____. / If a body _____ a body, / Need a body _____"?

Answer: "rye" / "kiss" / "cry."

LANGUAGE

Which words complete the saying: "All _____ and no _____ makes Jack a _____ boy"?

Answer: "work" / "play" / "dull."

ARTS, RELIGION, & CULTURE

Which Biblical person's accidental "death" was staged by his jealous brothers, to which country was he taken, and what did he interpret for the Pharaoh to become a high official?

Answer: Joseph's / Egypt / dreams.

POTPOURRI

Identify 3 of the 5 W's of journalism, the traditional and essential questions a good reporter is expected to ask.

Answer: Who / what / when / where / why (*how* is considered a sixth essential question).

U.S. GEOGRAPHY

In which city is the Lincoln Park Zoo, in which city is Central Park, and in which city is Balboa Park, the site of a famous American zoo?

Answer: Chicago / New York / San Diego (the San Diego Zoo).

HISTORY

Which present-day city founded by which country was originally called New Amsterdam, and on the southern tip of which island was it founded in 1626?

Answer: New York City / Holland (or The Netherlands) / Manhattan.

LITERATURE

Which word completes the title of Jean Craighead George's _____ *of the Wolves*, in which U.S. state is she alone and lost on its North Slope, and where does her pen pal live?

Answer: *Julie* / Alaska / San Francisco.

ENTERTAINMENT

What kind of an animal is the comic strip character Garfield, what is his favorite food, and what is the name of his master?

Answer: Cat / lasagna / Jon.

SPORTS AND GAMES

How often are the Olympic Games held, in which city were the first modern Games held in 1896, and which country's athletes traditionally march into the stadium first?

Answer: Every 4 years / Athens / Greece's.

SCIENCE AND NATURE

From which animal is cashmere obtained, from which one is wool primarily obtained, and from which one does angora come?

Answer: (Cashmere) Goat / sheep / (Angora) goat.

WORLD GEOGRAPHY
Denmark, Netherlands, Belgium, Luxembourg, Switzerland, and the Czech Republic are 6 of the 9 countries bordering Germany. Name the 3 largest countries bordering Germany.
Answer: France / Austria / Poland.

LEADERS & GOVERNMENT
Of which countries did P.W. Botha, Mikhail Gorbachev, and General Lopez de Santa Anna become the leaders?
Answer: South Africa / Soviet Union (accept Russia) / Mexico.

MUSIC & RHYMES
In the song "Peter Cottontail," which feast day is "on its way," when Peter comes "hopping down the bunny trail," what kind of beans does he have for Tommy, and what kind of eggs for sister Sue?
Answer: Easter / "jelly beans" / "colored eggs."

LANGUAGE
Complete the phrases: "Two's _____, three's a crowd," "Easy come, easy _____," and "Where there's a will, there's a _____."
Answer: "company" / "go" / "way."

ARTS, RELIGION, & CULTURE
In the Bible, who are the "Chosen People," which phrase derived from a parable means "a compassionate person who helps another unselfishly," and which person said he was the "Son of Man"?
Answer: Israelites / Good Samaritan / Jesus.

POTPOURRI
What are the standard legal male and female names used to represent persons whose names are unknown, and which signer's name on the Declaration of Independence today designates a signature?
Answer: John Doe / Jane Doe / John Hancock's.

U.S. GEOGRAPHY

What are the 2 names for the line that separates the waters draining into the Atlantic Ocean from those draining into the Pacific, and in which mountains is this Divide?

Answer: Great Divide / Continental Divide / Rocky Mountains.

HISTORY

Name the country Jawaharlal Nehru served as prime minister from 1947-1964, the country from which it gained its independence, and Nehru's daughter who later became prime minister.

Answer: India / Britain / Indira Gandhi.

LITERATURE

In a Hans Christian Andersen tale, who is the little girl an inch high, which animal captures her, and which animal proposes marriage?

Answer: Thumbelina (or Thumbelisa) / toad / mole.

ENTERTAINMENT

Give the surname of Dagwood in the comic strips, name his wife, and identify the man for whom he works.

Answer: Bumstead / Blondie / Mr. Dithers.

SPORTS AND GAMES

Europe and North and South America are 2 of the 5 continents represented by the Olympic symbol of 5 interlocking rings. Name the other 3.

Answer: Africa / Asia / Australia.

SCIENCE AND NATURE

Which honeybee lays eggs and is the colony's mother; which one gathers food, builds the colony, and cares for the young; and which one fertilizes the bee that lays the eggs?

Answer: Queen / worker / drone.

WORLD GEOGRAPHY
Which 2 countries border Sweden, and which gulf separates it from the country to the east?
Answer: Norway / Finland / Gulf of Bothnia.

LEADERS & GOVERNMENT
Who was queen of England from 1558 to 1603, who was queen from 1837 to 1901, and who became queen in 1952?
Answer: Elizabeth I / Victoria / Elizabeth II.

MUSIC & RHYMES
Which word completes the name of the dance called the "Peppermint _____," and which dances begin: "You put your right foot in; / You put your right foot out" and "Put your right foot forward; / Put your left foot out"?
Answer: "Twist" / "The Hokey-Pokey" / "The Bunny Hop."

LANGUAGE
According to the expressions, how many birds can be killed with one stone, what kind of circus is a place of confusion, and what dollar value is assigned to a most important question?
Answer: Two birds / three-ring circus / $64 question (accept $64,000 question).

ARTS, RELIGION, & CULTURE
In Christian theology, which kind of sin is so bad it causes the death of the soul, which minor kind of sin doesn't cause the death of the soul, and which sin did Adam transmit to mankind by eating from the tree of knowledge?
Answer: Mortal sin (accept unpardonable sin) / venial sin / original sin.

POTPOURRI
Identify the "Jacks" who are: "a handyman," "a personification of cold weather," and "a hollow pumpkin, cut to look like a human and used as a lantern."
Answer: Jack-of-all-trades / Jack Frost / jack-o'lantern.

U.S. GEOGRAPHY

Identify 3 of the 4 states whose names begin with the letter *A*.

Answer: Alabama / Alaska / Arizona / Arkansas.

HISTORY

Which year followed 1 B.C., and what are the meanings of B.C. and A.D.?

Answer: 1 A.D. / Before Christ / *anno Domini* or in the year of our Lord.

LITERATURE

On how many mattresses and eider-down beds does the fairy tale princess sleep, on what hard object does she sleep that makes her "black and blue," and what is the name of this fairy tale story?

Answer: 20 / pea / "The Princess and the Pea."

ENTERTAINMENT

The *C* in Walt Disney World's EPCOT Center means community. Give the meaning of the *E*, *P*, and *T*.

Answer: Experimental / Prototype / (Community of) Tomorrow.

SPORTS AND GAMES

Black and blue are 2 of the 5 colors of the interlocking rings used an the Olympic symbol. Name the other 3.

Answer: Green / red / yellow.

SCIENCE AND NATURE

Name 3 of the 4 major blood groups.

Answer: A / B / AB / O.

WORLD GEOGRAPHY

Name the 3 largest countries that border France.

Answer: Spain / Italy / Germany.

LEADERS & GOVERNMENT

Who were the leaders of France from 768 to 814, from 1643 to 1715, and from 1804 to 1814?

Answer: Charlemagne / Louis XIV / Napoleon I.

MUSIC & RHYMES

Complete the rhyme: "The eensy (or itsy), _____ spider / Went up the _____. / Down came the _____ / And washed the spider out."

Answer: "weensy" (or "bitsy") / "waterspout" / "rain."

LANGUAGE

Complete the expressions: "Red sky at morning, Sailor take _____, / Red sky at night, Sailor's _____" and "To take the wind out of someone's _____."

Answer: "warning" / "delight" / "sails."

ARTS, RELIGION, & CULTURE

What is the name given to the Sunday before Easter, and, according to John 12:15, who made a triumphal entry into which city on this day as people spread branches along the path?

Answer: Palm Sunday / Jesus / Jerusalem.

POTPOURRI

Traditionally, a bottle of which liquid is broken over the bow of a new ship, what is an actor in a play told to break when one wishes him good luck, and what is a person said to kick when he dies?

Answer: Champagne / a leg / the bucket.

U.S. GEOGRAPHY

Identify the 3 states whose names begin with the letter *C*.

Answer: California / Colorado / Connecticut.

HISTORY

In which year did the U.S. Civil War begin, and which fort in which state was fired upon on April 12 of that year?

Answer: 1861 / Fort Sumter / South Carolina.

LITERATURE

Of which city does the fairy tale Dick Whittington become mayor, with what does he think the streets of this city are paved, and which animal of his is sold to the King of Barbary for a fortune?

Answer: London / gold / his cat.

ENTERTAINMENT

Which general is sent to find the foe in the Disney film *Davy Crockett*, in which century does the fight take place, and how is Davy trying to kill a bear before a major interrupts him?

Answer: Andrew Jackson / 19th / "by grinning him to death."

SPORTS AND GAMES

Give the English translation of the 3-word Olympic Latin motto, *Citius, Altius, Fortius*.

Answer: "Faster" (or "Swifter") / "Higher" / "Stronger" (or "Braver").

SCIENCE AND NATURE

Identify 3 of the 4 kinds of taste the human tongue is traditionally thought to be able to distinguish.

Answer: Sweet / sour / salt / bitter.

WORLD GEOGRAPHY

Which 3 countries besides Bangladesh and Laos border Burma, or Myanmar?

Answer: India / China / Thailand.

LEADERS & GOVERNMENT

In which country did the *shah* sit on the Peacock Throne, in which one were the chief military commanders called *shoguns*, and in which land was the Dalai Lama the ruler and chief monk until he fled in 1959?

Answer: Iran / Japan / Tibet.

MUSIC & RHYMES

In the song, which words complete: "Row, row, row your _____ / Gently down the _____, / Merrily, merrily, merrily, merrily, / Life is but a _____"?

Answer: "boat" / "stream" / "dream."

LANGUAGE

Complete each of the following triplets: "King, Queen, and _____"; "Men, women, and _____"; and "No if's, and's, or _____."

Answer: "Jack" (accept "Knave") / "children" / "but's."

ARTS, RELIGION, & CULTURE

Which Jewish festival celebrates the flight of the Israelites from Egyptian slavery, in which book of the Bible is this story told, and what is the word for the unleavened bread eaten at this time?

Answer: Passover / Exodus / matzoh.

POTPOURRI

Which month of the year was named for the Roman god of beginnings and endings; which one for Octavian, the first Roman emperor; and which one for the Latin word for "ten"?

Answer: January / August (his official title was Augustus) / December.

U.S. GEOGRAPHY

Identify 3 of the 4 states whose names begin with the letter *I*.

Answer: Idaho / Illinois / Indiana / Iowa.

HISTORY

Name the 1954 case in which the Supreme Court ruled racial segregation in public schools unconstitutional, and identify the city and state being sued in the case.

Answer: *Brown v. Board of Education* / Topeka / Kansas.

LITERATURE

Complete the following Judy Blume titles: *Are You There, God? It's Me,* _____; *Tiger* _____; and *Then Again, Maybe I* _____.

Answer: *Margaret* / *Eyes* / *Won't*.

ENTERTAINMENT

What is the meaning of *E.T.* in the 1982 Steven Spielberg film, which boy befriends the creature so named, and how does this creature dress on Halloween?

Answer: Extra-Terrestrial / Elliott / as a ghost.

SPORTS AND GAMES

Name 3 of the 4 events in which Jesse Owens won a gold medal in the 1936 Olympic Games.

Answer: 100-meter / 200-meter / broad jump / member of the 400-meter relay team.

SCIENCE AND NATURE

The wedge, screw, and wheel (or wheel and axle) are 3 of the 6 simple machines. Name the other 3.

Answer: Lever / inclined plane / pulley.

WORLD GEOGRAPHY
Which 3 independent countries besides Nepal, Bhutan, and Bangladesh border India?
Answer: Pakistan / China / Burma (or Myanmar).

LEADERS & GOVERNMENT
Who were the rulers of Russia from 1696 to 1725 and from 1894 to 1917, and who was the leader of the Soviet Union from 1927 to 1953?
Answer: Peter the Great (or Peter I; he came to the throne in 1682 at age 10, but his half sister ruled the country) / Nicholas II / Joseph Stalin.

MUSIC & RHYMES
Complete the rhyme: "Ring around the _____, / A _____ full of _____, / A-tishoo! A-tishoo! ("Ashes! Ashes!") / We all fall down."
Answer: "rosey" ("roses") / "pocket" / "posey" ("posies").

LANGUAGE
Complete each of the following triplets: "Red, white, and _____"; "Tall, dark, and _____"; and "Snap, crackle, and _____."
Answer: "blue" / "handsome" / "pop."

ARTS, RELIGION, & CULTURE
What is the most solemn day in the Jewish calendar, how many days after the Jewish New Year does it occur, and what is the name for the Jewish New Year?
Answer: Yom Kippur / 10 / Rosh Hashanah.

POTPOURRI
Which musical instrument has the same name as a geometric figure, which indoor sport has the same name as a vegetable, and which kind of jumping insect has the same name as an English game?
Answer: Triangle / squash / cricket.

U.S. GEOGRAPHY

Identify the 3 states whose names begin with the letter *O*.

Answer: Ohio / Oklahoma / Oregon.

HISTORY

Which famous American Revolutionary War traitor helped capture which New York fort in May 1775, and which New York fort, now a military academy, was he planning to turn over to the British?

Answer: Benedict Arnold / Fort Ticonderoga / West Point.

LITERATURE

In Aesop's fables, what stops the goose from laying golden eggs, how much is the lion's share when he and others kill a stag, and what does the dog in the manger keep the cows from eating?

Answer: The farmer kills it / all of it / the hay.

ENTERTAINMENT

Give the names of the brother and sister of the fictional boy who befriends E.T., and then tell where E.T. lives while in their house.

Answer: Michael / Gertie / in the closet.

SPORTS AND GAMES

In 1985 and 1988, respectively, which players from which country became at 17 the youngest to win the Wimbledon Tennis Championship and the French Open?

Answer: Boris Becker / Steffi Graf / both from (West) Germany.

SCIENCE AND NATURE

Name the 2 bones of the lower arm, and then name the long, thin outer bone of the human leg between the knee and ankle.

Answer: Radius / ulna / fibula.

WORLD GEOGRAPHY

Which 3 independent countries besides Egypt border Israel?

Answer: Lebanon / Syria / Jordan.

LEADERS & GOVERNMENT

Identify the king of England who in 1936 abdicated for the woman he loved, name Queen Elizabeth's father who became king, and name her son who became heir apparent when she became queen.

Answer: Edward VIII / George VI / Prince Charles.

MUSIC & RHYMES

Complete the rhyme: "Little Robin _____ sat upon a _____, / Up went pussy cat, and down went he; / Down came pussy cat, and away Robin ran; / Says little Robin . . . , '_____ me if you can.'"

Answer: "Redbreast" / "tree" / "Catch."

LANGUAGE

Complete each of the following quadruplets: "Eye, ear, nose, and _____"; "Rain, hail, sleet, or _____"; and "Eeny, meeny, miney, _____."

Answer: "throat" / "snow" / "moe."

ARTS, RELIGION, & CULTURE

Identify the Greek and Roman goddesses of love and beauty, and identify the Roman god of love, the son of the Roman goddess of love.

Answer: Aphrodite / Venus / Cupid.

POTPOURRI

Which colors are associated with inexperience, with cowardice, and with royalty?

Answer: Green / yellow / purple.

U.S. GEOGRAPHY

Identify 3 of the 4 states whose names begin with the letter *W*.

Answer: Washington / West Virginia / Wisconsin / Wyoming.

HISTORY

Which American soldier at 23 became the youngest Union Army general, and at which battle in which territory was he defeated on June 25, 1876?

Answer: George Armstrong Custer / Little Big Horn / Montana Territory.

LITERATURE

In the Brothers Grimm fairy tale "Snow White and Rose Red," which animal is allowed into the house, who is actually entrapped as this animal, and who condemned him to be so?

Answer: Bear / the Prince / the wicked dwarf.

ENTERTAINMENT

Give the titles of the first 2 sequels to the 1977 film *Star Wars*, and identify the wise little old creature in these sequels who dies at 900 years of age.

Answer: *The Empire Strikes Back* / *Return of the Jedi* / Yoda.

SPORTS AND GAMES

Which sports were invented in Springfield and Holyoke, one by James Naismith in 1891 and the other by William G. Morgan in 1895, and in which state are these cities?

Answer: Basketball / volleyball / Massachusetts.

SCIENCE AND NATURE

Which animal is said to in the throat when one is hoarse, which insects are said to be in the stomach when one is nervous, and which insect is said to be in the bonnet when one is obsessed with an idea?

Answer: Frog / butterflies / bee.

WORLD GEOGRAPHY

Which 3 countries besides Afghanistan, Azerbaijan, Turkmenistan, and Armenia border Iran?

Answer: Turkey / Iraq / Pakistan.

LEADERS & GOVERNMENT

What was the name of the federal legislature of the 13 colonies of the U.S. from 1774 to 1789, which army did it create in 1775, and who was named its commander in chief?

Answer: Continental Congress / Continental Army / George Washington.

MUSIC & RHYMES

Complete the song lines: "Hush, little _____, don't say a _____; / Papa's gonna buy you a mockingbird. / If that mockingbird don't sing, / Papa's gonna buy you a _____ ring."

Answer: "baby" / "word" / "diamond."

LANGUAGE

Complete the following sayings: "All talk and no _____," "All well and _____," and "All wool and a yard _____."

Answer: "action" / "good" / "wide."

ARTS, RELIGION, & CULTURE

Identify the Greek and Roman supreme deities, and identify the Greek mountain regarded as the home of the Greek deities.

Answer: Zeus / Jupiter / Mount Olympus.

POTPOURRI

Proverbially, what killed the cat, what does a cowardly animal have between its legs, and which bird's appearance signals the end of winter?

Answer: Curiosity / its tail / robin's.

U.S. GEOGRAPHY

In which Western states are Puget Sound, Willamette Valley, and Central Valley?

Answer: Washington / Oregon / California.

HISTORY

In which year in which country was the Battle of Hastings fought, and who defeated Harold in this battle?

Answer: 1066 / England / William the Conqueror.

LITERATURE

In a Norse tale, how many Billy-Goats-Gruff are going to the hillside to get fat, which ugly creature lives under the bridge, and which Billy-Goat-Gruff kills this creature?

Answer: 3 / Troll / the Big Billy-Goat-Gruff.

ENTERTAINMENT

Name the following characters in the *Star Wars* films: the Dark Lord of the Sith, the Dark Lord's son, and one of the 2 robot companions.

Answer: Darth Vader / Luke Skywalker / C3-PO (or C-3PO) or R2-D2.

SPORTS AND GAMES

Name these Olympic gymnasts: Nadia _____, a 14-year-old who was the first to receive a perfect 10; Olga _____, who won 3 gold medals at 17; and Mary Lou _____, a gold medal winner at 16.

Answer: Comaneci / Korbut / Retton.

SCIENCE AND NATURE

How many hours, minutes, and seconds are there in a single day?

Answer: 24 hours / 1440 minutes / 86,400 seconds.

WORLD GEOGRAPHY

Which European cities are known by the nicknames "The City of Lights" and "The Eternal City," and which country is called "The Emerald Isle"?

Answer: Paris / Rome / Ireland.

LEADERS & GOVERNMENT

Name the 3 requirements a person must meet according to the U.S. Constitution in order to become President.

Answer: A natural-born citizen / at least 35 years of age / a resident of the U.S. for at least 14 years.

MUSIC & RHYMES

Complete the words to the song: "For he's a jolly good _____, / Which _____ can _____."

Answer: "fellow" / "nobody" / "deny."

LANGUAGE

Complete the sayings: "Add insult to _____," "At someone's beck and _____," and "The best laid schemes (plans) of mice and _____ often go astray."

Answer: "injury" / "call" / "men."

ARTS, RELIGION, & CULTURE

Identify the Greek and Roman gods of the sea, and give the word for the 3-pronged spear they carried.

Answer: Poseidon / Neptune / trident.

POTPOURRI

Proverbially, which bird delivers babies, which bird's breast was dyed red from blood after it took a thorn from Christ's crown, and which bird is said to be proud when it spreads it feathers?

Answer: Stork / robin's / peacock.

U.S. GEOGRAPHY

In which cities are Logan, Hartsfield, and John F. Kennedy International airports?

Answer: Boston / Atlanta / New York.

HISTORY

Which river did George Washington cross on December 25, 1776, and in which city in which state did he surprise the predominantly Hessian garrison?

Answer: Delaware River / Trenton / New Jersey.

LITERATURE

In which Charles Perrault tale does a cat pass the miller's son off as the Marquis de Carabas, and what 2 things does the cat ask for to secure a fortune and a royal wife for his master?

Answer: *Puss in Boots* / a sack / a pair of boots.

ENTERTAINMENT

Match the musicals *West Side Story*, *Bye Bye Birdie*, and *Chorus Line*, with these songs: "Kids," "Jet Song," and "One."

Answer: *Bye Bye Birdie* / *West Side Story* / *Chorus Line*.

SPORTS AND GAMES

In which Olympic sports did Carl Lewis win 4 gold medals, Eric Heiden 5 gold medals, and Mark Spitz 7 gold medals?

Answer: Track and field / speed skating / swimming.

SCIENCE AND NATURE

For which instruments are 29.92, 6.2, and 98.6 fairly typical readings?

Answer: Barometer / seismometer / thermometer.

WORLD GEOGRAPHY

On which 3 countries besides Somalia and Uganda does Kenya border?

Answer: Sudan / Ethiopia / Tanzania.

LEADERS & GOVERNMENT

Who nominates a person for a position on the U.S. Supreme Court, which body confirms this nomination, and how many members were on the first Supreme Court?

Answer: The President / The Senate / 6.

MUSIC & RHYMES

Complete the song lines: "Rain, rain, go _____. / Come again another _____. / Little Johnny wants to _____."

Answer: "away" / "day" / "play."

LANGUAGE

Complete the phrases: "Between a rock and a _____ place," "The birds and the _____," and "Share and share _____."

Answer: "hard" / "bees" / "alike."

ARTS, RELIGION, & CULTURE

Identify the Greek and Roman messengers of the gods, and identify the animals that entwined the staff, or caduceus, they carried.

Answer: Hermes / Mercury / serpents.

POTPOURRI

Which word completes the cheer: "Two bits, four bits, six bits, a _____," how much money is 2 bits, and how much is 12 bits?

Answer: "dollar" / 25 cents / $1.50.

U.S. GEOGRAPHY
Name the world's largest office building when it was opened in 1943, the government department with its headquarters there, and the Virginia city in which it is located.
Answer: Pentagon / Department of Defense / Arlington.

HISTORY
Name the ditch of water that surrounded medieval castles, name the bridge that could be raised or lowered by chains, and name the iron grating that protected the main entrance.
Answer: Moat / drawbridge / portcullis.

LITERATURE
In a Brothers Grimm fairy tale, what is the occupation of the brave little man who wore on his belt "Seven at one blow," what does he kill with the "one blow," and whose daughter does he marry?
Answer: Tailor / flies / the king's.

ENTERTAINMENT
Name the beautiful girl living in a little French village in the Disney film *Beauty and the Beast*, identify her favorite preoccupation, and name the handsome, conceited man who asks her to marry him.
Answer: Belle / reading / Gaston.

SPORTS AND GAMES
How many minutes are in an NBA quarter, how many minutes are in a half of college basketball, and what name is given to periods played at the end of regulation play in basketball?
Answer: 12 / 20 / overtime.

SCIENCE AND NATURE
Give the first 3 cardinal numbers, the first 3 ordinal numbers, and the first 3 prime numbers.
Answer: 1, 2, 3 (one, two, three) / 1st, 2nd, 3rd (first, second, third) / 2, 3, and 5.

WORLD GEOGRAPHY

On which 3 countries besides Algeria, Niger, and Chad does Libya border?

Answer: Tunisia / Sudan / Egypt.

LEADERS & GOVERNMENT

How many members are there in the U.S. House of Representatives, what is the minimum number of representatives each state must have, and how often are congressional seats reassigned by the Census Bureau?

Answer: 435 / one / every 10 years.

MUSIC & RHYMES

Complete the song: "This old _____, he played one; / He played knick-knack on my _____. / With a knick-knack, _____-whack, / Give a dog a bone; / This old man came rolling home."

Answer: "man" / "thumb" / "paddy."

LANGUAGE

Complete the expressions: "Someone's bread and _____," "Bright-eyed and bushy-_____," and "Chief cook and bottle _____."

Answer: "butter" / "tailed" / "washer."

ARTS, RELIGION, & CULTURE

Complete these lines from the song "O Come, All Ye Faithful": "Come and _____ Him, / Born the King of _____ / O come let us _____ Him . . . / Christ, the Lord."

Answer: "behold" / "Angels" / "adore."

POTPOURRI

In which month is flag day in the U.S., and which seamstress from which city is traditionally considered to have sewn the first U.S. flag?

Answer: June (14) / Betsy Ross / Philadelphia.

U.S. GEOGRAPHY

Name 3 of the 4 states bordering Texas.

Answer: New Mexico / Oklahoma / Arkansas / Louisiana.

HISTORY

Which person in which city at which memorial made his August 28, 1963, "I Have a Dream" speech?

Answer: Martin Luther King Jr. / Washington. D.C. / Lincoln Memorial.

LITERATURE

In which fairy tale by which author does a little boy watching a procession say, "He doesn't have anything on"; and what peculiar quality have the swindlers told the emperor their fabrics have?

Answer: "The Emperor's New Clothes" / Hans Christian Andersen / invisibility (can be seen only by those who are wise).

ENTERTAINMENT

Which Disney film features the song "The Sorcerer's Apprentice," which character plays the Sorcerer's Apprentice, and which objects does he magically get to fill the tub with water?

Answer: *Fantasia* / Mickey Mouse / brooms.

SPORTS AND GAMES

In basketball, what is the word for advancing the ball by bouncing it, how many points are awarded for a shot beyond the 23-foot, 9-inch mark in the NBA, and which type of defense is prohibited in the NBA?

Answer: Dribbling / 3 points / zone defense.

SCIENCE AND NATURE

What is the only marsupial native to North America, when does it hunt for food, and what does this animal do when it is in danger?

Answer: Opossum / at night / lies motionless and plays dead (or plays "possum").

WORLD GEOGRAPHY

On which 3 countries besides Mexico does Guatemala border?

Answer: Belize / Honduras / El Salvador.

LEADERS & GOVERNMENT

How many nations make up the U.N. Security Council, how many are permanent members of this council, and within 15, how many nations are members of the U.N.?

Answer: 15 / 5 / 188 (in the year 2000; accept 173 to 203).

MUSIC & RHYMES

Complete the song lines: "Lou, Lou, Skip to my Lou, . . . Skip to my Lou my _____ / Lost my _____, what'll I do . . . / Flies in my _____, shoo, fly, shoo."

Answer: "Darling" / "partner" / "buttermilk."

LANGUAGE

Which body parts complete the expressions: "To stick out like a sore _____," "To work one's _____ to the bone," and "To have it on the tip of one's _____"?

Answer: "thumb" / "fingers" / "tongue."

ARTS, RELIGION, & CULTURE

In the Old Testament, who was the wisest and most magnificent king of Israel, and who were his parents?

Answer: Solomon / David / Bathsheba.

POTPOURRI

Give the total number of days for April, June, and November; the total number for January, March, and July; and the total number in the years 1600 and 2000.

Answer: 90 / 93 / 732 (both are leap years).

U.S. GEOGRAPHY

Name the only 2 states bordering the state of Washington, and name one of the only 2 bordering Florida.

Answer: Oregon / Idaho / Georgia or Alabama.

HISTORY

Which airship or Zeppelin from which country crashed in which state in the town of Lakehurst on May 6, 1937?

Answer: The *Hindenburg* / Germany / New Jersey.

LITERATURE

Name the 3 Mrs. W's in Madeleine L'Engle's *A Wrinkle in Time*.

Answer: Mrs. Whatsit / Mrs. Who / Mrs. Which.

ENTERTAINMENT

Identify these *Sesame Street* characters: the 2-headed monster, the gigantic sheep dog, and the bright pink monster with a radish-shaped head who likes to watch TV.

Answer: Frank and Stein / Barkley / Telly Monster.

SPORTS AND GAMES

Which NBA team won 8 championships from 1959 to 1966, which player scored 100 points in a game in 1962, and which one was the first to score 37,000 points?

Answer: Boston Celtics / Wilt Chamberlain / Kareem Abdul-Jabbar.

SCIENCE AND NATURE

What word designates "a person who doesn't eat meat," and what do *carnivores* and *herbivores* eat?

Answer: Vegetarian / meat / plants.

WORLD GEOGRAPHY

On which 3 countries does Chile border?

Answer: Peru / Bolivia / Argentina.

LEADERS & GOVERNMENT

Which Cabinet position is held by the chief law officer of the U.S., which department does this person head, and who appoints this person with the approval of the Senate?

Answer: Attorney General / Department of Justice / President.

MUSIC & RHYMES

Complete the song lines: "Down in the _____ in a little bitty _____ / Swam three little fishies and mama fishie too . . . / And they swam and they swam all over the _____."

Answer: "meadow" / "pool" / "dam."

LANGUAGE

Complete the expressions: "Come hell or high _____," "Cross my heart and hope to _____," and "Cock and bull _____."

Answer: "water" / "die" / "story."

ARTS, RELIGION, & CULTURE

Identify the Greek god of light, healing, and music; the one of wine; and the one of the fields and flocks.

Answer: Apollo / Dionysus / Pan.

POTPOURRI

How many years are there in a decade, in a century, and in a millennium?

Answer: 10 / 100 / 1000.

U.S. GEOGRAPHY

Name the 3 states bordering California.

Answer: Oregon / Nevada / Arizona.

HISTORY

In which month on which day in which year did man first set foot upon the moon?

Answer: July / 20 / 1969.

LITERATURE

Which word completes the title of Margaret Wise Brown's *Goodnight* _____, what is the color of the great room, and what kind of animal is saying "Goodnight" to his room?

Answer: *Moon* / green / bunny.

ENTERTAINMENT

Identify 3 of the 4 kinds of animals involved in "The Dance of the Hours" in the Disney film *Fantasia*.

Answer: Hippopotamuses / elephants / ostriches / crocodiles.

SPORTS AND GAMES

In which sports did Carl Hubbell, George Mikan, and Edwin Moses become famous?

Answer: Baseball / basketball / track.

SCIENCE AND NATURE

What are the 2 tallest land animals, and what is their native continent?

Answer: Giraffe / elephant / Africa.

WORLD GEOGRAPHY

On which 3 countries does Paraguay border?

Answer: Bolivia / Brazil / Argentina.

LEADERS & GOVERNMENT

Which woman was the first to be pictured on a U.S. coin in general circulation, on which coin did her picture appear in 1979, and which Constitutional amendment is nicknamed after her?

Answer: Susan B. Anthony / $1.00 / 19th amendment.

MUSIC & RHYMES

Complete the song lines: "As I was walking down the _____ . . . / Buffalo _____ won't you come out tonight, / And dance by the light of the _____."

Answer: "street" / "gal" (or "gals") / "moon."

LANGUAGE

Complete the expressions: "Eat (us) out of house and _____," "Every nook and _____," and "Fight like cat(s) and _____."

Answer: "home" / "cranny" / "dog(s)."

ARTS, RELIGION, & CULTURE

According to the Bible, at which site on which day will the great and final conflict between the forces of good and evil take place, and in which book of the Bible is this site named?

Answer: Armageddon / Judgment Day / Revelation.

POTPOURRI

Give the meanings of the acronyms or initialisms SCUBA, ICBM, and SNAFU.

Answer: Self-Contained Underwater Breathing Apparatus / Intercontinental Ballistic Missile / Situation Normal All Fouled Up.

U.S. GEOGRAPHY

Identify 3 of the 4 states bordering Mississippi.

Answer: Louisiana / Arkansas / Tennessee / Alabama.

HISTORY

Name the 2 members on the U.S. mission that first set foot upon the moon, and then name the mission.

Answer: Neil A. Armstrong / Edwin E. "Buzz" Aldrin / *Apollo 11* (Michael Collins remained in the command module).

LITERATURE

What are the breeds of the 3 animals who make the trip in Sheila Burnford's *The Incredible Journey*, a story set in Canada?

Answer: Labrador retriever / bull terrier / Siamese cat.

ENTERTAINMENT

Identify the mythological goddess of the rainbow, the goddess of hunting and the Moon, and the god of the sun in the *Pastoral Symphony* section of the Disney film *Fantasia*.

Answer: Iris / Diana / Apollo.

SPORTS AND GAMES

What is a perfect score in a ten-pin bowling game, how many consecutive strikes are needed to achieve it, and how many frames are in a game?

Answer: 300 / 12 / 10.

SCIENCE AND NATURE

Name the 3 basic types of rocks.

Answer: Igneous / metamorphic / sedimentary.

WORLD GEOGRAPHY

On which 3 countries besides Brazil and Bolivia does Peru border?

Answer: Ecuador / Colombia / Chile.

LEADERS & GOVERNMENT

Which Cabinet level departments of the U.S. government are known as HUD, DOT, and DOE?

Answer: (Department of) Housing and Urban Development / Department of Transportation / Department of Energy.

MUSIC & RHYMES

Complete the song lines: "Goodnight _____ . . . / We're going to _____ you now. / Merrily we roll along, roll along, roll along / Merrily we roll along o'er the _____ blue sea."

Answer: "Ladies" / "leave" / "deep."

LANGUAGE

Complete the expressions: "As snug as a bug in a _____," "Footloose and fancy _____," and "Go in one _____ and out the other."

Answer: "rug" / "free" / "ear."

ARTS, RELIGION, & CULTURE

Which tower in which city was intended to reach heaven, and in which book of the Bible is its story told?

Answer: Babel / Babylon / Genesis.

POTPOURRI

Give the meanings of the acronyms LASER, RADAR, and ZIP.

Answer: Light Amplification by Simulated Emission of Radiation / Radio Detecting And Ranging / Zone (Zoning) Improvement Plan.

U.S. GEOGRAPHY

Identify 3 of the 4 states bordering Minnesota.

Answer: South Dakota / North Dakota / Iowa / Wisconsin.

HISTORY

In which country in which year did the failed invasion known as the Bay of Pigs take place, and who was the U.S. President in office at the time?

Answer: Cuba / 1961 / John Kennedy.

LITERATURE

Name the author of *Little Women*, give the number of girls in the family, and give their surname.

Answer: Louisa May Alcott / 4 (Meg, Jo, Beth, and Amy) / March.

ENTERTAINMENT

Name the king of the gods and the objects he hurls to earth in the *Pastoral Symphony* section of the Disney film *Fantasia*, and name the mythological home of these gods.

Answer: Zeus / thunderbolts / Mount Olympus.

SPORTS AND GAMES

Between which 2 pins in bowling is the pocket for a right-handed bowler, what is the term for a strike when a right-handed bowler hits on the left side, and what is the term for 3 strikes in a row?

Answer: 1 and 3 pins / Brooklyn / turkey.

SCIENCE AND NATURE

Which words are defined as "the remains of animals and plants that have lived and died on earth," "the study of the earth," and "the study of fossils"?

Answer: Fossils / geology / paleontology.

WORLD GEOGRAPHY

Which 3 countries border Venezuela?

Answer: Colombia / Brazil / Guyana.

LEADERS & GOVERNMENT

Which U.S. government agencies are known as the IRS, the FBI, and the CIA?

Answer: Internal Revenue Service / Federal Bureau of Investigation / Central Intelligence Agency.

MUSIC & RHYMES

Complete the words to the rhyme: "Polly, put the _____ on, / . . . And we'll all have _____. / _____ take it off again, / . . . They've all gone away."

Answer: "kettle" / "tea" / "Sukey."

LANGUAGE

Complete the expressions: "In this day and _____," "Keep body and _____ together," and "Land of milk and _____."

Answer: "age" / "soul" / "honey."

ARTS, RELIGION, & CULTURE

Identify the Biblical words that today mean "a scene of noise and confusion" and "riches or material wealth"; and identify the wife of Ahab whose name today means "a shameless woman."

Answer: Babel / mammon / Jezebel.

POTPOURRI

Which Indian name is shouted by paratroopers upon leaving a plane, which Indian was the main medicine man at the Battle of Little Big Horn, and which one won gold medals at the 1912 Olympic Games?

Answer: Geronimo / Sitting Bull / Jim Thorpe.

U.S. GEOGRAPHY

Name the only 2 states bordering South Carolina, and name one of the only 2 bordering Rhode Island.

Answer: North Carolina / Georgia / Connecticut or Massachusetts.

HISTORY

Which mail delivery service operated between St. Joseph and Sacramento from 1860 to 1861, and in which states are those cities?

Answer: Pony Express / Missouri / California.

LITERATURE

Which kind of animal is Moby Dick in a novel of the same name by Herman Melville, what color is this animal, and which captain pursues it?

Answer: Whale / white / Captain Ahab.

ENTERTAINMENT

Which cartoon character, who is "smarter than the average bear," steals picnic baskets from visitors, in which park does he do so, and what is the name of his sidekick?

Answer: Yogi Bear / Jellystone Park / Boo Boo Bear.

SPORTS AND GAMES

In automobile racing, green signals the start of the race. Which flags signal each of the following: caution—no passing; a pit stop; and the finish?

Answer: Yellow / black / white and black (accept checkered).

SCIENCE AND NATURE

Identify the 3 most common of all the elements in the earth's crust.

Answer: Oxygen / silicon / aluminum.

WORLD GEOGRAPHY

Which 3 South American countries lie along the equator?

Answer: Ecuador / Colombia / Brazil.

LEADERS & GOVERNMENT

Which Asian countries have legislatures called the Diet and the Knesset, and in which one was the Politburo created in 1917?

Answer: Japan / Israel / Soviet Union (accept Russia).

MUSIC & RHYMES

Which words complete the song lines: "He flies through the air with the greatest of _____, / The _____ young man on the flying _____"?

Answer: "ease" / "daring" / "trapeze."

LANGUAGE

Complete the expressions: "To leave high and _____," "To feed a cold and starve a _____," and "To make fish of one and _____ of the other."

Answer: "dry" / "fever" / "fowl."

ARTS, RELIGION, & CULTURE

Identify each of the following as a stringed, brass, or percussion instrument: tuba, cello, and xylophone.

Answer: Brass / stringed / percussion.

POTPOURRI

Which young animals are called "joeys," what is their native country, and which circus performers are nicknamed "joeys"?

Answer: Kangaroos (accept any marsupial) / Australia / clowns.

U.S. GEOGRAPHY

Name the 3 states bordering New Hampshire.

Answer: Maine / Massachusetts / Vermont.

HISTORY

Identify the Indian girl, daughter of Powhatan, who allegedly stopped the execution of an English soldier about 1609, name the soldier, and identify the colony in which this incident occurred.

Answer: Pocahontas / (Captain) John Smith / (Jamestown) Virginia.

LITERATURE

Which word completes the title of Louise Fitzhugh's *Harriet the* _____, in which city is it set, and which beloved person in her household does she call "Ole Golly"?

Answer: *Spy* / New York / her nursemaid.

ENTERTAINMENT

Which words complete the lines from Dr. Seuss's *Cat in the Hat*: "The sun did not _____. / It was too wet to _____. / So we sat in the house / All that cold, cold, wet _____"?

Answer: "shine" / "play" / "day."

SPORTS AND GAMES

Which U.S. states are associated with the Indy 500 automobile race, the Daytona Beach 24-hour race, and the Charlotte Motor Speedway?

Answer: Indianapolis / Florida / North Carolina.

SCIENCE AND NATURE

What is the name for the liquid part of the blood, which blood cells are called *erythrocytes*, and which ones are called *leukocytes*?

Answer: Plasma / red blood cells / white blood cells.

WORLD GEOGRAPHY

Which 3 continents have the most independent countries?

Answer: Africa / Asia / Europe.

LEADERS & GOVERNMENT

Of the 3 branches of the U.S. government, which one makes treaties with other nations, which one approves them, and which one settles questions about them?

Answer: Executive / legislative / judicial.

MUSIC & RHYMES

Which word completes the song title, "She'll Be Comin' Round the _____," how many white horses will she be driving, and what will we kill when she comes?

Answer: "Mountain" / "six white horses" / "the old red rooster."

LANGUAGE

Complete the sayings: "There's a time and a place for _____," "There's no time like the _____," and "Never put off till tomorrow what you can do _____."

Answer: "everything" / "present" / "today."

ARTS, RELIGION, & CULTURE

Traditionally, which flower with which color blossoms is used to decorate churches and homes on Easter, and which food representing the animal sacrificed on the first Passover is eaten on this day?

Answer: Lilies / white / lamb.

POTPOURRI

Which body of water did Paul Bunyan dig for drinking water for his ox, which one did he dig in Washington to float logs to the mill, and in which state did he open an iron mine for shoes for his ox?

Answer: Great Lakes / Puget Sound / Minnesota.

U.S. GEOGRAPHY

Name the 3 states bordering New Jersey.

Answer: Delaware / Pennsylvania / New York.

HISTORY

Identify the founder of the nursing profession, who was known as the "Lady With the Lamp"; her nationality; and the war in which she served in 1854.

Answer: Florence Nightingale / English / Crimean War.

LITERATURE

Identify Winnie-the-Pooh's gloomy donkey friend who likes to eat thistles, his tiger friend, and the animal that goes "lumping along."

Answer: Eeyore / Tigger / Heffalump.

ENTERTAINMENT

In Dr. Seuss's *Cat in the Hat*, what color is the big wood box the cat brings in, and what are the names of the 2 "Things" in the box?

Answer: Red / Thing One / Thing Two.

SPORTS AND GAMES

What is the French term meaning "large prize" for the series of races involving Formula One cars, and in which countries are the Monte Carlo Rally and the Le Mans 24-hour race held?

Answer: *Grand Prix* / Monaco / France.

SCIENCE AND NATURE

Identify the conifers that provide more lumber than any other variety of tree; name the wood used to line clothing chests and closets; and name the one often called the world's finest cabinet wood.

Answer: Pine / cedar / mahogany.

WORLD GEOGRAPHY

On which continent is the world's highest waterfall; on which one is the South Pole; and of which one is the world's largest island considered a part?

Answer: South America (Angel Falls) / Antarctica / North America (Greenland).

LEADERS & GOVERNMENT

Which official is the president of the U.S. Senate, on which occasions does he vote, and what title is given to the Senate's temporary president?

Answer: Vice President of the U.S. / only when there is a tie / president *pro tempore* (accept "president pro tem").

MUSIC & RHYMES

Do, *re*, *mi*, *fa*, and *so* (or doh, ray, me, fah, soh) are the singable names for 5 of the 8 notes of the musical scale. Name the other 3.

Answer: La / ti / do (or lah, te, doh).

LANGUAGE

Complete the phrases: "To separate the men from the _____," "To separate the grain from the _____," and "To separate the sheep from the _____."

Answer: "boys" / "chaff" / "goats."

ARTS, RELIGION, & CULTURE

In which city was Christ crucified, what is lighted on Easter to symbolize Jesus as the "Light of the World," and what is the familiar symbol of fertility associated with Easter?

Answer: Jerusalem / (paschal) candle / Easter egg (accept rabbit or bunny).

POTPOURRI

Identify the acronym AIDS; the acronym SIDS, also called crib death; and the official police abbreviation DUI or DWI.

Answer: Acquired Immune Deficiency Syndrome / Sudden Infant Death Syndrome / Driving Under the Influence or Driving While Intoxicated.

U.S. GEOGRAPHY
Name 3 of the 4 states bordering Maryland.
Answer: Pennsylvania / Delaware / Virginia / West Virginia.

HISTORY
Which Barbary pirate of the 1500s had a red beard, which 18th-century pirate was born Edward Teach, and which Scottish pirate's exploits were recounted in Poe's *The Gold Bug*?
Answer: Barbarossa / Blackbeard / Captain Kidd's.

LITERATURE
In which wood do Winnie-the-Pooh and his friends live, and what are the names of his kangaroo friend and her baby?
Answer: Hundred Acre Wood / Kanga / Baby Roo.

ENTERTAINMENT
In which city and at what address does Sherlock Holmes live, and who created this fictional detective?
Answer: London / 221 B Baker Street / Sir Arthur Conan Doyle.

SPORTS AND GAMES
In the game of pool, how many pockets are on the table, how many object balls are used in most pool games, and what is the term for hitting the cue ball into the racked balls to start a game?
Answer: 6 / 15 / break.

SCIENCE AND NATURE
Which naturalist from which country firmly established the theory of evolution through the process of natural selection, and on which ship did he set sail in 1831 on a 5-year voyage?
Answer: Charles Darwin / Britain / *Beagle*.

WORLD GEOGRAPHY

On which 2 oceans does Africa border, and which large sea borders Africa on the north?

Answer: Atlantic Ocean / Indian Ocean / Mediterranean Sea.

LEADERS & GOVERNMENT

Of the 3 branches of the U.S. government, which one chooses judges, which one approves judges, and which one may rule that officials have acted illegally?

Answer: Executive / legislative / judicial.

MUSIC & RHYMES

Complete the song lines: “Casey _____! Orders in his hand. / Casey . . . Mounted to the _____, / Took his farewell journey to that promised _____.”

Answer: “Jones” / “cabin” / “land.”

LANGUAGE

Complete the expressions: “To rob Peter to pay _____,” “Six of one and a half _____ of the other,” and “Someone near and _____.”

Answer: “Paul” / “dozen” / “dear.”

ARTS, RELIGION, & CULTURE

On which Thursday in November does the U.S. celebrate Thanksgiving, in which year did the Plymouth colonists first give thanks, and in which year was the first national Thanksgiving Day held?

Answer: 4th / 1621 / 1789.

POTPOURRI

Give the meaning of the initialisms AWOL, COD, and GMT.

Answer: Absent Without Leave / Collect (Cash) On Delivery / Greenwich Mean Time.

U.S. GEOGRAPHY

In each of the following pairs, which is the larger state in area: North Carolina or South Carolina; North Dakota or South Dakota; Virginia or West Virginia?

Answer: North Carolina / South Dakota / Virginia.

HISTORY

Give the meaning of the NAT in the acronym NATO, an organization established in 1949 to provide for the common defense of 16 Western nations.

Answer: North / Atlantic / Treaty (Organization).

LITERATURE

In which work by Lewis Carroll are 2 fat little men so alike as to be indistinguishable, and what are their names?

Answer: *Through the Looking Glass* / Tweedledum / Tweedledee.

ENTERTAINMENT

Who is Sherlock Holmes' assistant and colleague with whom he sometimes lives, which instrument does Holmes play, and which "Napoleon of Crime" is Holmes' archenemy?

Answer: Dr. John Watson / violin / Professor Moriarty.

SPORTS AND GAMES

In which sports did Pistol Pete Maravich, Earl Anthony, and Arnold Palmer become famous?

Answer: Basketball / bowling / golf.

SCIENCE AND NATURE

Name 3 of the 4 types of teeth in the human mouth.

Answer: Incisors / canines (or cuspids) / premolars (or bicuspids) / molars.

WORLD GEOGRAPHY

On which 3 oceans does North America border?

Answer: Atlantic / Pacific / Arctic.

LEADERS & GOVERNMENT

Which 2 U.S. Presidents were the first to win a Nobel Peace Prize, and which President won a Pulitzer Prize for his *Profiles in Courage*?

Answer: Theodore Roosevelt / Woodrow Wilson / John Kennedy.

MUSIC & RHYMES

In the song "If I Had a Hammer," what 3 things would be hammered out?

Answer: "danger" / "warning" / "love between my brothers and my sisters."

LANGUAGE

Complete the phrases: "Spic and _____," "Stand up and be _____," and "Strange but _____."

Answer: "span" / "counted" / "true."

ARTS, RELIGION, & CULTURE

On which date does Valentine's Day occur, which god of love is depicted as a chubby infant with wings, and which weapon does he use to cause a person to fall in love?

Answer: February 14 / Cupid (or Amor) / bow and arrow.

POTPOURRI

How many numbers are there in a zip code, which state has the lowest zip code, and which one has the highest?

Answer: 5 (accept 9) / Massachusetts / Alaska.

U.S. GEOGRAPHY

Which state flag features a grizzly bear and a red star, which one features a pelican feeding its young, and which one features a white bison?

Answer: California / Louisiana / Wyoming.

HISTORY

What name is given to the raid by American colonists on British ships in Boston Harbor on December 16, 1773; how many ships were attacked; and how were the colonists dressed?

Answer: Boston Tea Party / 3 / Indians (as Mohawks).

LITERATURE

Complete the book titles: *Caddie* _____ by Carol Ryrie Brink, *The Witch of* _____ *Pond* by Elizabeth Speare, and *My Friend* _____ by Mary O'Hara.

Answer: *Woodlawn* / *Blackbird* / *Flicka*.

ENTERTAINMENT

Which Japanese word for "pocket monsters" identifies a game built on many characters with names like Jigglypuff, how many cards are there, and which mouse-like creature triggers electrical disturbances in the atmosphere?

Answer: Pokémon / 151 / Pikachu.

SPORTS AND GAMES

How many holes comprise a round of golf, what is the term for the area of mowed grass between the teeing ground and the putting surface, and what is the term for the putting surface?

Answer: 18 / fairway / green.

SCIENCE AND NATURE

Which extinct animals are named from the Greek for "terrible lizard" and "breast tooth," and which extinct giant cat had 2 long, fanglike teeth?

Answer: Dinosaur / mastodon / saber-toothed tiger.

WORLD GEOGRAPHY

Which area in Asia, whose name means "the land between two rivers," is known as the "Cradle of Civilization," and between which 2 rivers is it located?

Answer: Mesopotamia / Tigris / Euphrates.

LEADERS & GOVERNMENT

Of the 2 chambers of the U.S. Congress, which one is known as the *upper house*, which one is called the *lower house*, and how many members make up the *upper house*?

Answer: Senate / House of Representatives / 100 (2 per state).

MUSIC & RHYMES

Complete the words to "Taps": "_____ is done, gone the _____; / From the lake, from the hills, / From the sky; / All is well, safely rest, / _____ is nigh."

Answer: "Day" / "sun" / "God."

LANGUAGE

Complete the expressions: "Live and _____," "Through thick and _____," "To fight tooth and _____."

Answer: "learn" (or "let live") / "thin" / "nail."

ARTS, RELIGION, & CULTURE

What are the traditional "Three R's" all school children should know?

Answer: Readin' / 'Ritin' / 'Rithmetic.

POTPOURRI

Proverbially, what is hard to find in a haystack, where is it said a snowball has no chance, and which "horse" is considered to be an unlikely winner in an election?

Answer: Needle / in Hell / dark horse.

U.S. GEOGRAPHY

Which city in each of the following groups is farthest south: San Francisco, San Diego, or Los Angeles; Houston, Dallas, or Austin; and Jacksonville, Tallahassee, or Tampa?

Answer: San Diego / Houston / Tampa.

HISTORY

Which massacre took place on March 5, 1770; which black leader of a patriot mob died in this incident; and which country's soldiers did the killing?

Answer: Boston Massacre / Crispus Attucks / Britain's.

LITERATURE

Complete the following lines from an Ernest L. Thayer poem: "And somewhere men are laughing and somewhere children _____, / But there is no joy in _____: Mighty _____ has struck out."

Answer: "shout" / "Mudville" / "Casey" (from "Casey at the Bat").

ENTERTAINMENT

In the Disney film *Song of the South*, which animal is boarding up his home as Uncle Remus passes; which animal catches this animal in a trap; and which animal is tricked into trading places?

Answer: Brer Rabbit / Brer Fox / Brer Bear.

SPORTS AND GAMES

Give the nicknames of the athletic teams at Wake Forest, Wisconsin, and Vanderbilt.

Answer: Demon Deacons (or Deacs) / Badgers / Commodores.

SCIENCE AND NATURE

Identify the 3 most common elements in the atmosphere.

Answer: Nitrogen (78%) / oxygen (21%) / argon (1%).

WORLD GEOGRAPHY
In which country does the 820-mile-long Rhine River rise in a glacier, through which country does it last flow before emptying into the sea, and into which body of water does it empty?
Answer: Switzerland / The Netherlands (or Holland) / North Sea.

LEADERS & GOVERNMENT
National begins the name of the U.S. government agency called NASA. What do the other 3 initials of this acronym stand for?
Answer: Aeronautics / (and) Space / Administration.

MUSIC & RHYMES
"In Dublin's fair city," what was "sweet" Molly Malone's occupation, what did she drive "Through streets broad and narrow," and which word completes her cry, "_____ and mussels, alive, alive-o"?
Answer: Fishmonger / wheelbarrow / "Cockles."

LANGUAGE
Which punctuation marks are used to separate items in a series, to introduce lists, and to separate independent clauses linked by a conjunctive adverb?
Answer: Comma / colon / semicolon.

ARTS, RELIGION, & CULTURE
Which legendary person brings gifts to children on Christmas Eve, where does he live, and which creatures help him make toys?
Answer: Santa Claus (accept Saint Nicholas or Father Christmas) / North Pole / elves.

POTPOURRI
What kind of a "horse" did the Indians call a locomotive, whom did they call the "Great White Father," and what is the popular name for the North American *bison*?
Answer: An iron horse / U.S. President / buffalo.

U.S. GEOGRAPHY
Name the 3 states bordering Lake Superior.
Answer: Minnesota / Wisconsin / Michigan.

HISTORY
On which continent was the Zulu Empire founded in the 1820s, in which country did the Boers make The Great Trek in 1836-37, and in which country was the Manchu Dynasty overthrown in 1911?
Answer: Africa / South Africa / China.

LITERATURE
In Tolkien's *The Fellowship of the Ring*, which hobbit is the finder of the One Ring; who is the chosen Ring-bearer; and who is the maker of the One Ring, the supreme agent of evil?
Answer: Bilbo Baggins / Frodo Baggins / Sauron.

ENTERTAINMENT
Who tells the young boy "You can't run away from trouble" in Disney's *Song of the South*, with which "baby" does Brer Rabbit get entangled, and where does he ask not to be thrown?
Answer: Uncle Remus / Tar Baby / in the briar patch.

SPORTS AND GAMES
Which 3 pieces surround a king at the beginning of a chess match?
Answer: Queen / bishop / pawn.

SCIENCE AND NATURE
Give the word for "the earliest known inhabitants of Australia," name the wild dog they brought there, and identify the tree-dwelling marsupial animal that feeds mostly on eucalyptus leaves.
Answer: Aborigines / dingo / koala (or native bear).

WORLD GEOGRAPHY

Which body of water is the world's largest lake, which is the largest of the former Soviet Republics bordering it, and which Asian country other than a former Soviet Republic borders it?

Answer: Caspian Sea / Russia / Iran.

LEADERS & GOVERNMENT

Give the meaning of the initials INF in the INF Treaty signed by the leaders of the U.S. and the Soviet Union in 1987, and identify these leaders.

Answer: Intermediate-range Nuclear Force treaty / Ronald Reagan / Mikhail Gorbachev.

MUSIC & RHYMES

In the song "If I Had a Hammer," which words complete, "the _____ of justice," the _____ of freedom," and "the _____ about love"?

Answer: "hammer" / "bell" / "song."

LANGUAGE

Complete each of the following triplets: "Don't fold, spindle, or _____," "White tie, top hat, and _____," and "Race, creed, or _____."

Answer: "mutilate" / "tails" / "color" (accept "national origin").

ARTS, RELIGION, & CULTURE

Name the traditional "Three Bs" of classical music.

Answer: Johann Sebastian Bach / Ludwig van Beethoven / Johannes Brahms.

POTPOURRI

What color thumb are you said to have if you are a good gardener, what are you wearing if you are wearing your birthday suit, and what kind of car do you have if you bought a "lemon"?

Answer: Green / nothing / a defective one.

U.S. GEOGRAPHY
Name the only state bordering Lake Ontario, the only one bordering Lake Huron, and the only one bordering Alberta, Canada.
Answer: New York / Michigan / Montana.

HISTORY
How many lanterns would be shown from the steeple if the British went by land and how many if they went by sea; and from which city's Old North Church on April 18, 1775, was the signal flashed?
Answer: One if by land / two if by sea / Boston's.

LITERATURE
Complete these lines from "The Charge of the Light Brigade": "Theirs not to make reply, / Theirs not to reason _____, / Theirs but to do and _____. / Into the Valley of Death / Rode the six _____."
Answer: "why" / "die" / "hundred."

ENTERTAINMENT
In Disney's *Song of the South*, which word completes the song title, "Everybody's Got a _____ Place"; who leads Brer Fox and Brer Bear to that place; and what is found there?
Answer: "Laughing" / Brer Rabbit / a giant beehive.

SPORTS AND GAMES
Which words complete the following phrases derived from sports and games: "To flex one's _____," "To keep a poker _____," and "To play both ends against the _____"?
Answer: "muscles" / "face" / "middle."

SCIENCE AND NATURE
How many chambers are in a bird's heart, what is the saclike enlargement of its gullet or esophagus, and what is the thick-walled digestive organ it uses for grinding?
Answer: 4 / crop / gizzard.

WORLD GEOGRAPHY

Identify the world's largest body of fresh water and second largest lake and the 2 countries that border it.

Answer: Lake Superior / United States / Canada.

LEADERS & GOVERNMENT

Give the surname of each of the following Chief Justices of the U.S. Supreme Court: William Howard _____, Earl _____, and Warren E. _____."

Answer: Taft / Warren / Burger.

MUSIC & RHYMES

Complete the song lines: "I've been working on the _____ / All the _____ day . . . / Just to pass the time away. / Don't you hear the _____ blowing? / Rise up so early in the morn."

Answer: "railroad" / "livelong" / "whistle."

LANGUAGE

Give the meaning of the following Greek word elements: *-ectomy*, *-mania*, and *-phobia*.

Answer: "Surgical removal of" / "madness" or "passion for" / "abnormal fear" or "hatred of."

ARTS, RELIGION, & CULTURE

Complete the following song lines, "I've got a mule, her name is _____, / _____ miles on the Erie _____. / She's a good old worker and a good old pal."

Answer: "Sal" / "Fifteen" / "Canal."

POTPOURRI

Which phrase designates the western U.S. during lawless pioneer days, which word completes the phrase "Pikes Peak or _____," and which article of clothing did cowboys want to be wearing when they died?

Answer: Wild West (accept Wild and Woolly West) / "Bust" / their boots.

U.S. GEOGRAPHY

Name the 3 largest Hawaiian islands according to area.

Answer: Hawaii / Maui / Oahu (listed from largest to smallest).

HISTORY

What part of the U.S. was known as "Seward's Icebox," and from which country in which year was this land purchased?

Answer: Alaska / Russia / 1867.

LITERATURE

What is the name of the bull who doesn't want to fight in a story by Munro Leaf, what does this bull prefer to smell, and in which country does he live?

Answer: Ferdinand / smell the flowers / Spain.

ENTERTAINMENT

Give the number that completes the Disney film title _____ *Dalmatians*, and name the dogs in this film that take silent vows outside the church as Roger and Anita Radcliff take them inside.

Answer: 101 / Pongo / Perdita.

SPORTS AND GAMES

Which words complete the following phrases derived from sports and games: "To give someone a run for his _____," "To keep one jump _____," and "To keep an eye on the _____"?

Answer: "money" / "ahead" / "ball."

SCIENCE AND NATURE

What is the Latin name for the brightest star seen from Earth at night, which animal's name is given to this star, and in which constellation of the Southern Hemisphere is it located?

Answer: Sirius / dog's (Dog Star) / Canis Major (or Great Dog).

WORLD GEOGRAPHY

What are the 3 colors of the French flag?

Answer: Blue / white / red (or *bleu* / *blanc* / *rouge*).

LEADERS & GOVERNMENT

What are the 3 unalienable rights of the people asserted by the Declaration of Independence?

Answer: Life / Liberty / Pursuit of Happiness.

MUSIC & RHYMES

Which words complete the song lines: "Don't you hear the _____ shouting, / 'Dinah, blow your horn'? . . . / Someone's in the _____ with Dinah; / Strumming on the old _____"?

Answer: "captain" / "kitchen" / "banjo" (from "I've Been Working on the Railroad").

LANGUAGE

In a manuscript, how are foreign words or book titles indicated; how are the titles of short stories, poems, and songs indicated; and what does a writer use to enclose incidental explanatory material?

Answer: Underlining or italics / quotation marks / parentheses.

ARTS, RELIGION, & CULTURE

Which oratorio by which composer from which country includes the famous "Hallelujah" chorus?

Answer: *Messiah* / George Frideric Handel / England (accept Germany).

POTPOURRI

Traditionally, what does one throw into a wishing well, what color is a flag of truce or surrender, and which animal allegedly buries its head in the sand when it is frightened?

Answer: Money (coins) / white / ostrich (it is not true for this bird is really just rearranging the eggs in its nest with its bill).

U.S. GEOGRAPHY
On which rivers are the Grand Coulee, the Hoover, and the Fort Peck dams?
Answer: Columbia / Colorado / Missouri.

HISTORY
Which American frontiersman and soldier during which war led the "Green Mountain Boys," and which state did his military force represent?
Answer: Ethan Allen / Revolutionary War / Vermont.

LITERATURE
Under which favorite tree did Ferdinand the Bull like to sit, what did he sit on that caused him to puff and snort and paw the ground as if he were mad, and to which city was he taken to fight?
Answer: Cork tree / a bumblebee / Madrid.

ENTERTAINMENT
Identify the city in which the Disney film *101 Dalmatians* is set, the Radcliffs' housekeeper who helps deliver the puppies, and the wealthy villainess who steals the puppies with the help of Horace and Jasper.
Answer: London / Nanny (or Nanny Cook) / Cruella De Vil.

SPORTS AND GAMES
Which words complete the following phrases derived from sports and games: "A feather in one's _____," "Monday-morning _____," and "A full court _____"?
Answer: "cap" / "quarterback" / "press."

SCIENCE AND NATURE
From which animals do veal, ham, and pork come?
Answer: Calf (cattle) / pigs (hogs) / pigs (hogs).

WORLD GEOGRAPHY
Between which 2 continents is the Strait of Gibraltar, and which of the 2 countries separated by this strait has the larger area?
Answer: Europe / Africa / Spain (Morocco is the other country).

LEADERS & GOVERNMENT
How many delegates signed the U.S. Constitution, and in which building in which city is the original Constitution displayed?
Answer: 39 / National Archives Building / Washington, D.C.

MUSIC & RHYMES
Complete the song lines: "Oh! I come from _____, / With my _____ on my knee, / I'm going to _____, / My true love for to see."
Answer: "Alabama" / "banjo" / "Louisiana" (from "Oh, Susanna!").

LANGUAGE
Which words complete the expressions: "That's the way the _____ crumbles," "That's the way the _____ bounces," and "To see which way the _____ blows"?
Answer: "cookie" / "ball" / "wind."

ARTS, RELIGION, & CULTURE
Complete the saying: "_____ may work from sun to _____, / But _____'s work is never done."
Answer: "Man" / "sun" / "woman."

POTPOURRI
On which part of the chicken or turkey does one traditionally make a wish, what do 2 people do with this part when they make a wish, and which person supposedly will have his wish answered?
Answer: Wishbone (or the furcula) / they pull and break it / the one who gets the longer piece.

U.S. GEOGRAPHY

Name the 2 oceans that border Alaska, name both the ocean and the gulf that border Florida, and name the 2 bodies of water bordering the Baja or Lower California Peninsula.

Answer: Pacific Ocean and Arctic Ocean / Atlantic Ocean and Gulf of Mexico / Gulf of California (formerly called the Sea of Cortés and the Vermilion Sea) and the Pacific Ocean.

HISTORY

In which month, on which day, in which year at Pearl Harbor did Japan accomplish a sneak attack that brought the U.S. into World War II?

Answer: December / 7 / 1941.

LITERATURE

Identify the captain of the Plymouth settlement whose name completes the title of the Longfellow poem *The Courtship of Miles* _____, and identify the pair on whose marriage the poem is centered.

Answer: *Standish* / John Alden / Priscilla Mullens.

ENTERTAINMENT

Which Disney films feature these songs: "Never Smile at a Crocodile," "Bella Notte," and "The Walrus and the Carpenter"?

Answer: *Peter Pan* / *Lady and the Tramp* / *Alice in Wonderland*.

SPORTS AND GAMES

In which sport was the World Cup first won by Uruguay in 1930, which player in this sport was known as the "Black Pearl," and which country did he lead to the world championship in 1958, 1962, and 1970?

Answer: Soccer / Pelé / Brazil.

SCIENCE AND NATURE

What did Marco Polo describe as "black stones" that could burn all night, black liquid that could be burned, and black powder that was used for fireworks?

Answer: Coal / oil / gunpowder.

WORLD GEOGRAPHY

Which country holds Gibraltar as a dependency, and which 2 bodies of water are connected by the Strait of Gibraltar?

Answer: Britain / Atlantic Ocean / Mediterranean Sea.

LEADERS & GOVERNMENT

Give the full names of the U.S. Presidents related as grandfather and grandson, and give the surname of the ones who were 5th cousins.

Answer: William Henry Harrison / Benjamin Harrison / Roosevelt (Theodore and Franklin).

MUSIC & RHYMES

Which words complete the song lines: "The men will cheer, the boys will _____, / The _____, they will all turn out, / And we'll all feel gay when _____ comes marching home"?

Answer: "shout" / "ladies" / "Johnny."

LANGUAGE

Which animal's name completes each of the expressions: "A wolf in _____'s clothing," "To place one's head in the _____'s mouth," and "A big _____ in a little pond"?

Answer: "sheep" / "lion" / "fish."

ARTS, RELIGION, & CULTURE

Which words complete the song lines: "I'm _____ of a White Christmas, / Just like the ones I used to _____," and what do children "listen to hear in the snow"?

Answer: "dreaming" / "know" / "sleigh bells."

POTPOURRI

Which candy bar was named after the daughter of President Grover Cleveland, which one was named after Alexandre Dumas' fictional characters, and which one was named after a galaxy?

Answer: Baby Ruth / Three Musketeers / Milky Way.

U.S. GEOGRAPHY
Which West Coast volcano in which year blew its top in a huge eruption on May 18, and in which state is this volcano located?
Answer: Mount Saint Helens / 1980 / Washington.

HISTORY
Which U.S. state became the 50th state, in which year did it join the Union, and who was the President at the time?
Answer: Hawaii / 1959 / Dwight Eisenhower.

LITERATURE
Which word completes the title of Thomas Rockwell's *How to Eat _____ Worms*, how many worms does Billy bet Alan he can eat, and how much money does he bet?
Answer: *Fried* / 15 (in 15 days) / $50 (Billy wins).

ENTERTAINMENT
Which Disney films feature these songs: "That's What Uncle Remus Said," "You Can Fly, You Can Fly, You Can Fly," and "Painting the Roses Red"?
Answer: *Song of the South* / *Peter Pan* / *Alice in Wonderland*.

SPORTS AND GAMES
Which words complete the following phrases derived from sports and games: "To take the bull by the _____," "To cash in one's _____," and "To be out in _____ field"?
Answer: "horns" / "chips" / "left."

SCIENCE AND NATURE
Name the part of the human body associated with each of the following adjectives: optical, nasal, and pectoral.
Answer: Eye / nose / chest.

WORLD GEOGRAPHY

Which body of water is called *La Manche* in French, to which body is it connected by the Strait of Dover, and in which countries are Calais and Dover, the major ports located on opposite sides of the strait?

Answer: English Channel / North Sea / France and England.

LEADERS & GOVERNMENT

Which U.S. President promoted his Fourteen Points, which one addressed the people in his "Fireside Chats," and which one was in office at the start of the Great Depression?

Answer: Woodrow Wilson / Franklin D. Roosevelt / Herbert Hoover.

MUSIC & RHYMES

Complete the lines to the song: "Should auld acquaintance be _____, / And never bro't to _____? / . . . And days of auld lang _____."

Answer: "forgot" / "mind" / "syne."

LANGUAGE

In English grammar, which kinds of words are used "to name a person, place, or thing," "to modify a noun or pronoun," and "to replace one or more nouns"?

Answer: Noun / adjective / pronoun.

ARTS, RELIGION, & CULTURE

Complete these lines from "The New Colossus": "The wretched _____ of your teeming shore, / Send these, the _____, tempest-tost, to me: / I lift my _____ beside the golden door."

Answer: "refuse" / "homeless" / "lamp."

POTPOURRI

Which dog says, "Take the Bite Out of Crime," which owl says, "Give a hoot; don't pollute," and which bear says, "Only you can prevent forest fires"?

Answer: McGruff the Crime Dog / Woodsy Owl / Smokey the Bear.

U.S. GEOGRAPHY

In which cities were World's Fairs or Expositions held in Washington in 1974, in Tennessee in 1982, and in Louisiana in 1984?

Answer: Spokane / Knoxville / New Orleans.

HISTORY

Before the Civil War, which line was regarded as the dividing line between free and slave states, and which 2 states did this line originally separate?

Answer: Mason-Dixon Line / Maryland / Pennsylvania.

LITERATURE

Which flower does Antoine de Saint-Exupéry's Little Prince cover up before leaving home; which planet is the 7th, and last, he visits; and which animal does he encounter who is "no thicker than a finger"?

Answer: Rose / Earth / snake.

ENTERTAINMENT

Which Disney films feature these songs: "Kanine Krunchies Commercial," "The Siamese Cat Song," and "Ev'rybody Wants to Be a Cat"?

Answer: *One Hundred and One Dalmatians* / *Lady and the Tramp* (the song is better known as "We Are Siamese If You Please") / *The Aristocats*.

SPORTS AND GAMES

Which words complete the following phrases derived from sports and games: "To put one's cards on the _____," "To throw one's hat into the _____," and "To keep the ball _____"?

Answer: "table" / "ring" / "rolling."

SCIENCE AND NATURE

What percent of the Earth's surface is covered with water—50, 60, or 70%; what percent of all water is in the ocean—87, 93, or 97%; and what percent of all water is fresh (unsalty)—3, 13, or 23%?

Answer: 70% / 97% / 3%.

WORLD GEOGRAPHY

Which mountain chain is called the "Backbone of South America," which country on this continent is known as the "Stringbean Country," and which one is called "Half a Continent"?

Answer: Andes / Chile / Brazil.

LEADERS & GOVERNMENT

Which words complete the statement, "I believe this government cannot endure . . . half _____ and half _____," and which future U.S. President said this in 1858?

Answer: "slave" / "free" / Abraham Lincoln.

MUSIC & RHYMES

Complete the lines from the song: "The old gray _____ she ain't (isn't) what she used to _____, / Many long years _____."

Answer: "mare" / "be" / "ago."

LANGUAGE

Name the 3 words in the English language that end in *-ceed.*

Answer: Exceed / proceed / succeed.

ARTS, RELIGION, & CULTURE

According to the Bible, which prophet was thrown overboard and swallowed by a great fish, which type of fishlike mammal is traditionally said to have swallowed him, and how many days did he live in the fish?

Answer: Jonah / whale / 3 days.

POTPOURRI

Which animal owned by which lady allegedly started a great fire on October 8, 1871, by kicking over a lighted lantern, and in which city did this fire take place?

Answer: Cow / Mrs. O'Leary / Chicago.

U.S. GEOGRAPHY

Identify the highest mountain and the lowest point in the U.S., and identify the highest mountain in the contiguous 48 states.

Answer: Mount McKinley / Death Valley / Mount Whitney.

HISTORY

Which country built a 3,500 mile long wall to keep out invaders, across the northern part of which country did Hadrian build a wall, and in which country was the "Wall of Shame" built in 1961?

Answer: China (Great Wall) / England / East Germany.

LITERATURE

Which letter and number identify the asteroid of the Little Prince in a work by Antoine de Saint-Exupéry, and in which desert on which continent is this work set?

Answer: B-612 / Sahara Desert / Africa.

ENTERTAINMENT

Which professor in which Disney film invents flying rubber, and what name does he give to this substance?

Answer: Ned Brainerd / *The Absent-Minded Professor* / Flubber.

SPORTS AND GAMES

Which words complete the following phrases derived from sports and games: "To have the ball in one's _____," "To have the ball at one's _____," and "A whole new ball _____"?

Answer: "court" / "feet" / "game."

SCIENCE AND NATURE

Give the words for "the rapid union of oxygen with any substance," "the slow union of oxygen with iron," and "the physical process by which a substance changes from a gas to a liquid."

Answer: Combustion (accept burning) / rusting (accept corrosion) / condensation.

WORLD GEOGRAPHY

On which continent is the major part of the Great Rift Valley, and in which countries on this continent are the Valley of the Tombs of the Kings and the Kimberley Mines?

Answer: Africa / Egypt / South Africa.

LEADERS & GOVERNMENT

Which U.S. governmental position has been described as being only a heartbeat away from the most powerful elective office in the world, and which 2 men have resigned this position?

Answer: Vice Presidency / John C. Calhoun / Spiro Agnew.

MUSIC & RHYMES

Complete the song lines: "My Bonnie lies over the _____, / My Bonnie lies over the _____, / Oh! bring back my Bonnie to _____."

Answer: "ocean" / "sea" / "me."

LANGUAGE

Give the common names for animals referred to by the words *canine*, *feline*, and *leonine*.

Answer: dog / cat / lion.

ARTS, RELIGION, & CULTURE

Complete the lines to the spiritual: "Go down, _____, / Way down in _____'s land, / Tell old _____, / Let my people go."

Answer: "Moses" / "Egypt" / "Pharaoh."

POTPOURRI

Which U.S. state was named for France's King Louis XIV, which Asian island country was named for Spain's King Philip II, and which South American country was named for Simón Bolívar?

Answer: Louisiana / Philippines / Bolivia.

U.S. GEOGRAPHY

Name the largest bodies of water on which Savannah, Georgia; Mobile, Alabama; and Memphis, Tennessee, are directly located.

Answer: Atlantic Ocean / Gulf of Mexico / Mississippi River.

HISTORY

Which words complete these U.S. slogans: "Remember the _____" in 1836, "Remember the _____" in 1898, and "Remember _____" in 1941?

Answer: "Alamo" / "Maine" / "Pearl Harbor."

LITERATURE

What is the title of Margaret Mitchell's only published novel, in which state is it set, and who is this novel's heroine?

Answer: *Gone With the Wind* / Georgia / Scarlett O'Hara.

ENTERTAINMENT

Name the golden candelabra in a forbidding castle in the Disney film *Beauty and the Beast*, name the teapot who lives there with her son, Chip, and name the clock.

Answer: Lumiere / Mrs. Potts / Cogsworth.

SPORTS AND GAMES

Which words complete the following phrases derived from boxing: "To box someone's _____," "To hit below the _____," and "To take it on the _____"?

Answer: "ears" / "belt" / "chin."

SCIENCE AND NATURE

What is the cube of 3, what is the cube root of 8, and what is the sum of all the factors of six?

Answer: 27 / 2 / 12 (1 + 2 + 3 + 6).

WORLD GEOGRAPHY

In which country is Baffin Island the largest island, in which ocean is New Guinea the largest island, and what is the largest island in the U.S.?

Answer: Canada / Pacific Ocean / Hawaii.

LEADERS & GOVERNMENT

Which word is defined as "government by the people," on which sheet of paper are votes marked during an election, and which word derived from a voting practice of dropping colored balls into a box means "to exclude"?

Answer: Democracy / ballot / blackball.

MUSIC & RHYMES

Which words complete these song lines: "There's a yellow rose in _____, I'm going there to see," and "Her eyes are bright as _____, They sparkle like the _____"?

Answer: Texas / "diamonds" / "dew."

LANGUAGE

Which animals are referred to by the words *equine*, *porcine*, and *taurine*?

Answer: Horse / pig / bull.

ARTS, RELIGION, & CULTURE

Which musical instrument is known as a "squeeze box," which one is called a "licorice stick," and which one is called a "mouth organ"?

Answer: Accordion / clarinet / harmonica.

POTPOURRI

In which cemetery in which state is the Tomb of the Unknown Soldier, now called the Tomb of the Unknowns, located, and how many graves are included as a part of the memorial?

Answer: Arlington National Cemetery / Virginia / 4 (WWI, WWII, Korean War, and Vietnam War; in 1999, with the Vietnam crypt left empty because of modern means of identification, the inscription "Honoring and keeping faith with America's missing servicemen/1958-1975" was placed on the tomb).

U.S. GEOGRAPHY

In which states are the Everglades, Petrified Forest, and Sequoia national parks?

Answer: Florida / Arizona / California.

HISTORY

Which American frontiersman founded the settlement of Boonesborough, in which state was this settlement, and which trail did he blaze through the Cumberland Mountains to get there?

Answer: Daniel Boone / Kentucky / Wilderness Road.

LITERATURE

Which author from which country wrote the historical novel *The Three Musketeers*, and what is the motto of this group?

Answer: Alexandre Dumas (père) / France / "All for one, one for all."

ENTERTAINMENT

In the Disney film *Beauty and the Beast*, to which part of the castle is the girl forbidden to go; which container holds the glowing rose; and which room does the Beast show the girl for her surprise?

Answer: West Wing / bell jar / library.

SPORTS AND GAMES

Name the first black player to quarterback a team in the Super Bowl, the team for which he played, and the team that he helped defeat in Super Bowl XXII, 42-10.

Answer: Doug Williams / Washington Redskins / Denver Broncos.

SCIENCE AND NATURE

Give the words for "the fleshy part of the human body between the waist and the upper thigh," "the place at which 2 or more bones meet," and "the framework of bones that supports the lower part of the abdomen."

Answer: Hip / joint (or articulation) / pelvis.

WORLD GEOGRAPHY

Which countries control Easter Island, Staten Island, and Bermuda?

Answer: Chile / United States / Great Britain.

LEADERS & GOVERNMENT

Which countries award the decorations known as the Iron Cross, the Legion of Honor, and the Victoria Cross?

Answer: Germany / France / Great Britain.

MUSIC & RHYMES

Complete the following rhyme: "One misty, moisty _____, / When cloudy was the _____, / I met a little old man / Clothed all in _____."

Answer: "morning" / "weather" / "leather."

LANGUAGE

Identify the one definite and the 2 indefinite articles in English grammar.

Answer: The / a / an.

ARTS, RELIGION, & CULTURE

In which months are Washington's Birthday, Mother's Day, and Father's Day celebrated in the U.S.?

Answer: February / May / June.

POTPOURRI

Which fairy tale person supposedly makes children sleepy, which mythical creature leaves a child money after taking a baby tooth, and where has the child placed this tooth?

Answer: Sandman / tooth fairy / under the pillow.

U.S. GEOGRAPHY

In which states are Shenandoah, Yosemite, and Zion national parks?

Answer: Virginia / California / Utah.

HISTORY

Which "Father of the American Navy" during which war said to the Captain of the *Serapis*, "I have not yet begun to fight," and which country was he fighting?

Answer: John Paul Jones / Revolutionary War / Britain.

LITERATURE

Name the Three Musketeers.

Answer: Athos / Porthos / Aramis.

ENTERTAINMENT

Name the quarrelsome, hunchbacked puppet and his wife in a show which derives its name from the Neapolitan Punchinello, and name their dog.

Answer: Punch / Judy / Toby.

SPORTS AND GAMES

How many wheels do a unicycle and a tricycle have; and how many people normally ride a tandem bike?

Answer: 1 / 3 / 2.

SCIENCE AND NATURE

Which transparent body is used for refracting light, what is the name for the band of colors formed when light passes through this body, and which English scientist discovered this band?

Answer: Prism / spectrum / Sir Isaac Newton.

WORLD GEOGRAPHY

What are the world's 3 largest seas in area?

Answer: South China Sea / Caribbean Sea / Mediterranean Sea.

LEADERS & GOVERNMENT

With which African country was the policy of *apartheid* associated, what is the meaning of this word, and from which language does it come?

Answer: (Republic of) South Africa / (strict racial) "segregation" (of the non-white population) / Afrikaans.

MUSIC & RHYMES

Complete the phrases in the theme song from *Man of La Mancha*: "to dream _____," "to fight _____," and "to bear _____."

Answer: "the impossible dream" / "the unbeatable foe" / "with unbearable sorrow" ("to run where the brave dare not go").

LANGUAGE

Spell the words *February*, *Wednesday*, and *Saturday*.

Answer: F-E-B-R-U-A-R-Y / W-E-D-N-E-S-D-A-Y / S-A-T-U-R-D-A-Y.

ARTS, RELIGION, & CULTURE

Avarice (covetousness), lust (lechery), sloth (laziness), and anger (wrath) are 4 of the 7 Deadly or Capital Sins. Name the other 3.

Answer: Pride / envy / gluttony.

POTPOURRI

Give the year of the first day of the 21st century, identify the first leap year in the 21st century, and name the West Coast city where Century City, a planned community, is located.

Answer: (January 1) 2001 / 2004 / Los Angeles.

U.S. GEOGRAPHY

In which 2 Southern states is Great Smoky Mountains National Park, and in which New England state is Acadia National Park?

Answer: North Carolina / Tennessee / Maine.

HISTORY

Arrange in chronological order: establishment of Jamestown, Virginia; Pilgrims' signing of the Mayflower Compact; and De Soto's discovery of the Mississippi River.

Answer: De Soto (1541) / Jamestown (1607) / Mayflower Compact (1620).

LITERATURE

Which character says, "I was exceedingly surprised with the print of a man's naked foot on the shore," what name does he give to the person he finds on his island, and who is this book's author?

Answer: Robinson Crusoe (in *Robinson Crusoe*) / Man Friday (accept Friday) / Daniel Defoe.

ENTERTAINMENT

Complete the name of Johnny Gruelle's doll character Raggedy _____, identify her brother, and complete the name of the fairyland in Marcella's backyard, _____ Deep Woods.

Answer: Ann / Raggedy Andy / Deep.

SPORTS AND GAMES

A player in which position in which sport wins the Cy Young Award, and which player in this sport is known as a "Fireman"?

Answer: Pitcher / baseball / a relief pitcher.

SCIENCE AND NATURE

Which disease is known as the "kissing disease," which one is called the "Royal disease," and which one is known as "consumption"?

Answer: Mononucleosis / hemophilia / tuberculosis.

WORLD GEOGRAPHY

On which continent are the Pyrenees Mountains, and between which 2 countries do they form a natural barrier?

Answer: Europe / France / Spain.

LEADERS & GOVERNMENT

Name the 3 highest ranking positions in order of succession if a U.S. President dies while in office.

Answer: Vice President / Speaker of the House / President *pro tempore* of the Senate.

MUSIC & RHYMES

Complete the song lines: "John _____ was a little baby, / Sittin' on his gran'ma's _____; / Oh, he lift up a hammer and a little chunk of _____, / Said, 'This hammer's gonna be the death of me.'"

Answer: "Henry" / "knee" / "steel."

LANGUAGE

Spell the words *bookkeeper*, *athletics*, and *inoculation*.

Answer: B-O-O-K-K-E-E-P-E-R / A-T-H-L-E-T-I-C-S / I-N-O-C-U-L-A-T-I-O-N.

ARTS, RELIGION, & CULTURE

Complete the words to the spiritual: "Nobody knows the _____ I've seen, / Nobody knows but _____. / . . . Glory, _____."

Answer: "trouble" / "Jesus" / hallelujah."

POTPOURRI

Which bird symbolizes peace, which one symbolizes war, and what kind of branch traditionally symbolizes peace?

Answer: Dove / hawk / olive branch.

U.S. GEOGRAPHY

In which states are Vicksburg, Shiloh, and Gettysburg national military parks?

Answer: Mississippi / Tennessee / Pennsylvania.

HISTORY

Arrange in chronological order: Dutch purchase of Manhattan Island; Marquette-Joliet's exploration of the Mississippi; and Salem witch trials.

Answer: Dutch purchase (1626) / Marquette and Joliet (1673) / Witch trials (1692).

LITERATURE

Identify the author of *Uncle Tom's Cabin*, the character whose name today means "any cruel taskmaster," and the character who says, "I 'spect I growed."

Answer: Harriet Beecher Stowe / Simon Legree / Topsy.

ENTERTAINMENT

Name the wizard and the evil witch in the Disney film *The Sword in the Stone*, and identify the wise animal friend of the wizard Archimedes.

Answer: Merlin / Madame Mim / owl.

SPORTS AND GAMES

Identify the 3 types of weapons used in fencing.

Answer: Foil / Épée / the sabre.

SCIENCE AND NATURE

How many feet are in a 3rd of a yard, how many feet are in a 10th of a mile, and how many yards are in a 10th of a mile?

Answer: 1 / 528 / 176.

WORLD GEOGRAPHY

Which Italian cities are nicknamed the "City of Seven Hills," the "Queen of the Adriatic," and the "Leaning Tower City"?

Answer: Rome / Venice / Pisa.

LEADERS & GOVERNMENT

Name the 3 requirements a person must meet according to the U.S. Constitution in order to become a member of the House of Representatives.

Answer: At least 25 years of age / a citizen for at least 7 years / a resident of the state in which elected.

MUSIC & RHYMES

Complete the song lines: "John Henry drove through _____ feet, / The _____ drill only drove nine; / But he drove so hard that he broke his poor heart, / And he laid down his _____ and he died."

Answer: "fourteen" / "steam" / "hammer."

LANGUAGE

Give the feminine counterparts for a duke, a hero, and a master.

Answer: Duchess / heroine / mistress.

ARTS, RELIGION, & CULTURE

On which date is International Labor Day celebrated, and on which Monday in which month does the U.S. celebrate Labor Day?

Answer: May 1 / first Monday / September.

POTPOURRI

Which animal is said to be "Man's Best Friend"; which animal completes the phrase "There's more than one way to skin a _____"; and which animals are you not supposed to swap while crossing a stream?

Answer: Dog / cat / horses.

U.S. GEOGRAPHY

In which states are Horseshoe Bend, Fredericksburg, and Chattanooga national military parks?

Answer: Alabama / Virginia / Tennessee.

HISTORY

Arrange in chronological order: Boston Tea Party; Boston Massacre; and Battles of Lexington and Concord.

Answer: Boston Massacre (1770) / Boston Tea Party (1773) / Lexington and Concord (1775).

LITERATURE

Who is the author of *Black Beauty*, which kind of animal is Black Beauty, and who is the narrator of this story?

Answer: Anna Sewell / horse / the horse.

ENTERTAINMENT

Which country was to be ruled by the person who pulled out the sword in the Disney film *The Sword in the Stone*, who pulls it out, and which night bird saves this person from being eaten by the Pike?

Answer: England / Arthur (nicknamed Wart) / the owl.

SPORTS AND GAMES

In which sport are falcons trained to hunt other birds; what is another name for the duck hawk, the fastest falcon; and what is the term for a falcon's claws?

Answer: Falconry / peregrine falcon / talons.

SCIENCE AND NATURE

Give the words for "the molten rock under the earth's surface," "the molten rock that reaches the surface," and "the hard, black, smooth, shiny volcanic glass formed when molten rock cools quickly."

Answer: Magma / lava / obsidian.

WORLD GEOGRAPHY

What are the largest islands in the Mediterranean Sea, the Caribbean Sea, and the Indian Ocean?

Answer: Sicily / Cuba / Madagascar.

LEADERS & GOVERNMENT

Name the first 3 U.S. Presidents to serve 2 full terms.

Answer: George Washington / Thomas Jefferson / James Madison.

MUSIC & RHYMES

Complete the song lines: "John Brown's body lies _____ in the _____, / His _____ is marching on. Glory, glory, hallelujah."

Answer: "a-mouldering" / "grave" / "soul."

LANGUAGE

Give 3 of the 4 kinds of sentences classified according to grammatical structure.

Answer: Simple / compound / complex / compound-complex.

ARTS, RELIGION, & CULTURE

Which musical instrument do angels traditionally play, which word completes the phrase, "Acts of _____" to describe quakes and floods, and which one completes the proverb, "Virtue is its own _____"?

Answer: Harp / "God" / "reward."

POTPOURRI

Complete the following sayings of Benjamin Franklin: "Remember time is _____," "There never was a good war or a bad _____," and "A penny saved is a penny _____."

Answer: "money" / "peace" / "earned."

U.S. GEOGRAPHY

In which states are Antietam, Manassas, and Cowpens national battlefields?

Answer: Maryland / Virginia / South Carolina.

HISTORY

Arrange in chronological order: adoption of U.S. Declaration of Independence; signing of Revolutionary War peace treaty; and ratification of Articles of Confederation.

Answer: Independence (1776) / Articles (1781) / Peace treaty (1783).

LITERATURE

Which words complete the titles "The Masque of the Red _____" and "The Murders in the Rue _____," and who wrote these short stories?

Answer: "Death" / "Morgue" / Edgar Allan Poe.

ENTERTAINMENT

What is the name of the boy living in the jungle in Disney's *The Jungle Book*, and which animals are named Bagheera and Baloo?

Answer: Mowgli / panther / bear.

SPORTS AND GAMES

What is the name of the sport of mountain climbing, which famous mountain was first climbed in 1953 for the first time, and which New Zealander made it to the top of this mountain in that year?

Answer: Mountaineering (or Alpinism) / Mount Everest / Sir Edmund Hillary.

SCIENCE AND NATURE

Which gem is nature's hardest substance, which one comes from a mollusk, and which one comes from the skeletons of tiny sea animals?

Answer: Diamond / pearl / coral.

WORLD GEOGRAPHY

In which capital cities are the statues of the Manneken-Pis and the Little Mermaid, and with which country is the story of the boy holding back the sea with his finger in the dike associated?

Answer: Brussels / Copenhagen / The Netherlands (or Holland).

LEADERS & GOVERNMENT

Name the first 3 U.S. Presidents in the 20th century to serve at least 2 full terms.

Answer: Woodrow Wilson / Franklin D. Roosevelt / Dwight Eisenhower.

MUSIC & RHYMES

Complete the song lines: "Jim Crack _____, I don't _____, / My master's gone away," and then identify the fly that caused the pony to throw his rider, resulting in his death.

Answer: "corn" / "care" / "blue-tail fly."

LANGUAGE

Name the 3 verbals.

Answer: Gerund / infinitive / participle.

ARTS, RELIGION, & CULTURE

Outside which fort in which city was which person inspired to write the "Star-Spangled Banner"?

Answer: Fort McHenry / Baltimore / Francis Scott Key.

POTPOURRI

Complete the following sayings of Benjamin Franklin: "Little strokes fell great _____," "God helps those that help _____," and "He that falls in love with himself will have no _____."

Answer: "oaks" / "themselves" / "rivals."

U.S. GEOGRAPHY
In which 3 states is Cumberland Gap National Historical Park?
Answer: Kentucky / Tennessee / Virginia.

HISTORY
Arrange in chronological order: moving of the U.S. capital to Philadelphia; writing of the U.S. Constitution; and first meeting of the U.S. Congress.
Answer: Constitution (1787) / Congress (1789) / Capital moved (1790).

LITERATURE
Give the first names of the fictional Montague son and Capulet daughter who love each other in spite of the hatred between their families, and identify the author of a 1595 play concerning them.
Answer: Romeo / Juliet / William Shakespeare.

ENTERTAINMENT
What is the name of the king of the apes in Disney's *The Jungle Book*, and which kinds of animals are Kaa and Shere Khan?
Answer: King Louie / python (accept snake) / tiger.

SPORTS AND GAMES
Identify the hard rubber disk used in ice hockey, the area outlined in red in front of each cage, and the color of the lines on either side of the centerline or red line.
Answer: Puck / (goal) crease / blue.

SCIENCE AND NATURE
What is 1/2 of 1/2 of 1/2, what is 4 divided by 1/2, and how many surfaces does a Möbius strip have?
Answer: 1/8 / 8 / 1.

WORLD GEOGRAPHY

Identify the largest bodies of water on which the French cities of Le Havre, Biarritz, and Nice are located.

Answer: English Channel / Atlantic Ocean (accept Bay of Biscay) / Mediterranean Sea.

LEADERS & GOVERNMENT

Identify each of the following Presidents from the commonly used initials: W.W., H.H., and C.C.

Answer: Woodrow Wilson / Herbert Hoover / Calvin Coolidge.

MUSIC & RHYMES

Complete the tongue twisters: "Moses supposes his toeses are _____, / But Moses supposes _____," and "She sells sea shells by the _____."

Answer: "roses" / "erroneously" / "seashore."

LANGUAGE

What is the term for "a word formed by omitting one or more letters," which punctuation mark shows the omission of a letter from a word, and which mark divides a word at the end of a line?

Answer: Contraction / apostrophe / hyphen.

ARTS, RELIGION, & CULTURE

In the song "Day by Day" from *Godspell*, what 3 things are prayed for to the "dear Lord"?

Answer: "To see Thee more clearly" / "love Thee more dearly" / "follow Thee more nearly."

POTPOURRI

In which country did which woman allegedly ride naked through the town of Coventry protesting a tax increase, and who allegedly peeped at her and went blind as she rode?

Answer: England / Lady Godiva / Peeping Tom.

U.S. GEOGRAPHY

In which states are Cape Canaveral, Cape Cod, and Cape Hatteras national seashores?

Answer: Florida / Massachusetts / North Carolina.

HISTORY

Arrange in chronological order: John Adams' move into White House; Lewis and Clark exploration; and Louisiana Purchase.

Answer: John Adams (1800) / Louisiana Purchase (1803) / Exploration (1804-1806).

LITERATURE

Which character in a novel by Miguel de Cervantes lives in the province of La Mancha, in which country is the novel set, and which objects does he think are giants?

Answer: Don Quixote / Spain / windmills.

ENTERTAINMENT

In which city does the rich Madame Adelaide Bonfamille live in the Disney film *The Aristocats*, who is the mother cat, and how many kittens does she have?

Answer: Paris / Duchess / 3 (Berlioz, Marie, and Toulouse).

SPORTS AND GAMES

Which New England team became the first U.S. team to join the NHL, which U.S. team won 4 consecutive championships from 1980-1983, and which Canadian team won 5 championships from 1956-1960?

Answer: Boston Bruins / New York Islanders / Montreal Canadiens.

SCIENCE AND NATURE

What is the world's largest deer, what is the name for the wild reindeer of North America, and what is the more common name for the North American deer called the wapiti?

Answer: (North American) moose / caribou / elk.

WORLD GEOGRAPHY

Identify the largest bodies of water on which the following African cities are located: Algiers, Algeria; Dakar, Senegal; and Dar es Salaam, Tanzania.

Answer: Mediterranean Sea / Atlantic Ocean / Indian Ocean.

LEADERS & GOVERNMENT

Which words ending in *-archy* mean "rule by a single ruler," "rule by no government," and "absolute rule by one person"?

Answer: Monarchy / anarchy / autarchy.

MUSIC & RHYMES

Complete the rhyme: "Here is the _____, and here is the _____; / Open the door and here are the _____. / Here is the parson going upstairs, / And here he is a-saying his prayers."

Answer: "church" / "steeple" / "people."

LANGUAGE

Give the abbreviations for the words *ounce*, *pound*, and *teaspoon*.

Answer: Oz. / lb. / tsp.

ARTS, RELIGION, & CULTURE

In which month is "Presidents' Day" celebrated, on which date is the Epiphany, and in which month is Memorial Day?

Answer: February / January 6 / May.

POTPOURRI

Which nicknames with the word "Bill" were given to 19th-century Americans named James Butler Hickok, William Frederick Cody, and William H. Bonney?

Answer: "Wild Bill" / "Buffalo Bill" / "Billy the Kid."

U.S. GEOGRAPHY
On which Great Lakes are Chicago, Illinois; Cleveland, Ohio; and Rochester, New York?
Answer: Lake Michigan / Lake Erie / Lake Ontario.

HISTORY
Arrange in chronological order: Battle of New Orleans; capture and burning of Washington, D.C.; and the British *Leopard*'s firing on the U.S. *Chesapeake*.
Answer: *Leopard* v. *Chesapeake* (1807) / Washington burned (1814) / New Orleans (1815).

LITERATURE
Identify the son of Jacob Stubbins who narrates many of the Dr. Dolittle stories, name this doctor's 2-headed llama, and identify the type of animal known as Chee-Chee or Dab-Dab.
Answer: Tommy Stubbins / Pushmi-Pullyu / monkey or duck.

ENTERTAINMENT
Identify the beautiful princess with whom Aladdin falls in love in the Disney film *Aladdin*, her pet tiger and bodyguard, and the evil vizier in the Sultan's palace who plots to get a magic lamp.
Answer: Jasmine / Rajah / Jafar.

SPORTS AND GAMES
In which sports did Bill Russell, Gary Player, and Bobby Orr become famous?
Answer: Basketball / golf / ice hockey.

SCIENCE AND NATURE
Identify the following branches of mathematics: the study of chance; the collection, organization, and interpretation of data; and the study of points, lines, planes, and their relationships.
Answer: Probability / statistics / geometry.

WORLD GEOGRAPHY

Identify the seas on which the Asian cities of Beirut, Lebanon, and Bombay, India, are located, and identify the sea of which Manila Bay in the Philippines is an extension.

Answer: Mediterranean Sea / Arabian Sea / South China Sea.

LEADERS & GOVERNMENT

Name 3 of the 4 U.S. Presidents carved in granite on Mount Rushmore.

Answer: George Washington / Thomas Jefferson / Theodore Roosevelt / Abraham Lincoln (listed from left to right).

MUSIC & RHYMES

In a song from *Oklahoma*, what kind of a "mornin'" is it, what kind of a "day" is it, and what line follows the words "I got a beautiful feelin'"?

Answer: "beautiful mornin'" / "beautiful day" / "Ev'rything's goin' my way."

LANGUAGE

Give the correct spelling of each of the following: "He had only (to, two, too) books," "John visited the monument, (to, too, two)," and "Give the book (to, too, two) your sister."

Answer: T-w-o / t-o-o / t-o.

ARTS, RELIGION, & CULTURE

How many years did the Trojan War last, who fought the Trojans, and which wood figure taken inside the city caused the city to fall?

Answer: 10 years / Greeks / Trojan (or wooden) horse.

POTPOURRI

Which American pioneer planted many apple trees along the early frontier, in which state did he do most of his planting, and what was his real name?

Answer: Johnny Appleseed / Ohio / John Chapman.

U.S. GEOGRAPHY

Name 3 of the 4 states that are known as the "Sunshine State."

Answer: Florida / South Dakota / California / New Mexico.

HISTORY

Arrange in chronological order: opening of the Erie Canal; Monroe Doctrine; and Missouri Compromise.

Answer: Missouri Compromise (1820) / Monroe Doctrine (1823) / Erie Canal (1825).

LITERATURE

Which word completes the title of the short story, "The Ransom of Red _____," what is the pen name of the story's author, and what is his real name?

Answer: "Chief" / O. Henry / William Sydney Porter.

ENTERTAINMENT

Which words beginning with *C* name "a merry-go-round," "a keyboard instrument having a series of steam whistles," and "a percussion instrument," also called *tubular bells*?

Answer: Carousel / calliope / chimes.

SPORTS AND GAMES

Identify the 132' x 54' rectangle in front of a soccer goal, the boundary lines on the sides of the field, and the manner in which the ball is put back in play from there.

Answer: Penalty area (box) / touch (side) lines / throw-in.

SCIENCE AND NATURE

How many eyes does a bee have, what is the name of the shelter where domestic bees live, and what is the name for the 6-sided celled structure built to hold their honey?

Answer: 5 (3 simple eyes and 2 compound eyes) / hive (or beehive) / honeycomb.

WORLD GEOGRAPHY

Identify the largest bodies of water on which Valparaíso, Chile, and Rio de Janeiro, Brazil are located, and identify one of the 2 capital cities located on the Río de la Plata.

Answer: Pacific Ocean / Atlantic Ocean / Montevideo (Uruguay) or Buenos Aires (Argentina).

LEADERS & GOVERNMENT

Which U.S. President developed the W.I.N. button; which one commanded a PT boat during WWII; and which one was the first to have starred in a Hollywood movie?

Answer: Gerald Ford / John F. Kennedy / Ronald Reagan.

MUSIC & RHYMES

Which U.S. cities complete these song lines: "I left my heart in _____," "_____, that toddling town," and "It don't rain in _____ in the summertime"?

Answer: "San Francisco" / "Chicago" / "Indianapolis."

LANGUAGE

Identify these poetic devices: "the sound device in which the beginning sounds of words are repeated"; "the repetition of vowel sounds"; and "the use of words that sound like the actions they name."

Answer: Alliteration / assonance / onomatopoeia.

ARTS, RELIGION, & CULTURE

What are the symbols of the Zodiac associated with the signs Aries, Taurus, and Gemini?

Answer: Ram / Bull / Twins.

POTPOURRI

Which letter of the alphabet describes the shape of a chevron, what is the meaning of the *D* in 3-D, and which letter is Hester forced to wear in *The Scarlet Letter*?

Answer: V(-shaped) / Dimensional / A (for adultery).

U.S. GEOGRAPHY
Name the 2 oldest and largest mountain ranges in the U.S., and identify the mountain chain that extends between California's Lassen Peak and British Columbia's Fraser River.
Answer: Appalachian Mountains / Rocky Mountains / Cascade Range.

HISTORY
Arrange in chronological order: discovery of gold in California; Mexican War; and Samuel Morse's invention of the telegraph.
Answer: Morse (1837) / Mexican War (1846) / Gold discovered (1848).

LITERATURE
Who is the British author of *A Tale of Two Cities*, and in which 2 cities is the novel set?
Answer: Charles Dickens / London / Paris.

ENTERTAINMENT
Which Disney film features "the best doggone dog in the West," which animal does this dog chase in the film's beginning that wreaks havoc on the farm, and which animal is named Jumper?
Answer: *Old Yeller* / a rabbit / a mule.

SPORTS AND GAMES
Give the horse racing terms for the jacket and cap provided by the horse owners and worn by the jockey, for the prize money in a race, and for the distance of 1/8 of a mile.
Answer: Silks (or colors) / purse / furlong.

SCIENCE AND NATURE
Give the animal names for each of the following: for a person who is a coward, for a person who saves small useless items, and for a greedy and ruthless person who preys on others.
Answer: Chicken / pack rat (accept trade rat) / vulture.

WORLD GEOGRAPHY

In which cities are the airports of Heathrow, Leonardo da Vinci, and Charles de Gaulle located?

Answer: London / Rome / Paris.

LEADERS & GOVERNMENT

During which decade and during the administration of which U.S. President did the Watergate scandal take place, and which President subsequently pardoned him for all federal crimes he might have committed?

Answer: 1970s / Richard Nixon / Gerald Ford.

MUSIC & RHYMES

Regarding the children's song "Sur le Pont d'Avignon," what is a *pont*, what do the people in the song do on this *pont*, and in which country is Avignon?

Answer: Bridge / dance ("l'on y danse") / France.

LANGUAGE

Which verbal functions only as an adjective; which one begins with the word *to* and is used as a noun, adjective, or adverb; and which one ends in *-ing* and functions as a noun?

Answer: Participle / infinitive / gerund.

ARTS, RELIGION, & CULTURE

What are the symbols of the Zodiac associated with the signs Cancer, Leo, and Virgo?

Answer: Crab / Lion / Virgin.

POTPOURRI

Which war was called the "Great War," which New York street's theatre district is called the "Great White Way," and on which continent are the Great Plains?

Answer: World War I / Broadway's / North America.

U.S. GEOGRAPHY
On which Great Lakes are Duluth, Minnesota; Milwaukee, Wisconsin; and Buffalo, New York?
Answer: Lake Superior / Lake Michigan / Lake Erie.

HISTORY
Arrange in chronological order: John Brown's raid; assassination of President Lincoln; and Gadsden Purchase.
Answer: Gadsden Purchase (1854) / John Brown's raid (1859) / Lincoln shot (1865).

LITERATURE
What kind of animal is the yearling in Marjorie Kinnan Rawlings' novel, in which U.S. state is the novel set, and what is the name of the Baxter boy who cares for this animal?
Answer: Deer (fawn) / Florida / Jody.

ENTERTAINMENT
In Disney's *Old Yeller*, which animal does Old Yeller attack to save Arliss, which animals does he chase out of the corn field, and which one with an offspring does he attack to save Travis?
Answer: Bear / raccoons / cow (a heifer).

SPORTS AND GAMES
Which race features horses that have never won a race, which infield electronic board has the official results, and what is the name for the track area between the last turn and the finish line?
Answer: Maiden race / tote board (or totalizator board) / home stretch.

SCIENCE AND NATURE
Give the adjective used to describe a disease that is easily spread from person to person, and identify the diseases known as rubeola and rubella.
Answer: Contagious / measles / German measles.

WORLD GEOGRAPHY

Give the English names for the countries known as Deutschland, España, and Suisse.

Answer: Germany / Spain / Switzerland.

LEADERS & GOVERNMENT

Which U.S. First Lady headed the "Say No to Drugs" campaign, which one worked to improve care for the elderly and the mentally ill, and which one wrote a newspaper column entitled "My Day"?

Answer: Nancy Reagan / Rosalynn Carter / Eleanor Roosevelt.

MUSIC & RHYMES

Which word completes the title to the song, "Tie a _____ Ribbon Round the Ole Oak Tree," how many years has the lover been away according to the song, and on which vehicle is he coming home?

Answer: "Yellow" / 3 years / bus.

LANGUAGE

Which figure of speech is an exaggeration not meant to be taken literally, which one is a comparison using *like* and *as*, and which one is an implied comparison not using the words *like* and *as*"?

Answer: Hyperbole / simile / metaphor.

ARTS, RELIGION, & CULTURE

What are the symbols of the Zodiac associated with the signs Libra, Scorpio, and Sagittarius?

Answer: Scales (Balance) / Scorpion / Archer.

POTPOURRI

In marriage, what does the roundness of the ring represent, on which finger on which hand does a U.S. bride wear the ring, and what did Jesus turn into wine at the wedding feast in Cana?

Answer: Eternity (or longevity) / third finger of the left hand / water.

U.S. GEOGRAPHY

Which 3 states of the Lower 48 border the Pacific Ocean?

Answer: California / Oregon / Washington.

HISTORY

Arrange in chronological order: purchase of Alaska; completion of the First transcontinental railroad; and Battle of Little Big Horn.

Answer: Alaska (1867) / Railroad (1869) / Little Big Horn (1876).

LITERATURE

Which word completes the title *The Wind in the* _____, who wrote the story, and in which country is it set?

Answer: *Willows* / Kenneth Grahame / England.

ENTERTAINMENT

In the Disney film *Old Yeller*, from which pack of animals does the dog save Travis, which rabid animal attacks the dog, and which animal does his papa bring Travis?

Answer: Hogs / a wolf / horse.

SPORTS AND GAMES

In horse race betting, what are the 3 terms used to designate a bet on a horse to finish in first, second, and third place?

Answer: Win / place / show.

SCIENCE AND NATURE

Identify the vertebral column that helps support the body, the ringlike bones that make up this column, and the 24 bones that enclose the chest.

Answer: Spine (or spinal column) / vertebrae / ribs.

WORLD GEOGRAPHY

In which countries are Siberia, Bavaria, and Andalusia?

Answer: Russia / Germany / Spain.

LEADERS & GOVERNMENT

Identify the only U.S. President who didn't live in the White House, and name the 2 cities in which he lived as President, the first U.S. capital cities.

Answer: George Washington / New York / Philadelphia.

MUSIC & RHYMES

In the song with the line, "Ya can't have one without the other," which words complete the lines: "Love and _____ / Go together like a _____ and _____"?

Answer: "marriage / "horse" / "carriage."

LANGUAGE

Choose the grammatically correct word in parentheses for the following: "He's a better student than (I, me)"; "No one but (he, him) likes school"; and "Just between you and (I, me), they like this game."

Answer: I / him / me.

ARTS, RELIGION, & CULTURE

What are the symbols of the Zodiac associated with the signs Capricorn, Aquarius, and Pisces?

Answer: Goat / Water bearer / Fishes.

POTPOURRI

Which words complete the common statements: "Don't call us, we'll _____," "If you can't say something good about someone, don't say _____," and "Your check is in the _____"?

Answer: "call you" / "anything at all" / "mail."

U.S. GEOGRAPHY

Which 3 states other than California and Nevada border Arizona?

Answer: Utah / Colorado / New Mexico.

HISTORY

Arrange in chronological order: impeachment of President Johnson; Bell's invention of the telephone; and assassination of President Garfield.

Answer: Johnson impeached (1868) / Bell and telephone (1876) / Garfield shot (1881).

LITERATURE

Name the character who loves cars and joyrides in the story *The Wind in the Willows*, and name 2 of the other 3 River-Bankers that aid this character to overthrow the Wild Wooders, or the weasels and stoats.

Answer: Toad / Badger / Mole / Rat.

ENTERTAINMENT

Cowabunga! *Teenage Mutant Ninja Turtles* was a 1990 movie derived from the pages of a cult comic book. Identify 3 of the 4 pizza-eating turtles named for Renaissance painters.

Answer: Leonardo / Michaelangelo / Donatello / Raphael.

SPORTS AND GAMES

In which sports did Willie Shoemaker, Maurice Richard, and Walter Hagen became famous?

Answer: Horse racing / ice hockey / golf.

SCIENCE AND NATURE

Arrange the following minerals in order of increasing hardness according to the Mohs hardness scale: quartz, talc, and gypsum.

Answer: Talc / gypsum / quartz.

WORLD GEOGRAPHY
On which continents are Timbuktu, Mandalay, and Tipperary?
Answer: Africa / Asia / Europe.

LEADERS & GOVERNMENT
Which queens of England are known by the nicknames "Bloody Mary," the "Virgin Queen," and "The Widow of Windsor"?
Answer: Mary I / Elizabeth I / Victoria.

MUSIC & RHYMES
Which Austrian composer with the middle name Amadeus wrote an opera at age 12, which trumpet player known as "Satchmo" was playing at 13, and which singer known as "Little Stevie" had a hit at 13?
Answer: Wolfgang Amadeus Mozart / Louis Armstrong / Stevie Wonder.

LANGUAGE
According to the sayings, what part of your body "do you follow" when you use common sense, what kind of "tale" is an incredible one full of hyperbole, and where are you "reading" when you try to understand what someone is really saying?
Answer: Your nose / tall tale / between the lines.

ARTS, RELIGION, & CULTURE
Ancient scientists thought that all matter was made up of 4 "substances" called elements. Name 3 of these substances or basic elements of matter.
Answer: Air / earth / fire / water.

POTPOURRI
Identify the disease, the American corporation, and the English singing group nicknamed "The Big C," "Big Blue," and the "The Fab Four," respectively.
Answer: Cancer / IBM / The Beatles.

U.S. GEOGRAPHY

Name 3 of the 4 states bordering Kansas.

Answer: Colorado / Nebraska / Missouri / Oklahoma.

HISTORY

Arrange in chronological order: blowing up of the U.S. battleship *Maine*; assassination of President McKinley; and Klondike gold rush.

Answer: Klondike (1896) / *Maine* (1898) / McKinley (1901).

LITERATURE

Name the big, ugly, yellow dog in a story by Fred Gipson, the state where the story is set, and the 14-year-old whose father leaves him in charge of the household.

Answer: Old Yeller / Texas / Travis.

ENTERTAINMENT

Who left his shadow behind in the Disney film *Peter Pan*, who locks it up for safe-keeping, and whose pixie dust helps the children to fly?

Answer: Peter Pan / Wendy / Tinker Bell's.

SPORTS AND GAMES

In which sports did Larry Bird, Sammy Baugh, and Eddie Arcaro become famous?

Answer: Basketball / football / horse racing.

SCIENCE AND NATURE

With which senses are the adjectives *gustatory*, *olfactory*, and *ocular* associated?

Answer: Taste / smell / sight.

WORLD GEOGRAPHY

Which 2 South American countries do not share a border with Brazil, and which country is the continent's southernmost?

Answer: Chile / Ecuador / Chile.

LEADERS & GOVERNMENT

Which leaders of Israel and Egypt were the co-winners of the 1978 Nobel Peace Prize, and which Accords did they sign for Middle East peace?

Answer: Prime Minister Menachem Begin / President Anwar Sadat / Camp David Accords.

MUSIC & RHYMES

Which actress called "Little Miss Miracle" was singing and dancing in movies at the age of 6, which "Lady of Soul" recorded a song at 16, and who at 16 sang the lead song in *The Wizard of Oz*?

Answer: Shirley Temple / Aretha Franklin / Judy Garland.

LANGUAGE

Give the words for "please" in French, Spanish, and German.

Answer: *S'il vous plaît / por favor / bitte.*

ARTS, RELIGION, & CULTURE

Which mythological twin brothers founded the city of Rome, and which animal is said to have rescued them from the Tiber River?

Answer: Romulus / Remus / she-wolf (accept wolf).

POTPOURRI

Which small rodent has a day named for it; what is the date of that day; and, according to legend, how many more weeks of winter will there be if this animal sees his shadow?

Answer: Groundhog / February 2 / 6 weeks.

U.S. GEOGRAPHY
Which 3 states other than Oklahoma, Missouri, and Tennessee border Arkansas?
Answer: Mississippi / Louisiana / Texas.

HISTORY
Arrange in chronological order: opening of Panama Canal; San Francisco earthquake; and establishment of New Mexico and Arizona as states.
Answer: Earthquake (1906) / New Mexico and Arizona (1912) / Panama Canal (1914).

LITERATURE
Which fictional narrator of a series of animal fables was created by Joel Chandler Harris, which rabbit always outwits his foes in these stories, and in which state was Harris a journalist?
Answer: Uncle Remus / Brer Rabbit / Georgia.

ENTERTAINMENT
Who saves Peter Pan from a bomb in the Disney film *Peter Pan*, which pirate shaves the Captain every morning and obeys every order, and in whose ship do the children return home?
Answer: Tinker Bell / Smee / Captain Hook's.

SPORTS AND GAMES
In track and field, what are the names of the events once called the *broad jump* and the *hop, step, and jump*, and what is the name of the long spear thrown overhand?
Answer: Long jump / triple jump / javelin.

SCIENCE AND NATURE
Which Austrian discovered the basic principles of heredity, which Englishman discovered how the blood circulates in the body, and which Italian discovered the law of the pendulum?
Answer: Johann Gregor Mendel / William Harvey / Galileo.

WORLD GEOGRAPHY
In which countries are the Volga River, the Loire River, and the Po River?
Answer: Russia / France / Italy.

LEADERS & GOVERNMENT
The United States and Russia are 2 of the 5 permanent members of the United Nations Security Council. Name the other 3.
Answer: People's Republic of China (or China) / Great Britain (or Britain) / France.

MUSIC & RHYMES
In the rhyme "Going to St. Ives," how many were going to St. Ives, how many wives are mentioned in this rhyme, and what did the wives' sacks hold?
Answer: One / 7 wives / (7) cats.

LANGUAGE
For, *yet*, *nor*, *neither*, and *so* are sometimes considered coordinating conjunctions. Name the other 3 that are considered the most common.
Answer: And / but / or.

ARTS, RELIGION, & CULTURE
Which capital city is the home of the famed Bolshoi Theatre Ballet, which city, formerly named Leningrad, is the home of this country's other major ballet company, the Kirov, and what cathedral in this capital is known for its many colorful, onion-shaped domes?
Answer: Moscow (Russia) / Saint Petersburg / St. Basil's Cathedral.

POTPOURRI
Which gangster controlling the underworld in which city in the 1920s was known as "Scarface Al," and for which February 1929 massacre was his gang blamed?
Answer: Al Capone / Chicago / St. Valentine's Day Massacre.

U.S. GEOGRAPHY

Name 3 of the 4 states bordering Indiana.

Answer: Illinois / Michigan / Ohio / Kentucky.

HISTORY

Arrange in chronological order: investigation of Teapot Dome scandal; Lindbergh's flight to Paris; and U.S. declaration of war on Germany in WWI.

Answer: Germany (1917) / Teapot Dome (1923) / Lindbergh (1927).

LITERATURE

What is the surname of the orphaned girl named Mary in Frances Hodgson Burnett's *The Secret Garden*, in which country did her parents die, and to which country does she go to live with her uncle?

Answer: Lennox / India / England.

ENTERTAINMENT

Which fox tells Chicken Little the sky is falling in a Disney short, which red cock is the supervisor of egg-collection, and which hen listens to the chicken and not to the fox?

Answer: Foxey Loxey / Cocky Locky / Henny Penny.

SPORTS AND GAMES

Give the number of events comprising a *heptathlon*, a *decathlon*, and a *pentathlon*.

Answer: 7 / 10 / 5.

SCIENCE AND NATURE

Which number is the base of the decimal system, how many zeroes are there in a million, and how many zeroes are in a trillion?

Answer: 10 / 6 / 12.

WORLD GEOGRAPHY

Name the 3 smallest continents in area.

Answer: Antarctica / Europe / Australia (listed from largest to smallest).

LEADERS & GOVERNMENT

Who became prime minister of Great Britain in 1979, which U.S. President took office in 1981, which Soviet leader came to power in 1985?

Answer: Margaret Thatcher / Ronald Reagan / Mikhail Gorbachev.

MUSIC & RHYMES

Which words complete the song lines: "On top of old _____, / All covered with _____, / I lost my true _____, / Come a-courtin' too slow"?

Answer: "Smoky" / "snow" / "lover."

LANGUAGE

Identify the physician who treats disorders of the nervous system, the one who treats mental and emotional illness, and the one who is an expert in mental and emotional processes.

Answer: Neurologist / psychiatrist / psychologist.

ARTS, RELIGION, & CULTURE

Which composer from which country wrote the ballet *Swan Lake*, and what is the French phrase for a group of dancers who perform as an ensemble in ballet?

Answer: Peter Ilich Tchaikovsky / Soviet Union (accept Russia) / *corps de ballet*.

POTPOURRI

After a wedding, what have guests traditionally thrown at the bride and groom to wish them fertility, which object does the bride toss to the single females, and what is expected to happen to the one who catches it?

Answer: Rice / bouquet / she will be the next to marry.

U.S. GEOGRAPHY

Which state flag includes the date December 7, 1787; which one features stars representing the Big Dipper and the North Star; and which state features a beehive and the motto "Industry"?

Answer: Delaware / Alaska / Utah.

HISTORY

Arrange in chronological order: Japanese bombing of Pearl Harbor; Amelia Earhart's first flight across the Atlantic; and President Roosevelt's Hundred Days.

Answer: Earhart (1928) / Roosevelt (1933) / Pearl Harbor (1941).

LITERATURE

Which kind of bird shows Mary how to enter the garden in Frances Hodgson Burnett's *The Secret Garden*, for which flower is the garden best remembered, and which boy can charm the wild animals?

Answer: Robin / roses / Dickon.

ENTERTAINMENT

Which type of factory does Willy Wonka own, where does Charlie find the money to purchase the item in which he finds a golden ticket, and which little men work in the factory?

Answer: Chocolate factory / in the gutter / Oompa Loompas.

SPORTS AND GAMES

Identify 3 of the 4 Olympic field events in which objects are thrown.

Answer: Shot-put / discus / javelin / the hammer throw.

SCIENCE AND NATURE

Which system includes the earth and the other planets, which galaxy includes the sun and the earth, and how many miles per second does light travel to cover 5.88 trillion miles in a year?

Answer: Solar System / Milky Way / 186,282 miles per second (accept 186,000).

WORLD GEOGRAPHY

On which continent is the active volcano Mount Vesuvius, and near which major city in which country is it located?

Answer: Europe / Naples / Italy.

LEADERS & GOVERNMENT

What is the meaning of the initialism SDI, what is the more common term for this U.S. government defensive system, and under which President was it initiated?

Answer: Strategic Defense Initiative / Star Wars / Ronald Reagan.

MUSIC & RHYMES

Complete these song lines: "Hail! Hail! the _____'s all _____, / Never mind the _____ / Here we are together, Hail!"

Answer: "gang" / "here" / "weather."

LANGUAGE

Identify the form of each of the following participles: talked, having talked, and talking.

Answer: Past participle / perfect participle / present participle.

ARTS, RELIGION, & CULTURE

Which Biblical Philistine warrior about 10 feet tall was killed by an Israeli youth, who was this youngster, and with what weapon did he kill the giant?

Answer: Goliath / David / a sling and a stone (accept slingshot).

POTPOURRI

September, October, November, and December are the 4 months that end in the letter *r*. Name the 3 months that begin with the letter *J*.

Answer: January / June / July.

U.S. GEOGRAPHY

Which cities are traditionally associated with Macy's Thanksgiving Day Parade, the Mardi Gras celebration, and the New Year's Mummers' Day Parade?

Answer: New York / New Orleans / Philadelphia.

HISTORY

Arrange in chronological order: bus boycott in Montgomery, Alabama; Marshall Plan; and Korean War.

Answer: Marshall Plan (1948) / Korean War (1950) / Montgomery (1956).

LITERATURE

From which state does Chester come in George Selden's *The Cricket in Times Square*, in which type of booth does he reside and sing songs, and in which city is Times Square?

Answer: Connecticut / newsstand / New York City.

ENTERTAINMENT

Who created the cartoon strip *Peanuts*, which character's famous line is "Good Grief," and what does he get in his bag when he goes out for "Tricks or Treats" on Halloween?

Answer: Charles Schulz / Charlie Brown / rocks.

SPORTS AND GAMES

Give the nicknames of the athletic teams at the U.S. Air Force Academy, the U.S. Military Academy, and the U.S. Naval Academy.

Answer: Falcons / Black Knights (accept Cadets) / Midshipmen.

SCIENCE AND NATURE

Which 2 body organs are associated with the word *cardiopulmonary*, and what part of the body is the *coccyx*?

Answer: Heart / lungs / tail bone.

WORLD GEOGRAPHY
Which 3 European countries are known as the "Benelux Countries"?
Answer: Belgium / Netherlands (or Holland) / Luxembourg.

LEADERS & GOVERNMENT
Which U.S. President is associated with the Teapot Dome Scandal, which one with the "Checkers" speech, and which one with the Iran-*contra* affair?
Answer: Warring Harding / Richard Nixon / Ronald Reagan.

MUSIC & RHYMES
Complete the song lines: "Six little ducks that I once knew, / _____ ones, _____ ones, fair ones too, / But the one little duck with the _____ on his back."
Answer: "Fat" / "skinny" / "feather" ("he led the others with a quack, quack, quack!").

LANGUAGE
Am, *is*, *are*, and *was* are 4 of the 7 forms of the verb *to be*. Name the other 3.
Answer: Were / being / been.

ARTS, RELIGION, & CULTURE
Who baptized Jesus; in which river did he baptize Him; and, according to tradition, which woman demanded this person's head on a platter?
Answer: John the Baptist / Jordan River / Salome.

POTPOURRI
What is the motto of the Boy Scouts, what is the slogan for the Boy Scouts method of learning, and what is the nationality of Robert Baden-Powell, the organization's founder?
Answer: "Be Prepared" / learn by doing / British.

U.S. GEOGRAPHY

Which 2-word phrases identify "a region of the U.S. prairie states with eroded topsoil," "a region of the U.S. where fundamentalist beliefs prevail," and "a region where the soil is rich and black"?

Answer: Dust Bowl / Bible Belt / Black Belt.

HISTORY

Arrange in chronological order: assassinations of Martin Luther King and Bobby Kennedy; Cuban Missile Crisis; and Watergate scandal.

Answer: Cuban Missile Crisis (1962) / assassinations (1968) / Watergate (1972).

LITERATURE

Which fictional detective who lives in Idaville was created by Donald Sobol, how much does he charge per day, and what is his father's profession?

Answer: Encyclopedia (Leroy) Brown / 25 cents (plus expenses) / chief of police.

ENTERTAINMENT

Which character in the comic strip *Peanuts* always needs his security blanket, which one admires Beethoven and wants to be a concert pianist, and which character is in love with this pianist?

Answer: Linus / Schroeder / Lucy (van Pelt).

SPORTS AND GAMES

Give the nicknames of the athletic teams at Michigan, Michigan State, and Mississippi.

Answer: Wolverines / Spartans / Rebels (accept Ole Miss).

SCIENCE AND NATURE

Name the 2 parallels of latitude along which most deserts lie, and give the word for the sand hills formed by the wind in a desert.

Answer: Tropic of Cancer / Tropic of Capricorn / dunes.

WORLD GEOGRAPHY

In which country is Istanbul, and what were this city's 2 previous names?

Answer: Turkey / Byzantium / Constantinople.

LEADERS & GOVERNMENT

Of President, Prime Minister, or Chancellor, which one designates the heads of government of Australia, Germany, and France, respectively?

Answer: Prime Minister / Chancellor / President.

MUSIC & RHYMES

Complete the lines from the song: "Hickety, pickety, my black hen, / She lays _____ for _____; / Sometimes nine and sometimes _____, / Hickety, pickety, my black hen."

Answer: "eggs" / "gentlemen" / "ten."

LANGUAGE

Which words complete the phrases describing "anger": "Hot under the _____," "Bent out of _____," and "Fit to be _____"?

Answer: "collar" / "shape" / "tied."

ARTS, RELIGION, & CULTURE

Which Biblical person was known for his great strength, which part of his body was the source of his strength, and which woman deprived him of it and delivered him as a slave to the Philistines?

Answer: Samson / his hair / Delilah.

POTPOURRI

Name 3 of the 4 *C*'s that describe the value of a diamond.

Answer: Carat / clarity / color / cut.

U.S. GEOGRAPHY

Which river makes up about 1,200 miles of the border between the U.S. and Mexico, what is the English translation of this river's name, and in which Rocky Mountain state does this river rise?

Answer: Rio Grande / "great (large) river" / Colorado.

HISTORY

Arrange in chronological order: first recorded Olympic Games; building of the Great Pyramids; and exodus of Moses and Israelites from Egypt.

Answer: Pyramids (c. 2500 B.C.) / Moses (c. 1250 B.C.) / Olympic Games (776 B.C.).

LITERATURE

Which word completes the title of Patricia MacLachlan's *Sarah, Plain and* _____, what did Mama do "every-single-day," and from which state does Sarah come?

Answer: *Tall* / sing / Maine.

ENTERTAINMENT

Who is Charlie Brown's pet beagle in the comic strip *Peanuts*, which plane does he fly, and what is the nickname of the WWI German aviator he sometimes fights?

Answer: Snoopy / Sopwith Camel / "The Red Baron."

SPORTS AND GAMES

Give the nicknames of the athletic teams at Arizona, Arizona State, and Colorado.

Answer: Wildcats / Sun Devils / Buffaloes (or Buffs).

SCIENCE AND NATURE

Which protein molecule speeds up the chemical reactions of food, which fluid in the mouth aids swallowing and digestion, and what is the term for the stomach's digestive juice?

Answer: Enzyme / saliva / gastric juice.

WORLD GEOGRAPHY

Name the 3 Prairie Provinces of Canada.

Answer: Manitoba / Alberta / Saskatchewan.

LEADERS & GOVERNMENT

In which countries were Leonid Brezhnev the chairman of the Presidium, Deng Xiaoping the general secretary, and Ferdinand Marcos the president?

Answer: Soviet Union (accept Russia) / China / Philippines.

MUSIC & RHYMES

Which words complete the rhyme: "Star light, star bright, / _____ star I see tonight, / I wish I _____, I wish I _____, / Have the wish I wish tonight"?

Answer: "First" / "may" / "might."

LANGUAGE

Give the meaning of the words *calligraphy*, *euphony* and *cacophony*.

Answer: Beautiful handwriting (especially as an art) / pleasant sounds / discordant or harsh sounds.

ARTS, RELIGION, & CULTURE

Give the words derived from mythology for each of the following: "a long voyage," "a book of maps," and "a handsome young man."

Answer: Odyssey / atlas / Adonis (accept Apollo and Narcissus).

POTPOURRI

How many sizable, or main, islands—4, 8, 12, or 16—make up the state of Hawaii, how many goals designate a "hat trick" in sports, and how many witches are in a coven?

Answer: 8 / 3 / 13.

U.S. GEOGRAPHY

Identify 3 of the 4 Great Lakes bordering the state of Michigan.

Answer: Lake Superior / Lake Michigan / Lake Huron / Lake Erie.

HISTORY

Arrange in chronological order: Punic Wars; sacking of Rome by Visigoths; and rule of Alexander the Great.

Answer: Alexander (336-323 B.C.) / Punic Wars (264-146 B.C.) / Rome sacked (A.D. 410).

LITERATURE

What is the surname of Ramona in works written by Beverly Cleary; what is Ramona's age in the title *Ramona* _____, *Age* _____; and what is the name of her older sister?

Answer: Quimby / *8* (*Ramona Quimby, Age 8*) / Beezus (accept Beatrice).

ENTERTAINMENT

Which *Peanuts* character is always surrounded by a cloud of dust, which one often falls asleep in class, and what is the name of Charlie Brown's sister?

Answer: Pig Pen / Peppermint Patty / Sally.

SPORTS AND GAMES

Give the nicknames of the athletic teams at Florida, Florida State, and Georgia.

Answer: Gators / Seminoles / Bulldogs.

SCIENCE AND NATURE

What is the unit used to measure the intensity of sound, which narrow tube connects the middle ear to the back of the throat, and which thin membrane separates the middle ear from the outer ear?

Answer: Decibel (accept bel) / eustachian tube / eardrum (or tympanic membrane).

WORLD GEOGRAPHY

Identify the Canadian provinces abbreviated N.B., P.E.I., and N.S.

Answer: New Brunswick / Prince Edward Island / Nova Scotia.

LEADERS & GOVERNMENT

Identify the countries in which the leaders live in the Federal Chancellor's Office, the Elysée Palace, and at 24 Sussex Drive.

Answer: Germany / France / Canada.

MUSIC & RHYMES

Which words complete the song lines: "_____, here I come, / "Right back where I started _____," and which bridge's name completes, "Open up that _____ Gate"?

Answer: "California" / "from" / "Golden."

LANGUAGE

Complete each of the following expressions: "To be bound hand and _____," "By leaps and _____," and "From the bottom of one's _____."

Answer: "foot" / "bounds" / "heart."

ARTS, RELIGION, & CULTURE

Which orchestral instrument gives the tuning note to the rest of the musicians, to which pitch is an orchestra tuned, and which device helps a pianist maintain regular tempo when practicing?

Answer: Oboe / A / metronome.

POTPOURRI

Identify the branch of the U.S. military that uses the Latin *Semper Fidelis* as its motto, give the English translation of this motto, and identify one of this branch's 2 official colors.

Answer: U.S. Marine Corps / "Always (Ever) Faithful" / scarlet or gold.

U.S. GEOGRAPHY

Identify 3 of the 4 states that Lake Erie borders.

Answer: Michigan / Ohio / Pennsylvania / New York.

HISTORY

Arrange in chronological order: Battle of Hastings; start of the First Crusade; and crowning of Charlemagne as king.

Answer: Charlemagne (800) / Battle of Hastings (1066) / Crusades (1096).

LITERATURE

In the story *Ben and Me* by Robert Lawson, what is Ben's full name; which animal is the *Me* in the title; and what is his name?

Answer: Ben Franklin / mouse / Amos.

ENTERTAINMENT

Which substance derived from rock fragments on Superman's planet is capable of weakening and killing him, what color is this substance, and what are the 3 colors of Superman's costume?

Answer: Kryptonite / green / red, blue, and yellow.

SPORTS AND GAMES

Give the nicknames of the athletic teams at Iowa, Iowa State, and Kansas.

Answer: Hawkeyes / Cyclones / Jayhawks.

SCIENCE AND NATURE

Of the 4 planets closest to the sun, which 2 have no satellites, and which one has 2?

Answer: Mercury / Venus / Mars.

WORLD GEOGRAPHY

Identify the Canadian provinces abbreviated Alta., Man., and Nfld.

Answer: Alberta / Manitoba / Newfoundland.

LEADERS & GOVERNMENT

Name the first and the last of the original 13 colonies to ratify the Constitution, and give the year either joined the Union.

Answer: Delaware / Rhode Island / 1787 or 1790.

MUSIC & RHYMES

In the song, "School Days," which words complete the lines: "Dear old _____-rule days, / Readin' and 'ritin' and '_____ / Taught to the tune of a _____ stick"?

Answer: "golden" / "rithmetic" / "hick'ry."

LANGUAGE

Complete each of the following expressions: "Don't bite off more than you can _____," "To hit the nail on the _____," and "Birds of a feather flock _____."

Answer: "chew" / "head" / "together."

ARTS, RELIGION, & CULTURE

In a cathedral, give the words for "the long central aisle"; "the semicircular domed projection, especially the altar or the east end of the church"; and "the steep, pointed roof on a tower"?

Answer: Nave / apse / spire (or steeple).

POTPOURRI

Chemistry, economics (economic science), and physiology or medicine are 3 of the 6 categories for which a Nobel Prize is awarded. Name the other 3.

Answer: Literature / peace / physics.

U.S. GEOGRAPHY

Which states are nicknamed the "Quaker State," the "Wolverine State," and the "Old Dominion"?

Answer: Pennsylvania / Michigan / Virginia.

HISTORY

Arrange in chronological order: beginning of the Hundred Years War; establishment of Inca civilization at Cuzco in Peru; and King John's signing of Magna Carta.

Answer: Incas (1200) / Magna Carta (1215) / Hundred Years War (1337-1453).

LITERATURE

Which character in William Pène Du Bois' *The Twenty-one Balloons* travels around the world, which noted volcano does he visit, and how does he travel across the country after his flight?

Answer: Professor Sherman / Krakatoa / (Presidential) train.

ENTERTAINMENT

What is Superman's adopted name, and in which city in Illinois and for which newspaper does he begin working at age 26?

Answer: Clark Kent / Metropolis / *Daily Planet*.

SPORTS AND GAMES

Give the nicknames of the athletic teams at North Carolina, North Carolina State, and Oklahoma.

Answer: Tar Heels / Wolfpack / Sooners.

SCIENCE AND NATURE

Name the innermost layer of the tooth; name the hard, yellow substance that surrounds this layer; and name the substance, the body's hardest tissue, that covers this yellow layer.

Answer: Pulp / dentin / enamel.

WORLD GEOGRAPHY

Identify the Canadian provinces abbreviated Ont., Que., and Sask.

Answer: Ontario / Quebec / Saskatchewan.

LEADERS & GOVERNMENT

Name the President of the U.S. during the American Civil War, and name both the President and the Vice President of the Confederacy.

Answer: Abraham Lincoln / Jefferson Davis / Alexander H. Stephens.

MUSIC & RHYMES

Complete these lines from "The Marines' Hymn": "From the halls of _____ to the shores of _____, / We fight our country's battles on the _____ as on the sea."

Answer: "Montezuma" / "Tripoli" / "land."

LANGUAGE

Complete the following traditional jingle learned by schoolchildren: "Write *i* before *e* / Except after _____ / Or when sounded as *a* / As in _____ and _____."

Answer: "c" / "neighbor" / "weigh."

ARTS, RELIGION, & CULTURE

In which cities are the Smithsonian Museums, the American Museum of Natural History, and the Field Museum of Natural History?

Answer: Washington, D.C. / New York / Chicago.

POTPOURRI

In which state did the Girl Scouts have its beginning in the city of Savannah in 1912, who was its founder, and what is its motto?

Answer: Georgia / Juliette Gordon Low / "Be Prepared."

U.S. GEOGRAPHY

Which states are nicknamed the "Constitution State," the "Puritan State," and the "Equality State"?

Answer: Connecticut / Massachusetts / Wyoming.

HISTORY

Arrange in chronological order: Pizarro's conquest of Incas; beginning of Magellan's round-the-world voyage; and da Gama's voyage around Africa.

Answer: da Gama (1497) / Magellan (1519) / Pizarro (1531-33).

LITERATURE

Which color completes the L.M. Montgomery title *Anne of _____ Gables*, in which country is the novel set, and which family adopts Anne?

Answer: *Green* / Canada / Cuthberts.

ENTERTAINMENT

In a Dr. Seuss story, who steals Christmas; in which town does he do this; and which animal does he disguise as a reindeer?

Answer: Grinch / Who-ville / his dog (Max).

SPORTS AND GAMES

Give the nicknames of the athletic teams at Texas, Texas Tech, and Baylor.

Answer: Longhorns / Red Raiders / Bears.

SCIENCE AND NATURE

Identify the following forms of precipitation: masses of tiny translucent ice crystals, pellets of ice and hard snow, and transparent frozen raindrops.

Answer: Snow / hail / sleet.

WORLD GEOGRAPHY

Which Canadian province borders Maine and no other U.S. state, which one is the smallest in area, and what is the only one entirely separated from the North American mainland?

Answer: New Brunswick / Prince Edward Island / Prince Edward Island.

LEADERS & GOVERNMENT

Which U.S. Presidents were responsible for dropping the atom bomb on Japan, for creating NASA, and for creating the Peace Corps?

Answer: Harry S Truman / Dwight Eisenhower / John F. Kennedy.

MUSIC & RHYMES

Which words complete the song lines: "_____, row the _____ ashore, Hallelujah! / The River _____ is chilly and cold, Hallelujah! / Chills the body but not the soul, Hallelujah!"?

Answer: "Michael" / "boat" / "Jordan."

LANGUAGE

Complete each of the following expressions: "Better to be safe than _____," "You're barking up the wrong _____," and "_____ is nine-tenths of the law."

Answer: "sorry" / "tree" / "possession."

ARTS, RELIGION, & CULTURE

In which country was Pablo Picasso born, in which one did he live from 1904 until his death, and which continent's sculpture influenced his Cubist paintings?

Answer: Spain / France / Africa's.

POTPOURRI

Which Spanish clay figure filled with candy and gifts and hung from a ceiling is broken by blindfolded children with a stick, and what are the words for "Merry Christmas" in Spanish and French?

Answer: *Piñata / Feliz Navidad / Joyeux Noël.*

U.S. GEOGRAPHY

Which states are nicknamed the "Treasure State," the "Empire State of the South," and the "Cotton State"?

Answer: Montana / Georgia / Alabama.

HISTORY

Arrange in chronological order: Thirty Years War; defeat of Spanish Armada; and Great London Fire.

Answer: Spanish Armada (1588) / Thirty Years War (1618-1648) / Fire (1666).

LITERATURE

Which word completes Mildred Taylor's *Roll of Thunder, Hear My* _____, who is the independent black girl in this story, and in which state does she live during the Depression?

Answer: *Cry* / Cassie (Logan) / Mississippi.

ENTERTAINMENT

Which kinds of animals are Robin Hood and Maid Marian, Little John, and the narrator Allan-a-Dale in a Disney animated feature film?

Answer: Foxes / Bear / rooster.

SPORTS AND GAMES

Give the nicknames of the athletic teams at Tennessee, Kentucky, and Syracuse.

Answer: Volunteers (or Vols) / Wildcats / Orangemen.

SCIENCE AND NATURE

How many centimeters, decimeters, and millimeters are in one meter?

Answer: 100 / 10 / 1000.

WORLD GEOGRAPHY

On which continent is the Suez Canal, and which 2 seas does this canal connect?

Answer: Africa / Red Sea / Mediterranean Sea.

LEADERS & GOVERNMENT

Which U.S. Presidents were responsible for waging "a war on poverty," establishing relations with the People's Republic of China, and for pardoning Vietnam draft resisters?

Answer: Lyndon B. Johnson / Richard Nixon / Jimmy Carter.

MUSIC & RHYMES

Complete the lines to the song: "'Mid pleasures and palaces / Though we may roam, / Be it ever so _____, / There's no _____ like _____."

Answer: "humble" / "place" / "home."

LANGUAGE

According to the phrases, what is a person doing when he brings home the bacon, what are people doing when they tie the knot, and what does it mean to go back to the drawing board?

Answer: Earning money to support the family / getting married / start all over.

ARTS, RELIGION, & CULTURE

Which color is associated with St. Patrick's Day, which one with Valentine's Day, and which 2 colors are associated with Christmas?

Answer: Green / red / green and red.

POTPOURRI

Identify the volunteer community group known as the PTA, give the meaning of ETA in airline parlance, and give the meaning of PAT in a football game.

Answer: Parent-Teacher Association / Estimated Time of Arrival / Point(s) After Touchdown.

U.S. GEOGRAPHY

The northern borders of West Virginia and Kentucky are formed by the Ohio River. Name the 3 states whose southern borders are formed by this river.

Answer: Ohio / Indiana / Illinois.

HISTORY

Arrange in chronological order: French Revolution; proclamation of Monroe Doctrine; and defeat of Napoleon at Waterloo.

Answer: French Revolution (1789) / Waterloo (1815) / Monroe Doctrine (1823).

LITERATURE

Which kinds of animals are Buck in Jack London's *The Call of the Wild*, Gentle Ben in Walter Morey's work of the same name, and Misty in *Misty of Chincoteague* by Eric Knight?

Answer: Dog / (Alaskan brown) bear / pony.

ENTERTAINMENT

What is the name of the car in the Disney film *The Love Bug*, what kind of car is it, and what number is painted on the car?

Answer: Herbie / Volkswagen (Beetle) / 53.

SPORTS AND GAMES

Give the nicknames of the athletic teams at Oregon, Oregon State, and Utah.

Answer: Ducks / Beavers / Utes.

SCIENCE AND NATURE

What names are given to polygons with 4 sides, 8 sides, and 10 sides?

Answer: Quadrilateral / octagon / decagon.

WORLD GEOGRAPHY

Name the 3 divisions besides England that make up Great Britain or the United Kingdom.

Answer: Northern Ireland / Scotland / Wales.

LEADERS & GOVERNMENT

Which song is traditionally played for the U.S. President, what is the name of the President's plane, and which Maryland retreat is reserved for this leader?

Answer: "Hail to the Chief" / *Air Force One* / Camp David.

MUSIC & RHYMES

Which words complete the song lines: "La Cucaracha / All is fair in love and _____" and "_____ they adore," and what is the English translation of the Spanish word *cucaracha*?

Answer: "war" / "Senoritas" / cockroach.

LANGUAGE

Complete the following expressions: "To have an ace up one's _____," "To be tied to his mother's _____-strings," and "To have ants in one's _____."

Answer: "sleeve" / "apron" / "pants."

ARTS, RELIGION, & CULTURE

In which American city is the Guggenheim Museum, in which European city is the Georges Pompidou National Center of Art and Culture, and in which Russian city is the Hermitage Museum?

Answer: New York / Paris / Saint Petersburg (formerly Leningrad).

POTPOURRI

In which countries were gunpowder and the steam engine invented, and in which one did Archimedes invent a *screw* that raised water from a lower level to a higher one?

Answer: China / England / Greece.

U.S. GEOGRAPHY

Which city in which state is the oldest in the U.S., and which city founded in 1610 as the capital of a Spanish colony has been a seat of government longer than any other state capital?

Answer: St. Augustine / Florida / Santa Fe.

HISTORY

Arrange in chronological order: opening of Suez Canal; first battle of U.S. Civil War; and Crimean War.

Answer: Crimean War (1853-1856) / U.S. Civil War (1861) / Suez Canal (1869).

LITERATURE

Which animals are featured in Richard Adams' *Watership Down* and Barbara Brenner's *A Killing Season*, and which kind of animal is Eric Knight's Lassie?

Answer: Rabbits / (black) bears / dog (a collie).

ENTERTAINMENT

Identify Andy's pull-string cowboy doll, Andy's sweetheart, and the toy whose mission is to protect the galaxy from the threat of invasion by the Evil Emperor Zurg in Disney's *Toy Story*.

Answer: Woody / Bo Peep / Buzz Lightyear.

SPORTS AND GAMES

Give the nicknames of the athletic teams at Alabama, Auburn, and Miami (Florida).

Answer: Crimson Tide (accept Red Elephants) / Tigers (accept Plainsmen or War Eagles) / Hurricanes (accept 'Canes).

SCIENCE AND NATURE

What types of lenses are prescribed for people who are near-sighted and far-sighted, and what is the name for the divided spectacles for near and far vision?

Answer: Concave / convex / bifocals.

WORLD GEOGRAPHY

Which palace in which city has been the residence of British sovereigns since 1837, and which famous ceremony do the red-coated guards perform each day in front of the palace?

Answer: Buckingham Palace / London / the changing of the guard.

LEADERS & GOVERNMENT

Which U.S. Presidents were responsible for the start of the Social Security program, for forcing the Soviets to remove missiles from Cuba, and for the invasion of Grenada?

Answer: Franklin D. Roosevelt / John F. Kennedy / Ronald Reagan.

MUSIC & RHYMES

What is the title of the U.S. Navy's famous marching song, and which words complete its lines, "Sail on to victory / And sink their _____ to Davy _____, hooray"?

Answer: "Anchors Aweigh" / "bones" / "Jones."

LANGUAGE

Complete the following expressions: "To know on which side one's bread is _____," "To take with a grain (pinch) of _____," and "To sell like hot _____."

Answer: "buttered" / "salt" / "cakes."

ARTS, RELIGION, & CULTURE

Name 3 of the 4 main families of instruments in a modern orchestra.

Answer: Woodwind / brass / percussion / strings.

POTPOURRI

On the Western frontier, what weapons did a cowboy have if he had a Winchester, a Derringer, and a Bowie?

Answer: Rifle / handgun (or pistol) / knife.

U.S. GEOGRAPHY

Name the 2 states bordered by 8 other states, and name the only one bordered by just one state.

Answer: Tennessee / Missouri / Maine.

HISTORY

Arrange in chronological order: beginning of World War I; Spanish-American War; and sinking of *Lusitania*.

Answer: Spanish-American War (1898) / WWI (1914) / *Lusitania* (1915).

LITERATURE

Who is the hero in J.R.R. Tolkien's *The Hobbit*, in which "world" do the Hobbits live, and whom do they call "the Big Folk"?

Answer: Bilbo Baggins / Middle-Earth / men.

ENTERTAINMENT

Which kind of gem is Madame Medusa trying to obtain in the Disney film *The Rescuers*, which kind of animals are detectives Bernard and Bianca, and which kind of bird is Orville?

Answer: Diamond (Devil's Eye) / mice / albatross.

SPORTS AND GAMES

Give the nicknames of the athletic teams at Brigham Young, Purdue, and Clemson.

Answer: Cougars / Boilermakers / Tigers.

SCIENCE AND NATURE

What is another name for the star Polaris, over which pole is it presently located, and in which constellation is it the brightest star?

Answer: North Star (accept polestar) / North Pole / Ursa Minor (or Little Bear).

WORLD GEOGRAPHY

In which city is Big Ben, what is Big Ben, and in which building is it located?

Answer: London / great bell (in the Clock Tower) / Houses of Parliament.

LEADERS & GOVERNMENT

Of which countries did David Lloyd George, Hosni Mubarak, and Juan Péron become the leaders?

Answer: Great Britain / Egypt / Argentina.

MUSIC & RHYMES

Which words complete these lines from a song in *The Sound of Music*: "_____ ev'ry mountain," "_____ ev'ry stream," and "_____ ev'ry rainbow"?

Answer: "Climb" / "ford" / "follow."

LANGUAGE

According to the sayings, what is the sincerest form of flattery, what is the best medicine, and what do you do if you can't beat them?

Answer: Imitation / laughter / join them.

ARTS, RELIGION, & CULTURE

How many people make up each of the following chamber music groups: quintet, septet, and quartet?

Answer: 5 / 7 / 4.

POTPOURRI

Which type of hat was named after an English horse race, how many gallons are in the name of a hat worn by American cowboys, and which flat, round hat originated in the European Basque region?

Answer: Derby / ten-gallon / beret.

U.S. GEOGRAPHY

In which Eastern states are the Hudson, Lehigh, and Shenandoah valleys?

Answer: New York / Pennsylvania / Virginia.

HISTORY

Arrange in chronological order: signing of Treaty of Versailles to end World War I; Russian Revolution; and beginning of the Great Depression.

Answer: Russian Revolution (1917) / Versailles (1920) / Great Depression (1929).

LITERATURE

In William Steig's *Amos & Boris*, what kinds of animals are Amos and Boris, and what is the name of the boat Amos builds?

Answer: Mouse / whale / *Rodent*.

ENTERTAINMENT

Whose accomplice in the Disney film *The Rescuers* is Mr. Snoops, what kind of animal is the elderly Rufus, and what kind of "swamp critter" is Evinrude?

Answer: Madame Medusa's / cat / dragonfly.

SPORTS AND GAMES

Give the nicknames of the athletic teams at Illinois, Indiana, and Ohio State.

Answer: (Fighting) Illini / Hoosiers / Buckeyes.

SCIENCE AND NATURE

How many stars are in the Little Dipper, of which constellation is it a part, and near which pole is this group of faint stars located?

Answer: 7 / Ursa Minor (or Little Bear) / North Pole.

WORLD GEOGRAPHY

Which 2 countries are on the Iberian Peninsula, and which people now living in the northern part of the larger one are thought to be descendants of those called Iberians?

Answer: Spain / Portugal / Basques.

LEADERS & GOVERNMENT

Which tax is imposed on the money made by a person in a given period, which one is imposed on the property of a deceased person passed on to heirs, and which one is collected from the owners of land?

Answer: Income tax / inheritance tax (or estate tax or death tax) / property tax.

MUSIC & RHYMES

Which words complete these lines to the U.S. "Air Force Song": "Off we go into the _____ blue _____ / Climbing high into the _____"?

Answer: "wild" / "yonder" / "sun."

LANGUAGE

Give the Spanish for *Mr.*, *Mrs.*, and *Miss.*

Answer: *Señor* / *señora* / *señorita*.

ARTS, RELIGION, & CULTURE

Which mythological leader of the Argonauts set off to capture the wool of a golden ram, what was the name of his boat, and what was the name of this wool?

Answer: Jason / *Argo* / Golden Fleece.

POTPOURRI

What is the word for a person who, according to superstition, was turned into a wolf at night, when did the wolf have to shed his skin and return to human form, and what did these wolves eat?

Answer: Werewolf / at daybreak / human flesh.

U.S. GEOGRAPHY

Which President chose the site of Washington, D.C., which black surveyor assisted Major Andrew Ellicott in laying out the city's boundaries, and which Frenchman drew up the city's plans?

Answer: George Washington / Benjamin Banneker / Pierre L'Enfant.

HISTORY

Arrange in chronological order: beginning of Spanish Civil War; Hitler's rise to chancellor of Germany; and beginning of World War II.

Answer: Hitler (1933) / Spanish Civil War (1936) / WWII (1939).

LITERATURE

Which kind of animal is Ping in Flack and Wiese's *The Story About Ping*, and in which country on which river does Ping live?

Answer: Duck / China / Yangtze River.

ENTERTAINMENT

In the comics, what kinds of animals are Heathcliff, Marmaduke, and Pogo?

Answer: Cat / dog / opossum.

SPORTS AND GAMES

Give the nicknames of the athletic teams at Pittsburgh, Nebraska, and Arkansas.

Answer: Panthers / Cornhuskers / Razorbacks (or Hogs).

SCIENCE AND NATURE

How many stars are in the Big Dipper, of which constellation is it a part, and over which pole is this group of stars located?

Answer: 7 / Ursa Major (or Big Bear) / North Pole.

WORLD GEOGRAPHY

On which peninsulas are Denmark, Italy, and Norway and Sweden?

Answer: Jutland / Appenine / Scandinavian.

LEADERS & GOVERNMENT

Which U.S. President was wounded in an assassination attempt on March 30, 1981, in which city did the attack occur, and who was the would-be assassin?

Answer: President Ronald Reagan / Washington, D.C. / John W. Hinckley Jr.

MUSIC & RHYMES

Complete the lines to the song: "Oh, I went down South for to see my Sal, / _____ Polly-wolly-_____ all the _____."

Answer: "Sing" / "doodle" / "day."

LANGUAGE

Give the words that literally mean "one marriage," "two marriages," and "many marriages."

Answer: Monogamy / bigamy / polygamy.

ARTS, RELIGION, & CULTURE

Give the Italian word or phrase for "a leading female ballet dancer," the French one for "a male ballet dancer," and the English one for "the person who arranges the movements of a ballet."

Answer: Ballerina or prima ballerina / danseur / choreographer.

POTPOURRI

Which animals do the Hindus consider most sacred, which color elephant was once considered sacred in Siam, and which long-legged bird that nests on chimneys do the Germans consider sacred?

Answer: Cows / white elephant / stork.

U.S. GEOGRAPHY

What is the largest river that lies wholly in the state of New York, what is the largest city on this river, and into which body of water does this river empty?

Answer: Hudson River / New York City / Atlantic Ocean.

HISTORY

Arrange in chronological order: beginning of Korean War; First Arab-Israeli War; and launching of *Sputnik* by Soviet Union.

Answer: Arab-Israeli War (1948) / Korean War (1950) / *Sputnik* (1957).

LITERATURE

Which word completes the title *The Little Engine That* _____, where must the little engine carry the toys for the boys and girls, and which word completes the engine's refrain "I think I _____"?

Answer: *Could* / over the mountain / "can."

ENTERTAINMENT

Give the first names of the parents of the cartoon character Dennis the Menace, and give the surname of his neighbors George and Martha.

Answer: Henry / Alice / the Wilsons.

SPORTS AND GAMES

Give the nicknames of the athletic teams at Maryland, Louisiana State, and Boston College.

Answer: Terrapins (Terps) / (Fighting) Tigers / Eagles.

SCIENCE AND NATURE

Identify the following clouds: the delicate ones highest in the atmosphere; the lowest ones, those associated with stormy weather; and the fair weather ones with huge, fluffy, dome-shaped white piles.

Answer: Cirrus / stratus / cumulus.

WORLD GEOGRAPHY

Give the names by which Persia, Gaul, and Siam are known today.

Answer: Iran / France / Thailand.

LEADERS & GOVERNMENT

Which U.S. President acquired Florida in a treaty in 1819; during which one's administration did the Gadsden Purchase add new territory to the U.S. in 1853-1854; and which one purchased Alaska in 1867?

Answer: James Monroe / Franklin Pierce / Andrew Johnson.

MUSIC & RHYMES

Give the surnames of 3 of the 4 Beatles: John _____, Paul _____, George _____, and Ringo _____."

Answer: Lennon / McCartney / Harrison / Starr.

LANGUAGE

Which words ending in *-cide* mean "the killing of one human being by another," "the killing of oneself," and "the killing of a race"?

Answer: Homicide / suicide / genocide.

ARTS, RELIGION, & CULTURE

Give the ballet terms for "the practice bar in a ballet studio," "a full turn on one foot," and "a dance for 2 persons."

Answer: Barre / pirouette / pas de deux.

POTPOURRI

In the Western U.S., which kind of trousers are Levis, what leather trousers do cowboys wear to protect their legs, and what is the Spanish name for a cowboy hat with a broad brim?

Answer: Blue jeans (heavy denim trousers) / chaps / sombrero.

U.S. GEOGRAPHY

New Mexico, Colorado, Utah, and Wyoming are 4 of the 8 states through which the Rocky Mountains pass. Name 3 of the other 4.

Answer: Idaho / Montana / Washington / Alaska.

HISTORY

Arrange in chronological order: building of Berlin Wall; Soviet Union's invasion of Afghanistan; and Soviet Union's invasion of Hungary.

Answer: Hungary (1956) / Berlin Wall (1961) / Afghanistan (1979).

LITERATURE

Name the city in which the Grand Canal is located, the father of Little Toot, and the singing men who propel the gondolas in the story *Little Toot on the Grand Canal*.

Answer: Venice / Big Toot / gondoliers.

ENTERTAINMENT

What is the surname of the comic strip character Dennis the Menace, what is the name of his dog, and what is the name of the young girl with red curls and glasses featured in this strip?

Answer: Mitchell / Ruff / Margaret (Wade).

SPORTS AND GAMES

Give the nicknames of the athletic teams at Duke, UCLA, and Southern California.

Answer: Blue Devils / Bruins / Trojans.

SCIENCE AND NATURE

Identify the following, each of which has the same name as a planet: an element, a candy bar, and a Disney cartoon dog.

Answer: Mercury / Mars / Pluto.

WORLD GEOGRAPHY
Of which oceans are the Coral Sea, the Sargasso Sea, and the Arabian Sea a part?
Answer: Pacific Ocean / Atlantic Ocean / Indian Ocean.

LEADERS & GOVERNMENT
Which U.S. Presidents were responsible for the annexation of Texas in 1845, for the annexation of Hawaii in 1898, and for the purchase of the Virgin Islands from Denmark in 1917?
Answer: John Tyler / William McKinley / Woodrow Wilson.

MUSIC & RHYMES
What is the English translation of the song title "Que Será, Será," and which words complete: "When I was just a little _____, / I asked my mother, / 'What _____ I be?'"
Answer: "Whatever Will Be, Will Be" / "girl" (accept "boy") / "will."

LANGUAGE
Complete each of the following phrases with an animal's name: "As poor as church _____," "As mad as a March _____," and "As mad as a wet _____."
Answer: "mice" / "hare" / "hen."

ARTS, RELIGION, & CULTURE
Identify the mythological woman married to Menelaus whose abduction started a war, identify the war, and identify the person who allegedly abducted her.
Answer: Helen of Troy / Trojan War / Paris.

POTPOURRI
Which American doctor, known as the "Baby Doctor," wrote *Common Sense Book of Baby and Child Care*, and which colors are traditionally associated with boy and girl babies?
Answer: Dr. Benjamin Spock / blue / pink.

U.S. GEOGRAPHY

What was the name of the longest overland route used by explorers and pioneers, in which state did it begin in Independence, and in which state did it end at Fort Vancouver?

Answer: Oregon Trail / Missouri / Washington.

HISTORY

Arrange in chronological order: Sadat's visit to Israel; Reagan and Gorbachev's signing of a treaty to reduce the size of their nuclear arsenals; and signing of Camp David Accords.

Answer: Sadat (1977) / Camp David (1979) / Reagan and Gorbachev (1987).

LITERATURE

In which New England city on which river is Robert McCloskey's *Make Way for Ducklings* set, and what name does the author give to the parents of the ducklings?

Answer: Boston / Charles River / Mr. and Mrs. Mallard.

ENTERTAINMENT

According to Linus, who rises out of the most sincere pumpkin patch each Halloween, what will he deliver to all the good little children, and whose ghost costume has lots of holes in it?

Answer: Great Pumpkin / toys / Charlie Brown's.

SPORTS AND GAMES

Give the nicknames of the athletic teams at Harvard, Princeton, and Yale.

Answer: Crimson / Tigers / Bulldogs (accept Elis).

SCIENCE AND NATURE

What is 2 to the 4th power, 4 to the 3rd power, and 7 squared?

Answer: 16 / 64 / 49.

WORLD GEOGRAPHY

In which country was the Trans-Siberian Railroad, the world's longest, built between 1891 and 1916, and what are the beginning and ending provinces of the Trans-Canada Highway?

Answer: Soviet Union (accept Russia) / Newfoundland / British Columbia.

LEADERS & GOVERNMENT

Which U.S. President was fond of playing touch football, which one was fond of eating jelly beans, and which one was fond of the "strenuous life" — riding, hunting, hiking, and boxing?

Answer: John F. Kennedy / Ronald Reagan / Theodore Roosevelt.

MUSIC & RHYMES

In the song "Put on a Happy Face" from *Bye Bye Birdie*, what kind of "skies are gonna clear up," and which words complete the line "Brush off the _____ and _____ up"?

Answer: "Gray" / "clouds" / "cheer."

LANGUAGE

Which words complete the expressions: "To talk off the top of one's _____," "Half a _____ is better than none," and "To have _____ on one's face"?

Answer: "head" / "loaf" / "egg."

ARTS, RELIGION, & CULTURE

Which mythological hero is noted for his strength and for the labors he accomplished, how many labors were there, and which multi-headed serpent did he kill as one of his labors?

Answer: Hercules (or Heracles) / 12 / hydra.

POTPOURRI

In English, which days of the week were named after the sun and the moon, and which is the only day named for a Roman god?

Answer: Sunday (sun's day) / Monday (moon's day) / Saturday (Saturn's day).

U.S. GEOGRAPHY
In which cities are the Metropolitan Opera House and Carnegie Hall; the High Museum of Art and Peachtree Center; and the Springer Opera House and Patrick's Press, the creator of the *Omniscience* game and book?
Answer: New York City / Atlanta / Columbus (Georgia).

HISTORY
Identify the Americans who said: "You may fire when you are ready, Gridley" and "The world must be made safe for democracy," and name the President whose motto was "The buck stops here."
Answer: Commodore George Dewey / Woodrow Wilson / Harry S Truman.

LITERATURE
Which words complete these lines from a Robert Frost poem: "The woods are _____, _____ and _____. / But I have promises to keep, / And miles to go before I sleep"?
Answer: "lovely" / "dark" / "deep" (from "Stopping by Woods on a Snowy Evening").

ENTERTAINMENT
Which fictional character, a "masked man," fights Western criminals; which superhero changes clothes in a phone booth; and which masked swordsman leaves the sign of the "Z" on his opponents?
Answer: Lone Ranger / Superman / Zorro.

SPORTS AND GAMES
What is the nationality of the men who created *Trivial Pursuit*, which American created *Omniscience*, and who hosted the TV quiz show *Who Wants to Be a Millionaire* on ABC?
Answer: Canadian / John Campbell / Regis Philbin.

SCIENCE AND NATURE
What is the meaning of the initialism IQ, which organization's members have IQs in the top 2 percent of the general population, and what is the meaning of the initialism ESP?
Answer: Intelligence quotient / Mensa / extrasensory perception.

WORLD GEOGRAPHY
In the year 2000, which country had a population of about 1.3 billion people, which one reached 1 billion, and which one had about 275 million?
Answer: China / India / United States.

LEADERS & GOVERNMENT
Who became in 1984 the first female Vice Presidential candidate chosen by a major political party, who chose her as his running mate, and who was the first Jew chosen on a major party's national political ticket?
Answer: Geraldine Ferraro / Walter Mondale / Joseph Lieberman (Al Gore's running mate in 2000).

MUSIC & RHYMES
Which words complete the song lines: "I want a girl, just _____ the girl / That _____ dear old _____"?
Answer: "like" / "married" / "Dad."

LANGUAGE
Complete the following expressions: "He who laughs _____, laughs best (longest)," "Jack-of-all-trades, _____ of none," and "Which came first, the chicken or the _____?"
Answer: "last" / "master" / "egg."

ARTS, RELIGION, & CULTURE
Which mythological creature lived in a maze on the island of Crete, which animal's head did its head resemble, and what was the maze called?
Answer: Minotaur / bull's / Labyrinth.

POTPOURRI
Identify the health care workers known by the abbreviations M.D., G.P., and R.N.
Answer: Doctor of Medicine (accept Medical Doctor) / General Practitioner (accept Graduate in Pharmacy) / Registered Nurse.